A
KILLER IN
THE
FAMILY

First published in 2013 by
New Holland Publishers
London • Sydney • Cape Town • Auckland
www.newhollandpublishers.com

The Chandlery, Unit 114, 50 Westminster Bridge Road, London, SE1 7QY
1/66 Gibbes Street Chatswood NSW 2067 Australia
Wembley Square First Floor Solan Road Gardens Cape Town 8001 South Africa
218 Lake Road Northcote Auckland New Zealand

ISBN: 9781742574547

10 9 8 7 6 5 4 3 2 1

Managing director: Fiona Schultz
Publisher: Alan Whiticker
Project editor: Kate Sherington
Designer: Kimberley Pearce
Production director: Olga Dementiev
Printer: Toppan Leefung Printing Limited

Follow New Holland Publishers on
Facebook: www.facebook.com/NewHollandPublishers

A KILLER IN THE FAMILY

Amanda Howard

NEW
HOLLAND

Books by the same author

Ritual: The Blood of Many (2013, KDP/CreateSpace)

Serial Killers and Philosophy: Being and Killing (2010, ed. Sara Waller, John Wiley & Sons)

Innocence Lost: Crimes that Changed a Nation (2009, New Holland)

Predators: Killers Without Conscience (2009, with Paul Wilson, New Holland)

Million Dollar Art Theft (2007, ticktock/Bearport)

Terror in the Skies (2007, ticktock/Bearport)

The Lottery Kidnapping (2007, ticktock/Bearport)

River of Blood: Serial Killers and Their Victims (2004, with Martin Smith, Universal)

A note from the author

You are about to embark on a journey into the childhoods, family lives and murderous violence of killers across the globe. I hope this book will help you understand a little about what makes and provokes a killer, whether it be a sex-crazed and murderous couple, a 10-year-old boy who is bored with life, or a maniac religious leader determined to condemn his flock. In the end, though, *A Killer in the Family* may raise more questions than it answers.

The book could not have been achieved without the support of my family, who again had to suffer my drowning in the depths of depravity to capture the essence of the killers described herein. They were there to offer me support and remind me that my investment in digging deep always pays off for the person I care about most – you, the reader.

I have had a long relationship with New Holland Publishers and it is always wonderful to work with such a professional team. Particular thanks go to Kate Sherington, my editor, who made a good book great, and Alan Whiticker, a fellow true crime author and commissioning editor at New Holland. Alan was the man with the vision.

A serial killer once asked me, 'Do you dream about me when you sleep?'[1] At the time, the question was terrifying, and for some nights to come I was scared to dream. So I would suggest that when reading *A Killer in the Family*, you keep the light on – just in case. Welcome to the journey.

Amanda Howard
August 2013

Contents

Introduction

I have worked with serial killers and violent criminals for 20 years and still there are days that are far too dark for me. As you will see in the pages that follow, human depravity knows no bounds, and killers are a species all their own, different from the rest of us. This knowledge allows us to continue in our daily lives, certain we would never commit such acts of evil.

I wrote in a previous book about serial killers crossing a line in the sand. While they are both bullies and the bullied, the strong and the weak, they lack an awareness and respect for the humane boundaries that keep our world civilised. The line in the sand that separates us from evil is obliterated in the mind of the killer; they not only cross that line, they wipe it from their own mind.

Ted Bundy, for example, was a successful young man in many ways – and the same could be said for his later killing spree. Although he came from a confusing home life, he blamed his early desire for pornography, not his family, for driving him to murder at least three dozen young women and girls. He saw nothing wrong with what he was doing. His line in the sand was crossed long before he started killing.

Other killers, like McVeigh and the Columbine boys, exploded in a frenzy of violence, killing many in a very short period of time, though in both cases they had taken years to prepare for that final onslaught, when they knew they would take that final step across the line. They felt as though society had pushed them into the shadows and the only way to garner the attention they wanted was through murder and violence. They sought to spread a message of government distrust and the violation of societal norms.

Jeffrey Dahmer and Marc Dutroux did not have a message. Instead, their motives were pure hedonistic pleasure. I have often read articles by Dahmer's father Lionel, who has been crushed by the realisation that he spawned one of society's greatest monsters. How does one live with that? In Lionel Dahmer's case, he appears to be torn between disgust at his son's crimes and love for his son in such an adverse situation. He, like everyone else, has wondered how a little blonde-haired boy could become such a heinous man. Where the warning signs were missing in Dahmer's case, though, Marc Dutroux's mother saw them as clear as day, and begged authorities to keep her son in jail. Her pleas fell on deaf ears and he was released to rape and murder young girls.

The killers in this book all have very different backgrounds, but their journeys through life brought them to the same place – the line drawn in the sand. They all chose to cross it. Why they did will become evident as you read on.

Chapter 1
The Wests

Claiming that deviant behaviour is 'what normal families do' is how sexual abuse and violence are often justified by family members. Warping a young child's understanding of what is normal can be achieved early in their life. Though not all child sexual abuse victims go on to become offenders themselves, almost one-third of them do. When two victims of child sexual abuse marry, the risk of their perpetuating such abuse is exponentially increased, such as in the case of Fred and Rose West, the serial-killing couple, both of whom were victims of childhood sexual abuse at the hands of their own parents.

Frederick Walter Stephen West was born in 1941 in Much Marcle, England, to Walter and Daisy West. Fred was the apple of his mother's eye, while his father, a stern man known for physically punishing his children, terrified Fred as a child. Living in a tiny English hamlet, with the family often sharing one large bed, Fred was sexually abused by his mother and witnessed his father sexually abusing his sisters and other local girls. After his incestuous start to life, a sexual awakening occurred in the young boy, which saw him become extremely aggressive with the local girls. He spent his teenage years coercing young girls to have sex with him, often giving them promise rings if they allowed him to bed them.[2]

Following a motorcycle accident in November 1958, which left him in a coma for eight days, a metal plate was inserted in his head to hold his smashed skull together as it healed. He also broke his arm and one of his legs, resulting in a permanent limp. Following the accident, the usually carefree, though sexually aggressive, young man was more morose, with an unpredictable temper, prone to sudden rages and striking out at those around him. Like his father, his violent streak was coupled with a voracious sexual appetite. It wasn't long before his behavior would get him into trouble.

In 1960, West suffered another brain injury following an attempt to have sex with a local girl. His victim had pushed him from a fire escape at a local youth club, causing him to fall and lose consciousness. It was also around this time that West was arrested for impregnating his 13-year-old sister.[3] At his trial for incestuous sexual assault, his sister refused to testify against him, leaving the police with little choice but to free him without a conviction. His father kicked him out of the house for bringing attention to the secret sexual deviance of the family, telling him never to return. West spent the next 18 months travelling the countryside, working odd jobs on construction sites.

In August 1962, the 20-year-old Fred met his future wife, 16-year-old pregnant runaway Catherine 'Rena' Bernadette Costello. Rena told Fred she had escaped a home for wayward girls where she had been sent following a brush with the law. Before meeting Fred, she had worked as a prostitute and stripper, and was also a convicted thief. The young couple were instantly attracted and became lovers, but before they could further their relationship, Rena abruptly returned to Scotland.

Fred went home and begged his parents to forgive him for the assault of his 13-year-old sister. They relented and let him return to live with them. When Rena returned to Much Marcle three month later, however, heavily pregnant with her first child, Fred convinced his parents that he was the father of the baby and Rena moved into the West's tiny home. During their numerous arguments, Fred routinely beat Rena; the couple also fought with Fred's parents, who did not like their son's choice of partner.

Fred and Rena secretly married on 17 November 1962, in a registry office in Ledbury, after which they moved to Scotland together. On 22

March of the following year, Rena gave birth to a daughter, Charmaine. While she was in hospital with her baby, Fred was at home, having sex with one of Rena's sisters.[4] He showed little interest in the baby, which wasn't his, preferring to spend his time bedding various local women.

Following the birth, Rena returned to her job as a stripper at a local club. There, Fred met Charmaine's Pakistani father, who according to Fred was also Rena's pimp. The man threatened West, telling him he was no longer allowed to have sex with Rena. As compensation, he supplied Fred with many other girls.

But Rena was already pregnant with West's baby. She tried to abort the unwanted pregnancy, without success, and in 1964 Anne-Marie West was born. Anne-Marie, like her older half-sister, would be subjected to decades of sexual torture and abuse at the hands of her father. Following the birth of Anne-Marie, West met 16-year-old Anna McFall, another teenage prostitute, who quickly fell under his spell. Anna moved into the home that West shared with Rena and worked as a nanny for the two babies.

Fred was working as an ice-cream truck driver to support his wife, nanny and children when tragedy struck – he reversed the truck over a four-year-old boy, killing him. Though the death was an accident, Fred packed up his belongings and, along with his lover Anna McFall and the children, returned home to Much Marcle, leaving his wife behind. He put the two girls into government care while he found a job in a slaughterhouse, honing the dissecting skills he later used on his victims.

By the time Rena attempted to win back her husband, she found that Anna McFall had taken on the full-time role of 'wife' to Fred and mother to the children, a domestic situation that made her furious. She stormed into the local constabulary, where she spoke to a young officer, Constable Hazel Savage, who recorded Rena's complaint that she believed Fred was molesting their children. It was one of the first encounters Constable Savage would have with the West family. She began investigating the accusations, but Rena soon withdrew her complaint. Nevertheless, the police now knew that the family was an unconventional one, requiring, at the very least, cursory monitoring. Savage would later be instrumental in uncovering the horrors that occurred in West's home at 25 Cromwell Street.

In 1967, Anna, pregnant with West's child, demanded that he divorce his wife and marry her. Yet Fred had no desire to yield to her demands. Instead, he just moved Anna into another caravan whenever Rena came to visit. The arrangement was less than appealing to Anna, who complained to her mother in letters about the treatment she received at Fred's hand. West would often rape and beat her, and try out various sadomasochistic sexual tortures on her, which would feature heavily in the later murders.

In August 1967, Anna McFall disappeared. She was eight months pregnant with Fred's child. According to Fred's later confession, he stabbed her through the heart, yet when her body was finally unearthed a quarter of a century later, it bore the hallmarks of a fatal torture session. Her hands were tied together behind her back and her body was clothed only in a light blue cardigan. Whether it was consensual or not will never be known, but the pregnant woman was certainly murdered by Fred. He then dismembered her body, removing several of her fingers and toes, as well as the full-term foetus from her womb, and buried her body in the green fields of Much Marcle. The specific land he chose, Fingerpost Field, was where he had worked as a boy, alongside his abusive father. From his home, he could look out over the field and see where he had buried Anna.

Fred later confessed to his father that he had killed his young girlfriend; he and his father shared many dark secrets over the years, including their sexual interference with the West sisters and other local girls. When Fred told his father about Anna's murder, Walter replied, 'I'm not going to turn you in or nothing. If you can live with it, I'll say nothing. Leave it.'[5] The body remained hidden until 1994.

Another young girl disappeared a few months later, in January 1968. Mary Bastholm, 15, disappeared while waiting for a bus in Gloucester. Though Fred never fully confessed to her murder,[6] it is likely she was murdered by West and buried somewhere near the body of Anna McFall.

14

In February 1968, Fred's mother Daisy had a heart attack and subsequently died. It hit Fred hard. He became more morose than ever, beating his wife and two children excessively, and molesting the little girls more frequently. The year was significant for another reason too – 1968 was the year he met Rosemary Letts, the young woman who would help to shape the man into an even more terrible monster.

Rosemary Pauline Letts was born in November 1953 in Devon, the fifth child of Bill and Daisy Letts. Bill was a sadistic schizophrenic and her mother Daisy was undergoing shock therapy for depression when she fell pregnant with the girl they would call 'Dozy Rosie'.[7] Daisy Lett's depression was related to the violence she suffered at the hands of her husband, who would also strike out at the children, with a ferocity only matched by his incestuous sexual appetite. As a child, Rosemary was known to rock herself so violently that she could fall into a catatonic state. This sort of unusual behaviour might have been the result of her conception during her mother's shock treatment, or due to the violent abuse she suffered later.

Like Fred West, Rosemary failed at school and left with only the fundamentals of reading and writing. When her older sisters left home, Rosemary's father turned all of his sexual attentions on her, and she, in turn, learned to win favour with her father through sexual promiscuity. This way, she would escape the beatings her other siblings suffered. She also inherited her father's violent and aggressive temper, beating her younger siblings or local children when the mood took her.

After years of abuse, Daisy Letts finally escaped the violent home, taking her daughter and two young sons with her. Yet the move did nothing to prevent Rosemary's sexually deviant behaviour. By the age of 14, she had seduced her younger brother, grooming him just as her father had done to her.

Following an affair with a man twice her age, Daisy moved again, this time leaving the teenage Rosemary behind to fend for herself. Rosemary went back to live with her father, where she took on the roles of both daughter and lover. During this time, she was sexually assaulted by a man who grabbed her from a bus stop while she waiting for a lift home. The man dragged her into a park and savagely raped her. Some suspect her attacker might have been none other than her future husband, Frederick West,[8] but the attack was never reported and Rosemary continued her life as her father's sexual plaything.

In summer 1968, Fred and Rosemary's lives officially collided. While working in a local bakery, West looked up to see Rosemary walk through the door. They were instantly attracted to one another and quickly began a sexual relationship. Their partnership would prove fatal for the young women of Gloucester.

In the early 1970s, Fred took a job driving a van through the country. He would often pick up young hitchhikers, whom he would rape and torture before letting them go. Rosemary, pregnant at home with Fred's baby, would babysit his two young daughters, often spending her days beating and whipping them. In October 1970, she gave birth to the couple's first child, Heather, but Fred went to prison on robbery charges in December, and would not be released until June the next year.

In June 1971, Rose murdered Charmaine West, Fred's step-daughter. Rose, still a child herself, was the primary carer of Charmaine, Anne-Marie and Heather while Fred was in prison. According to Fred's confession, his partner had lost her temper with the young child and struck out, killing her. Charmaine's body was buried under the kitchen of their rented home in 25 Midland Road, Gloucester, possibly after Fred's release from prison. She had been cut up prior to the haphazard burial; when later unearthed, she was missing her fingers and kneecaps.

In August 1971, Fred decided it was time to get rid of Rena, to prevent her raising questions about Charmaine's disappearance. He got his wife highly intoxicated and drove her to Much Marcle, where he had buried Anna McFall. According to his confession, he made love to her twice before the pair got into a fight. Then he claims to have killed her by smashing her into the iron gate that fenced the lush green paddocks from the roadway. He dismembered Rena's body and buried her in a shallow grave. Regardless of whether Rose played any part in the murder, she was aware that her lover had

16

murdered his wife, and this secret almost certainly cemented their deviant relationship.

Suspecting how far she would go, Fred pushed the boundaries with his promiscuous partner. He began advertising her sexual services in magazines, with photographs of Rose prominently featured. Fred allowed Rose to use their own bedroom to service her clients, many of them West Indian, as long as he was able to watch through a peephole in the wall. Fred would often have rough or kinky sexual intercourse with Rose following these sessions, which he also video-taped. He believed he could use the tapes not only spice up his own sexual fantasies, but possibly to blackmail the clients, who had families and wives of their own.

The pair, already bound by sex and murder, married in January 1972 at a Gloucester Registry Office. At the time, Rose was three months pregnant with Mae. After Mae's birth in June,[9] Fred moved his family into their final home, 25 Cromwell Street in Gloucester. In 1994, this house, where most of the victims' bodies were buried, would be dubbed 'the House of Horrors' in the press.

Fred chose the home specifically for its cellar. He had plans to convert it into a torture chamber where he could abuse his victims, including his own children, over the next 20 years. The first victim to be led to the cellar was his own daughter Anne-Marie. The eight-year old was lured into the dark hole by her parents. She was tied up and gagged before being savagely raped by her father. She was told that this would make her a better wife and mother later on.[10] The rape resulted in horrific injuries that required her to be away from school for several days while she recovered. It was only the beginning of the abuse she would endure at the hands of her parents.

Caroline Owens was the next victim of Fred's abuse. The 17-year-old accepted a job as a babysitter with the growing West family, but left the job in December 1972, due to Fred's incessant sexual pursuit. A few months later, while hitchhiking home, she accepted a lift from Fred and Rose. Taken to their house, she was bound and gagged before being raped and beaten with a belt buckle.[11] After hours of abuse, the teenager was allowed to leave, as long as she promised not to report them. She did report the attack, but the pair were let off with a nominal fine when Fred was able to convince the judge that Caroline had been a willing participant in their sexual games.[12]

Lynda Gough moved into the West house in April 1973. The 19-year-old had left a note for her parents saying she was going to move in with a nice couple to act as a babysitter to their children. Lynda began her time with the Wests as a willing accomplice in sex games with Rose, pregnant for a third time, and Fred. But one night Lynda found herself hanging by her ankles from the ceiling of the cellar's torture chamber. According to Fred's confession, the young woman enjoyed the bondage game she was playing with the kinky couple, but their games soon turned deadly. In the hours, even days, before her eventual death, Lynda Gough was slowly reduced to 'nothing more than a slab of meat'.[13]

Fred systematically sliced off pieces of the woman's body, in a torture method akin to the Chinese method of *ling chi*, which causes pain but does not kill quickly. Victims instead die from blood loss, over several days. Before she was buried, Lynda's fingers, hands and forearms had been removed. When her body was later discovered under the garage of 25 Cromwell Street, much later, 113 of her bones, including her fingertips and kneecaps, were missing.[14]

Four months after the murder of Lynda Gough, Rose gave birth to a son, Stephen. Yet having another baby in the house did little to stop the Wests' killing spree. Three months later, the couple chose their next victim, 15-year-old Carol Ann Cooper, who was last seen at a local pub. Fred picked up the young girl in November 1973. According to Fred, Rose was solely to blame for the young girl's murder in a 'kinky love session that went wrong'.[15] Carol was hung from a wooden beam in the cellar, Rose having placed a large elastic band around the girl's head and face to prevent her from calling out. Hanging helpless from the beam, she was beaten and abused for days, until she was finally murdered by the couple during one of their violent fantasy torture sessions, during which they severed the girl's head, possibly while she was still conscious. By the time her mutilated corpse was buried, the couple had removed nearly 50 of her bones, and many pounds of flesh.[16]

18

Lucy Partington disappeared on 27 December 1973, having been offered a lift by a friendly couple. They took her back to the West home, where she was made to perform various sexual acts with Fred and Rose before she also was tortured, mutilated and murdered. Lucy's body was buried with a knife that had been used in her murder, as well as a large piece of rope that was still knotted around her throat. Her remains were missing 72 bones.[17]

Four months later, they struck again. Therese Siegenthaler, a 21-year-old student, was picked up by Fred West while hitchhiking. Therese was tied up and taken down to the cellar, where she was tortured and mutilated, before her head was severed from her body and a further 37 bones removed. Her body was buried in a corner of the cellar. Fifteen-year-old Shirley Hubbard was the fifth girl to be murdered and buried at 25 Cromwell Street. On 14 November 1974, she had run away from her foster home, and ended up at Cromwell Street. Once she was inside the cellar, Fred West covered the girl's face with tape, creating a mask that covered her entire face. He fed two tubes into her nostrils so she could breathe. Shirley was left in the cellar for days, as the couple took turns beating and sexually assaulting her. Again, they sliced off pieces of her body until she finally died. According to Fred's confession, Shirley 'slipped off' the hook where she had been hung upside-down.[18]

Juanita Mott was the next to accept an offer to stay at Cromwell Street. The young girl had nowhere else to go and welcomed the invitation from the couple. In April 1975, though, her lodging arrangement proved fatal. She was tied up with rope, and abused and tortured before her death. She looked to have been struck 'as if a ball-ended hammer had been hit against the skin'.[19] The young woman was decapitated and almost 90 of her bones were removed before she was buried in the cellar with the other bodies.

Two years later, the next victim was murdered. Shirley Robinson, 18, rented one of the upstairs bedrooms in the West home in Cromwell Street. The pretty, green-eyed girl quickly became Fred's lover, often sharing a bed with both Fred and Rose. After Rose became pregnant to one of her Jamaican clients, Fred then impregnated Shirley.

Rose felt threatened by the younger and prettier woman who now took up most of Fred's attention, but in June 1977, Fred strangled Shirley while his wife slept. He buried the young woman and the unborn child he had cut from her womb in the back garden of Cromwell Street. Six months later, Rose gave birth to Tara.

In November 1978, another daughter, Louise, was born to Fred and Rose. At the same time, Anne-Maire suffered an ectopic pregnancy that required the removal of one of her fallopian tubes. Fred was believed to be the father of her unborn baby.

The Wests lured another victim to her death in September 1979. Alison Chambers was brought to the couple's bedroom, where she was tied down, with another belt tied around her face to stop her screaming. They tortured her for the next several days before finally murdering her. The girl's partial remains, missing 96 bones, were buried near the back steps of the Cromwell Street home.

Rosemary continued to have children. In June 1980, Barry West was born, followed two years later by Rosemary Junior, whose father was one of Rose's clients. A year after Rosemary Junior's birth came another mixed-race baby, Lucyanna, in July 1983. Anne-Marie had by then married and left the home, leaving Heather, one of the eldest children, to be sexually abused and harrassed by their lecherous father. The family unit was breaking down.

As stories of the abuse suffered by the West children began to filter throughout the neighbourhood, it was not long before police attention focused on Cromwell Street. By the time they searched the family home, however, it was too late for Heather. On 19 June 1987, she was killed, the final known victim of Fred and Rose West. Most observers of this case believe that no more murders occurred, though both Fred and Rose continued to threaten the other children with being buried in the garden like their sister.

Five years after Heather's disappearance, in August 1992, police executed a search warrant on 25 Cromwell Street. Complaints had been raised through child services, claiming that the West children were being kept in the cellar of the home, and were only brought up to be raped and sodomised. According to Fred's lawyer Howard Ogden, Anne-Marie claimed that during her childhood, she was brought from the cellar into the main house so she could be 'broken in' by her father.[20]

Thousands of video-tapes, recorded on the family's camera, were confiscated by investigators. As police went through the tapes, some of them showed the family on outings. Others showed Rose servicing clients from a bedroom in the West home, while yet more showed young women being raped and tortured in violent bondage sessions. The police had enough evidence to remove the children from the West household.

Fred was arrested for the molestation of Anne-Marie on 6 August 1992. He pleaded not guilty. Before the trial could proceed, Anne-Marie withdrew the complaints of rape and sodomy and refused to testify against her father. Later, once the 'House of Horrors' had been uncovered, police realised why she had done so. She did not want to end up under the house, like so many others had done over the years.

While viewing the tapes, DC Hazel Savage began working out the West family tree, and noticed there were gaps. Heather West was noticeably missing from the family videos after 1987. When the younger children were interviewed about the whereabouts of their older sister, many of them told the family joke 'that Heather was buried under the patio'.[21] After 18 months of looking for any evidence of Heather alive, police decided she was indeed dead, and probably buried at the West house.

Savage and four other officers arrived at 25 Cromwell Street, with a search warrant,on 14 February 1994. Mae West answered the front door to find Hazel Savage standing on the stoop. 'Mum, she's here again,' the young woman called out, towards the lounge room.

Rosemary West moved from the lounge, where she was watching an Australian soap opera, to the front door. She was wearing little more than a t-shirt. The house was a mess and its residents were in a similar state of disarray. So began the uncovering of one of the worst serial murder, rape and child abuse cases in history.

The warrant explained that officers were there to search the back garden for the body of Heather West. The police officers believed 16-year-old Heather had been murdered by her parents in 1986 or 1987. Rosemary told officers they were harassing her and yelled to her adult step-daughter Anne-Marie to call Fred, who was working on a nearby building site. Rose took the phone and barked down the line at her husband, 'Police are digging the garden up, come home quick.'[22]

When Fred arrived, he was taken straight to the local police station by DC Savage. He calmly told her that he had 'nothing to bloody hide'.[23] When faced with the children's comments about the family joke, Fred mocked police for acting on such a whim. He appeared confident that the true horrors of 25 Cromwell Street would remain hidden.

Both Rose and Fred told police the same story about Heather's whereabouts, claiming she had run away with a female lover. They said they hadn't seen her in years and did not know her current whereabouts. Meanwhile, police began to dig up the yard. The couple were released for what would be their final evening together. Fred decided that he would confess to killing Heather in the hopes that police would stop digging.

The following day, Fred admitted to police that, on 19 June 1987, while Rosemary was out, he'd had an argument with Heather and struck her across the face. He told police that when she laughed at him, he 'brought [his] two hands up and grabbed her round the neck'[24] and squeezed until she stopped moving. He claimed that he then tried to revive her by stripping her naked, placing her in the bathtub and running cold water over her, in the hope that the shock of the cold would wake her. When that failed, he dismembered her. He went into detail about the way he cut up his daughter's body: 'I looked around everywhere to try and find a knife or something … I looked at the axe … there was no way I could touch … her with it. I just couldn't do it. So I saw this knife sticking out with two prongs on the end … and I got that and I tried it with the big ones (bones) first and it was terrible … I finally managed to take her head off and then her legs. That was unbearable.'[25] The description was gruesome and shocking, yet Fred told it as though he was reading a story, not reliving his daughter's brutal murder. He said that after dismembering her, he put the pieces of his daughter into a garbage bag, and buried Heather's body in the garden after the rest of the West family had retired for the night.

For the next three days, as forensic experts continued to dig at Cromwell Street, investigators tried to get Fred to talk, specifically asking him if there were any other bones in the garden. After a lengthy pause, he replied, 'That's a peculiar question.'[26] He maintained that they would only find Heather. That's when investigators explained the problem they had with his story: Heather didn't have three legs.[27] When they told him they'd uncovered a third leg bone, and asked him who it belonged to, Fred replied, after drawing a deep breath: 'Shirley ... Shirley Robinson.'[28] The House of Horrors was finally giving up its secrets.

Five days into the investigation, Fred was losing count of the number of murders he had confessed to. When describing the interment of Shirley Robinson, he told police, 'I mean, where is this going to end? By this time I am realising that that is three ... two ... that's two, not three.'[29] He had made a monumental error and police noticed. While on a break with his lawyer, away from police, he confessed to the murder of a third woman. He named her only as 'Shirley's mate' and said that she too was buried in the yard, near the back step of the house.

Police took Fred back to Cromwell Street, which by now was swarming with media, to point out where the body was buried. From the yard, Fred could already see the uncovered body in a plastic bag. He later recalled, 'I looked straight across and I could see her. I think she is in a plastic bag ... you could actually see it in the corner ...'[30] According to Fred, he had strangled 'Shirley's mate' with a piece of flexible hosing.

When left alone with his lawyers again, they begged Fred to give police any further information; if there had been more murders, he should confess. Fred looked at his defence team and said, 'There is a fucking load more.'[31] He confessed to another five murders, eventually sitting down to write out a confession. In a childish scrawl, he wrote, 'I Frederick West ...

wish to admit to a further (approx) 9 killings, expressly, Charmaine, Reena [sic], Linda Gough, and others to be identified.'[32]

Fred, along with police investigators, returned to the house on Cromwell Street after 10pm on 5 March 1994. Down in the cellar of the terrace house, he pointed to the burial sites of six more bodies. Police continued to dig beneath the house and in the garden for days, uncovering body after body. What had begun as the search for one young girl had unearthed a pair of sadistic serial killers.

Yet as Fred West continued to confess to murdering his victims, he played down how he had killed them, claiming he had strangled each of them in a fit of rage, rather than during a session of sexual torture, which was evident in the bindings and tape found with many of the bodies, as well as their specific injuries and missing body parts. After months of interviews, he again changed his story. After seeing his wife in court after her own arrest on 24 April 1994, he realised she no longer considered him her partner, and knew that she would likely tell investigators her own story. Instantly, he turned on her. He told his lawyer that he had been prepared to take the blame for all of the murders before, but now wanted to clarify his wife's involvement in the killings. He also told police she was solely responsible for Heather's murder.

As the bodies continued to mount, Fred could see no way to escape the numerous murder charges. His wife and partner in crime had snubbed him; he was the most hated man in Britain, if not the world; and though some of his children chose to stand by him, he knew that was only temporary. On New Year's Day 1995, just before noon, Fred West was found dead in his cell. He had hanged himself with strips of his bedsheet, leaving Rose to face the charges alone.

Rose's trial for the sexual abuse, torture and murder of 10 of the victims opened in October 1995. While she denied any knowledge of the bodies that had been found beneath her family home, the prosecution were quick to point out what a perfect partner she had been for her murderous husband. The pair, both of whom had been abused by their own parents, had been a lethal combination together. Their relationship had stretched beyond the murders of wayward teens and hitchhikers to their own children. They had ritually and systematically abused their children from very young ages, attempting to skew their offsprings' beliefs about such practices, telling them that their early introduction into sexual abuse would help them in their adult lives – possibly this was what they had been told by their own parents, when they were children themselves. After a lengthy trial that produced dozens of witnesses and experts, many of whom gave evidence on the horrific injuries the victims had suffered, the jury took little time in finding Rose guilty. She was sentenced to 10 life terms.

Following the conclusion of the trial, the home at 25 Cromwell Street demolished and replaced with a park. The building's bricks and structures were buried at an undisclosed dumpsite to prevent macabre souvenir hunters from selling them.

According to David Canter, one of Britain's leading experts on criminology, the atrocities committed by Fred and Rose West would never have occurred had the two grown up in normal family circumstances.[33] The abuse the pair had endured themselves gave them both a skewed set of values, in which violence and sexual abuse was tolerated, even encouraged. During his confession, Fred claimed his own sexual appetite and values were shaped by the sexual abuse he received in the bed of his own mother. Incestuous relationships in both their childhoods would have been part of daily life, something that happened in every family as far as they knew. The 'normalcy' of the abuse was cemented and they grew up to become abusers themselves. The West children all suffered sexual and physical abuse at the hands of both of their parents, which meant the sins of the previous two generations had been passed on to the next.

The childhood abuse that made Fred and Rose killers was a great distance from the upbringing of Karla Homolka and Paul Bernardo. The young and beautiful couple were the polar opposites of the dowdy and uneducated Wests, yet both couples committed strikingly similar crimes. Bernardo, like Fred West, had a voracious sexual appetite that could not be sated by normal behaviour, and though there were problems in his childhood, nothing pointed to the serial killer he would become. Like West, he also became a rapist first before moving on to murder, fooling those around him with a convincing facade.

Chapter 2
Karla Homolka and Paul Bernardo

As one of the most gruesome cases in Canadian criminal history, the sexually motivated serial murders committed by Paul Bernardo and his wife Karla Homolka have been etched into the minds of all who know the case.

The story of their horrific crimes first broke when Homolka first went to hospital on 27 December 1992, having received a brutal beating at the hands of her husband. She said she had been in a car accident and was discharged l a few days later, returning to the home she shared with Bernardo. On 11 February 1993, though, she went to police and told them her husband had beaten her. Saying that she'd suffered abuse at his hands for the last time, she offered information about her husband regarding the Scarborough rapes and the schoolgirl murders, in exchange for immunity from prosecution herself. Questions were raised, however, about Homolka's participation in the killings and whether she was a victim of Battered Women's Syndrome, or an hybristophile – a person who gains pleasure from the sex crimes of another.[34]

Though many of the trial's details have been suppressed, there is enough information to create a profile of Bernardo as a brutal rapist who eluded police capture for many years and who, along with his wife, evolved into a serial killer not unlike the suave and sophisticated Ted Bundy.

Paul Bernardo was conceived in late 1963 when his mother Marilyn Bernardo sought the solace of an ex-boyfriend, having found her husband

Kenneth fondling their baby daughter and discovering he'd been charged with the sexual molestation of another small child. The separation was short-lived, however, and she returned to her violent husband once again. When Paul was born, he believed Kenneth was his father. It was only later, during a violent argument with his mother, that the teenage boy discovered the truth. The news shocked him deeply. He looked up to Kenneth, who, like Paul himself, was a peeping tom. That event remained etched in Paul's mind and forever made him doubt the honesty of his own family life; what he had believed to be healthy and whole was suddenly unstable.

As his voracious sexual appetite awoke, the teenaged Paul's behaviour shifted, from watching neighbourhood girls changing from the bushes outside their windows to bedding as many of them as possible. He knew what to say to get them into bed: he would proclaim his love and commitment to them, a certainty he had lost in his own life, and his angelic blue eyes and blonde hair hid the truth about his appetites. By the time he was enrolled in university, Paul had grown bored with normal sex and preferred to dominate submissive women. He chose women he knew would not reject his demands for anal sex and fellatio. Many of his girlfriends complained that he beat them, or urinated and defecated on them during sex.[35]

In October 1987, when he was working at a large Toronto accounting firm, the 23-year-old Paul Bernardo met Karla Homolka. At 17, Homolka was the eldest of three daughters born to Dorothy and Karel Homolka. Her childhood had been unremarkable. The pretty young girl was popular and intelligent and had many friends. She adored animals, which saw her take a job at a veterinary clinic after high school. Karla was attending a veterinary conference in Toronto when Bernardo spotted her across a restaurant. The 17-year-old was instantly charmed by the attention she received from the older man, and from that very first evening, their sexual chemistry was evident. They spent their first night together in a hotel room, having rough, fervent sex. According to Karla, the night was extremely passionate, and she actually poured ice water over Bernardo to cool him down at one point.[36] This sex session gave a small glimpse into the appetites they shared.

When Homolka returned home, she was eager to tell everyone about her new boyfriend, yet the fairytale quickly began to show cracks. Bernardo had given Homolka a list of demands and instructions about how she should behave and dress, included sexually explicit requests. He would often degrade her in public, calling her names like bitch and slut, and made her call herself degrading names during sex. And when the pair were not together, he continued to satisfy his sexual desires by assaulting woman in Scarborough, Toronto.[37]When he failed the exam to become a certified accountant, he told his family and friends he no longer wanted to work in the field, as he could earn more money in other ways. He soon began trafficking stolen goods across the American–Canadian border, his regular travels giving him more freedom to attack women.

The two soon became engaged, and Homolka made plans for a wedding to match the fairytale romance she was living, even as the sexual relationship between the pair grew more sadistic. According to Stephen Williams, Homolka started to encourage Bernardo's deviant behaviour: 'Karla, handcuffed, on her knees and begging for him, was scratching an itch. Paul asked her what she would think if he was a rapist. She would think it was cool. Their love deepened. He started raping women in earnest.'[38]

Since May 1987, Bernardo had savagely raped several women. He would often attack his victims from behind, grabbing them after they had stepped off a bus in a secluded area. He anally raped most his victims and forced them to perform fellatio before letting them go. While the attacks began sporadically, once he had Homolka's approval, the number of rapes escalated. According to one of Bernardo's victims, a young woman had been sitting in a car nearby, using a camera to record the rape. She was yelling out encouragement as he sodomised the victim. Bernardo loved the fact that his girlfriend revelled in the rapes.

When a rape victim finally managed to get a good look at Bernardo, he savagely bashed the woman and fled to Homolka's parents' home in Saint Catherines in the middle of the night.[39] He arrived hysterical and told Homolka about the rape. He said the victim had seen him and would no doubt tell the police, which indeed she had. An Identikit picture of the rapist was soon published all over Canada. Bernardo's friends joked about how much the picture looked like him, but few took it seriously.

During the investigations, Bernardo's name did come up and he was asked to provide saliva, blood and semen samples for DNA comparison.[40] Bernardo complied, sure it would only be a matter of days before he was arrested, but his sample was lost in the backlog. Then an anonymous hotline was set up, and one woman called in about her ex-boyfriend, Paul Bernardo. She told them about the sexual abuse to which he had subjected her, gave police his description and offered information about the car he drove.[41] The information was similar to accounts from victims of the ongoing sexual attacks, but with hundreds of calls coming in, there was not enough manpower to investigate every piece of information received and Bernardo's ex-girlfriend was overlooked.

By December 1990, Karla's parents were happy that their eldest daughter had found such a handsome and successful young man. Karla's younger sister Tammy was also thrilled. She really liked Paul; he was always nice to her and would bring her little presents. One evening when Bernardo went out to get more drinks for a family party, Tammy went with him. During the trip, Paul hugged Tammy, telling her how pure and innocent she was. The pair spent several hours kissing before they returned to the party, and faced the accusations of an extremely drunk Karla.

Karla's other sister, Lori, wasn't so sure about her sister's fiancée. She didn't trust Paul's smooth demeanour and was suspicious of his motives, especially towards Tammy, unaware that Bernardo had already set his sights on her. He had always hated that he was not Karla's first sexual partner, and spent many nights trying to persuade his fiancée to let him deflower Tammy as compensation. It didn't take long for Homolka to comply.

On 23 December 1990, after a Christmas feast at the Homolka family home, Karla slipped animal sedatives, stolen from the veterinary clinic where she worked, into Tammy's drinks. Tammy began slurring her words as Bernardo poured her more glasses of drug-laced wine. Once the rest of the family had retired for the night, Bernardo set up a video camera to record the night's events, and he and Homolka set about taking Tammy's virginity. Karla held a cloth soaked in halothane – an animal anaesthetic – over her young sister's nose and mouth, and Tammy passed out quickly. Bernardo began the attack while Homolka monitored Tammy's breathing, maintaining the cloth over her sister's nose and mouth to keep her unconscious. Bernardo undressed her, noticing that the teenager was menstruating. Homolka encouraged Bernardo to rape her sister, commenting on how well the girl's body was developing as she matured. Bernardo positioned the camera so it could record him penetrating the 15-year-old. After climaxing, he then sodomised her. Homolka became agitated and told Bernardo to hurry up, as she was worried others in the house might hear them.[42]

Bernardo pushed Homolka's face towards her sister's vagina and told her to perform cunnilingus. Homolka refused several times before Bernardo became abusive, hitting her over the back of the head as he forced her closer to her sister's vagina. As Karla began licking her unconscious sister's genitals, Tammy started to vomit. Her head lolled forward and she stopped breathing. As Tammy choked on the vomit pooling in her throat, Homolka redressed her sister and turned her upside down in an attempt to clear her airways. Unfortunately Tammy had by then fallen into a coma.

After hiding the camera and cleaning up the evidence, the couple called paramedics and woke the family. The ambulance team arrived and attempted to revive the comatose girl, without success. The family was questioned as to whether Tammy had ingested something besides alcohol – she had a huge purple stain around her mouth that suggested drugs. The couple claimed Tammy had only been drinking 'screwdrivers', but had had quite a few. In the end, Tammy's death was declared an accident and no toxicology tests were conducted. The purple stain was explained away as an acid burn from vomiting.

In fear that the family might find out what had happened, the couple purchased their own house and moved in soon after Tammy's funeral. Homolka, though grateful to be away from her parents' home, was fearful of life under Bernardo's control. He beat her often, but always in places where no marks would show. He made her sleep on the floor and would have her stand outside in the snow for hours, just to amuse himself.

Bernardo continued to earn money by smuggling cigarettes across the border. The illegal work was lucrative, but Homolka was concerned that it would bring unwanted attention from the police. Bernardo also spent a lot of time away from their new home and continued to rape women and girls he found walking home at night. One evening, sick of her fiancée stalking the streets, Homolka decided to bring him home. She rang his mobile and told him she had a gift waiting for him. Bernardo arrived home to find a pretty teenage girl unconscious in their house. Homolka had coerced a friend of Tammy's to come over and drugged her, reasoning that if she could find virginal victims for her fiancée, he might stay home and treat her better.

Bernardo enjoyed his gift, first making Homolka perform cunnilingus on their sleeping victim, then vaginally raping the virgin teenager before sodomising her brutally. But Karla's plan did not work. Bernardo began raping more women and, still unidentified, the suspect was dubbed 'the Scarborough Rapist' in the media.

On Friday 14 June 1991, Leslie Mahaffy spent the evening with friends, ignoring her parents' 10pm curfew. They had asked her to be home early and to remain in a group, as the Scarborough rapist was attacking victims more frequently and they were naturally concerned for their daughter's safety. Yet Leslie did not share their worry and it was not until 2am that she decided to head home. When she arrived at her front door, she found her parents had locked her out in an attempt to teach her a lesson. Unsure of what to do, she called a friend, whose mother told her to face the consequences at home, but Leslie was hoping to avoid any conflict. She tried to break in and failed, then decided to go for a wander along the street. Little did she know that at the same time, the most wanted man in Canada – the Scarborough Rapist – was also prowling the streets.

Bernardo spotted Leslie and knew she was his next victim. He got out of his car and crossed the road in front of Leslie, who was unaware that she was being watched. Hiding behind a tree, he sprang out and grabbed her at knifepoint as she walked by. He told her to get in the car, threatening her if she screamed, and eventually drove the teenager to his home. Once he had her inside the house, Bernardo forced Leslie to strip naked and filmed the terrified girl. He blindfolded the teenager and made her lie down. As he prepared to penetrate her vaginally, he climaxed. Furious at himself for ejaculating so quickly, he took his anger out on the young woman, beating her savagely across her back and head.

Homolka heard the commotion in the lounge room and went to see what Bernardo was doing. Bernardo was pleased that Homolka had woken, as he now had two women in his control. He grabbed the video camera and directed his fiancée to engage in various sexual positions with their captive while he filmed it, a scene that aroused Bernardo. He quickly gave the camera to Homolka so he could sodomise Leslie as she sobbed hysterically. He forced Leslie to tell the camera how much she loved him and how she was not worthy of his attention. She begged for him not to hurt her as he raped her three more times. When Bernardo grew tired of his captive, he drugged her with champagne and sleeping pills and went to sleep beside her.

The following morning Homolka and Bernardo continued their sexual assault. Leslie was raped and sodomised by Bernardo several more times, with Karla again filming the violations. The couple changed positions, with Karla performing numerous sex acts for the camera at Paul's direction. And finally, when the pair had finished torturing Leslie, the camera was turned off and the girl was murdered.

Later, Bernardo and Homolka blamed each other for the girl's murder, and there is no way of knowing who actually killed her. They both, however, shared the chore of cutting the girl's body into pieces. Each piece was placed in a cardboard box, which was then filled with concrete. When the blocks had set, the couple drove to a bridge on Lake Gibson and threw the pieces into the water, where they were eventually found.[43]

On the same day the remains of Leslie were fished out of Lake Gibson, Bernardo and Homolka were celebrating their marriage. The wedding was an extremely big occasion with all the trimmings, down to a horse-drawn carriage and huge bridal party. The couple were unaware of the discovery of Leslie's remains until they returned from their Hawaiian honeymoon and Homolka's family told them the news – the discovery had been front-page news during their time abroad. Later that evening, Bernardo and Homolka had a huge argument, both panicking about the possibility of being caught. But police again failed to identify them.

On 30 November 1991, five months after Leslie's murder, 14-year-old Terri Anderson disappeared. The young girl's naked body was found in the waters of Port Dalhousie six months later. Though no one was ever charged with Terri's murder, many investigators believe Bernardo and Homolka could have been to blame.[44]

Tammy's girlfriend, who had previously been drugged and raped by Bernardo and Homolka, was also called to their home again. Bernardo attempted to have sex with the teenager but she refused, claiming she was a virgin, unaware that she had previously been raped by Bernardo while unconscious. She did, however, submit to his demands for fellatio. Another night, the young girl was invited over and drugged again, as she had been that first night. This time, however, she stopped breathing for a moment. It was enough to scare Bernardo and Homolka and they stopped using animal tranquilisers.[45]

The girl's mother found out about Bernardo's inappropriate demands and the young girl was no longer allowed to see the couple, a situation that made Bernardo furious. He needed young girls to satisfy his lust and his wife, at 21, was too old to sexually attract him anymore. Homolka knew she had to do something to keep her husband's interest in her alive.

Kristen French was a beautiful girl, with long, brown hair and a gorgeous smile. On 16 April 1992, she was abducted from a church parking lot. Homolka lured the lovely brunette over to her car on the pretense of asking for directions, before Bernardo appeared, brandishing a knife and forcing Kirsten into the car. Like Leslie before her, Kristen was raped and sodomised by Bernardo and Homolka for the next several days. The entire abuse was caught on tape as the couple beat and assaulted the teenager. Kristen tried to keep her wits about her and went along with everything they suggested, even pretending to enjoy the deviant sex with both her male and female captors. The more she pretended to enjoy it, the more perverse her captors became. In one video, Bernardo is recorded saying, 'Don't make me mad. Don't make me hurt you,' as he rubs his groin into her face. 'Don't worry, I won't piss in your face.'[46] Finally, he stands over her and urinates. Then he moves, squatting his buttocks into her face, trying to defecate on her without success. 'You're a fucking piece of shit. But I like you,' he tells her. 'You look good covered in my piss.'[47]

These indignities went on for a day or two, all meticulously captured on video for the future enjoyment of the newlyweds. The assaults upon Kristen were intolerable. She had her teeth knocked out one at a time and was fed her own chopped off hair. Finally, when the couple tired of her, she was murdered and her body was dumped in a ditch, where it was later found. She had not been dismembered, which led investigators to erroneously conclude that the two murders were not connected.[48]

With the composite sketch of the rapist in every post office and frequently flashed on television, police began receiving more and more calls about a man named Paul Bernardo, who resembled the picture. Detectives who interviewed him at his home noted that he was clean-cut, handsome, polite and cooperative. Yes, he agreed, it was rather inconvenient and embarrassing that he looked like the Identikit drawing. They noticed the car in his driveway, a Nissan, which looked nothing like a Capri. Yet again, Paul was not pursued as a suspect.

By February 1993, Bernardo had raped more women and murdered several teen girls, yet police were no closer to catching him. When Karla Homolka walked into the police station, however, accusing Bernardo of beating her and demanding he be charged with assault and battery, the case finally came to an end. Using Homolka as a punching bag had proved to be Bernardo's fatal mistake. The physical abuse had been going on for years, but this time he had blackened both her eyes, knocked out several teeth, and fractured her ribs. Police took the badly beaten woman to the hospital, where detectives interviewed her at length. She began to tell them about the life she had led under the control of her husband and piece by piece the jigsaw that depicted Paul Bernardo as a serial killer began to fall into place.

Bernardo was arrested on 10 February, charged with the Scarborough rapes and the murders of Leslie and Kristen. But as the investigation continued, Homolka became afraid of being pursued as an accomplice to the terrible crimes that had occurred. On 19 February, police obtained a search warrant for the couple's home, and forensic teams combed the couple's Port Dalhousie home for 71 days. They were flabbergasted to find a complete directory of all the rapes and murders, written in Paul's own handwriting, as well as piles of violent sexual magazines and books. They did not, however, find the video recordings of the attacks. Homolka then made her deal – she would be found guilty of manslaughter, in exchange for the tapes, which she had in her possession, and testimony against her husband. Only once Homolka had been sentenced to 12 years did the full extent of her involvement become known. The tapes showed Homolka was heavily involved in sex acts with two captives, proving that she was an enthusiastic partner in the crimes.

At his trial two years later, Bernardo pleaded not guilty on all counts. He was found guilty and sentenced to life in prison, under a 'dangerous offender' classification, meaning there is no possibility of parole. Since his incarceration, he has been questioned about a number of other missing and murdered girls. He continues to play with police, posing hypothetical questions in response to direct requests for information.

Bernardo outwardly appeared to be a typical Canadian man with his life and career ahead of him, yet when they scratched away at the surface, those closest to him saw the monster he had become. His home life was unstable from the beginning. His mother, unhappy with her marriage, would often leave the children unsupervised while she visited other family members, even when Bernardo was as young as six. Within a few years, he was setting fires, using the skills he had learned at boy scout camps, where he found the companionship of friends. Though Bernardo was a good achiever in school, he never did well enough in his parents' eyes, and would be criticised for the work he had done. The resentment between him and his parents hit a peak when his mother told him he was not his father's son.

That turning point set the course for the rest of Bernardo's life, as his hatred of his mother manifested itself in a lack of respect for women. He began to refer to his mother as a slut and a whore, words he would later make Homolka call herself while he had sex with her. After several girlfriends refused to submit to his deviant demands, he turned to rape, before finally escalating to murder, encouraged by his wife, Homolka.

Homolka herself, though originally painted as a battered woman who succumbed to her partner's deviance, was not an innocent pawn. She played an active role in the abuse and torture of the victims and the recordings of the Mahaffy and French murders showed she participated willingly in her husband's fantasies. Bernardo and Homolka fed off each other's fantasies. She would submit to his paraphilias, such as choking and sodomy, while he was turned on by her encouragement, and when Homolka felt as though her husband was looking elsewhere for a deviant partner, she summoned him home with a victim at the ready. Their shared fantasies pushed the boundaries of the relationship, which was cemented with the death of Homolka's younger sister, in a planned attack.

Bernardo's compulsion to rape may have led to many more murders had he not been caught following a violent attack on his wife. He could easily have become another Ted Bundy, a handsome and intelligent young man who, like Bernardo, raped and murdered his way across state lines for years. Bundy's childhood was far from normal, although he considered it to be. In fact, it bred one of the most prolific serial killers of the past few decades.

Chapter 3
Ted Bundy

According to Ted Bundy, he was raised in a 'healthy home.'[49] He felt safe and secure in the life he had with those he believed to be his parents. Unlike the childhoods of other murderers, there was no religious mania, and no sexual, physical or psychological abuse in his home. He was shown love and encouragement and the family he knew remained settled through most of his young life. Ted Bundy's early years gave very few clues to the monster he would become.

Until the very end, Bundy was able to find people who adored him. Even the trial judge, Justice Edward Cowart, showed admiration and sympathy for the prolific serial killer when passing his death sentence, saying, 'Take care of yourself, young man. I say that to you sincerely; take care of yourself, please. It is an utter tragedy for this court to see such a total waste of humanity as I've experienced in this courtroom. You're a bright young man. You'd have made a good lawyer, and I would have loved to have you practice in front of me, but you went another way, partner. Take care of yourself. I don't feel any animosity toward you. I want you to know that. Once again, take care of yourself.'

Ted Bundy was born Theodore Robert Cowell on 24 November 1947. Unbeknownst to him, he was the illegitimate son of Eleanor 'Louise' Cowell. On Bundy's birth certificate, Lloyd Marshall was named as his father, but Eleanor also though another man, Jack Worthington, was a possible candidate. Claims have since surfaced that Bundy's grandfather – Louise's father – could in fact have been his father.[50]

To avoid any scandal and to hide the truth from Ted, Louise moved in with her parents, and Ted was brought up believing himself to be their son, and his biological mother Louise his older sister. While this could not be described as the perfectly healthy home Bundy later claimed it to be, he always maintained that his early life was quite normal, and that he was raised in 'a wonderful, loving home where he was the focus of his parents' lives'.[51] He was quick to turn blame for his crimes away from his family, instead pointing to external forces that may have led to him becoming one of the world's most prolific killers.

In 1951 Louise moved with Ted to another relative's place. A year later, she met and married an army cook called John Bundy, and Ted took Bundy's name, though he still did not know Louise was his real mother. As a boy of 12 about to embrace puberty, Bundy discovered pornography on magazine stands at local supermarkets, at news agencies, and discarded in rubbish bins on collection days. Yet Bundy soon found that the semi-clothed women of the soft porn magazines he stole no longer fuelled his sexual fantasies. He sought out more explicit images and went in search of harder pornography periodicals, including detective magazines that combined violence with sexually explicit stories and images. He would search through rubbish bins and dumps, looking for material to suit his violent tastes. Much later, in an interview in prison, he mused, 'Sex and violence brings about behaviour that is too terrible to describe. I'm not blaming porn, it did not cause me to go out and do those terrible things, the issue is how this type of literature contributed, moulded and shaped my violent behaviour. In the beginning it fuels the thought processes that crystallise as a separate entity.'[52]

At the same time that his sexual deviance was rising to the surface, Bundy learned he was an illegitimate baby, but still was not told that Louise was his mother. He threw himself into his studies, doing well at school and becoming popular. Psychologists later described him as 'intelligent, high achievement-oriented, had the acumen necessary for a political career'.[53]

At school, Bundy always felt a little out of place, yearning to be more like the wealthy students. He was suspected of committing several robberies to try and obtain things his family could not afford, but was never caught or charged with any offences.[54]

After graduating high school in 1965, he was accepted to the University of Washington, where he commenced studying for a degree in psychology, a weapon he would use to gain the trust of the women he abducted and later murdered, and to play with the psychologists who tried to study him in prison. He claimed that his stealing became more prolific at this time, too.

Bundy sent applications to several law schools between 1969 and 1972 and became actively involved in politics for the first time. He carried out volunteer work at a crisis clinic in Washington, then took a job with the King County Law and Justice Planning Office in Washington State, tracking habitual criminals. During this period, he discovered that his older sister was his real mother, and his mother and father were really his grandparents.

This information forced Bundy to close down part of his life. What he had believed to be a normal and loving family was more dysfunctional than he could have imagined. The shock destroyed his view of his 'normal' upbringing, and he turned his back on his family, returning to his studies with vigour. It was at this time that he learned to use disassociation, a behaviour people display when they are faced with uncomfortable feelings or emotions.[55]

Bundy returned to Washington University and graduated, and in September 1973 went to University of Puget Sound in Tacoma to study law. He started seeing Stephanie Brooks, a young woman he had dated before – she had broken up with when he became belligerent, but seeing his new drive and ambition, she was willing to give him another chance.

On 4 January 1974, Bundy brutally attacked his first victim. Eighteen-year-old student Joni Lenz was found unconscious and bleeding in her apartment bedroom the morning after the attack. Bundy had broken into the woman's room, tearing a rod from the bedhead and savagely raping her with it, causing horrific internal injuries. He had also beaten the woman around the head. Joni was taken to hospital, where she remained in a coma for several months. She survived the attack but was left with brain damage.

Bundy broke up with his girlfriend, Stephanie, in February 1974, purely to make her suffer the same grief he had done when she broke up with him originally. He was angry about the relationship, and found a way to act on those emotions, coupled with the violent fantasies he had been having since puberty – he began raping and murdering young women who looked like his ex-girlfriend.

On the night of 31 January 1974, 21-year-old Lynda Healy was murdered by Bundy in her basement level room at Washington State. Her room showed signs of their struggle and her bed, where Bundy had cut her throat after raping and sodomising her, was covered in blood. The top sheet was missing; Bundy had used it to bundle up his victim and remove her from the room. She was listed as missing for two months before police took the case seriously, having originally believed that she had suffered a bad nosebleed and gone to hospital, disappearing afterwards.

Having murdered his first victim, Bundy commenced a savage killing spree that would last four years. Though he was arrested several times, he would subsequently escape and continue to kill. Initially, he ensured that he remained in control. He was careful to hide his victims' bodies so that it would take months to find them and forensic evidence would be lost to the elements.

On 8 February 1974, Carol Valenzuela, aged 20, disappeared in Vancouver. Her body was found in October, along with the remains of another female who was never identified. The two murders have generally been attributed to Bundy, but the women may also have been the victims of Warren Leslie Forrest, another serial killer operating in the region at the time.[56] Then on 12 March 1974, another college student disappeared. Nineteen-year-old Donna Manson left her dorm room around seven in the evening to walk to a jazz concert on campus. Along the route, she was charmed by Bundy, who possibly offered to walk with her or give her a lift to the concert in the drizzling rain. Either way, he was able to take off with the young Evergreen State student, and Donna wasn't reported missing for six days, as she had a habit of travelling with little notice. She was never seen alive again.

Like Donna, 18-year-old Susan Rancourt disappeared as she walked across her college campus. On the evening of 17 April 1974, Susan had made plans with a friend to see a German film at Central Washington State College, but never arrived. She was last seen leaving a meeting with one of her advisers after nine that evening. It was the one and only time Susan had gone out at night alone, as she had been concerned about the disappearances in the area. Sadly, the risk she took that night cost her life.

Just a few weeks later, on 6 May, Bundy abducted another victim. Roberta 'Kathy' Parks, 21, decided to walk to another dorm to have coffee with friends. Along her way, she met with Bundy, who pretended to have a broken arm. He dropped his books near the young woman, who offered to pick them up for him. He then convinced her to carry them to his car, where he struck her over the head and abducted her.

Twenty-two-year-old Brenda Ball was next to disappear. She was last seen at Flame Tavern in Burien on 1 June 1974. She had told friends she was going to find a ride to Sun Lakes. Toward closing time, she asked one of the musicians at the tavern for a ride, but he was unable to help. She was last seen talking to Bundy in the parking lot. He had his arm in a sling, just as he had done with previous victims. It took Brenda's friends 19 days to realise she had not made it to Sun City and call police to report her missing.

On 11 June 1974, 18-year-old Georgann Hawkins was abducted from behind her sorority house, Kappa Alpha Theta, in Seattle. Georgann had been to a party and was on her way to say goodnight to her boyfriend, and to borrow some textbooks for a Spanish exam she was going to cram for. A friend of Georgann's saw her walking across campus and called out to her from a window. The two students chatted for a few minutes, they said goodnight, and Georgann walked toward her dormitory. When she had not arrived home two hours later, the alarm was raised. Given the recent abductions in the area, the Seattle police took action immediately.

A dorm mother had heard some screams, but thought it was students mucking around outside and did not look to see what was going on. Had the dorm mother looked, she might have noticed Bundy using his broken arm ruse on Georgann. Ted had asked her for help carrying his briefcase to his car and she had obliged. He knocked her unconscious, bundled her into the car and sped away. Bundy later recalled that Georgann had regained consciousness in the car and in her confused state thought he'd been sent to help her with her Spanish exam. He knocked her out again, then pulled over near Lake Sammamish, where he strangled her before raping her.

Bundy was becoming an expert at killing, having got away with at least eight murders. None of the bodies had been found and police were no closer to identifying the person responsible for the abductions. He felt so confident in his abilities and began escalating his crime spree – next, he killed two women on the very same day.

Janice Ott was the first. On 14 July 1974, she was missing her husband, who had stayed on at his practice in Riverside. She left a note for her roommate saying she was going to go for a bike ride around the park at Lake Sammamish. Witnesses told police they saw a girl matching Janice's description talking to a friendly-looking man with a broken arm. It was the last time she was seen alive. Ted abducted her in front of everyone at the park, without raising any suspicions. He took her into the woods, where she was raped and murdered, like the other victims before her.

Janice's murder had happened so quickly and easily that he went back to the same park to abduct another victim. Nineteen-year-old Denise Naslund was having a picnic with friends on Lake Sammamish that day as well. While the others fell asleep in the summer sun, Denise wandered off to the bathrooms, where she was spotted by Bundy. He asked her for help to get something from his car, pointing again to his broken arm, and she was happy to oblige. At his car, she was forced inside and then driven away to Bundy's dump-site, where she was bashed over the head and raped.

With the murders on his mind, Bundy's 'normal' life quickly began to lose its excitement. He soon left his position with Emergency Services and looked to study again. By 30 August 1974, he was a student at the University of Utah College of Law. A week after Bundy started studying for his law degree, bones were found scattered along a 4km stretch near Lake Sammamish State Park, which turned out to be the remains of Georgann Hawkins, Janice Ott and Denise Naslund. This discovery did little to dampen Bundy's drive to kill, but he did decide to find new dumping grounds for subsequent victims.

On 2 October 1974, he abducted 16-year-old Nancy Wilcox in Holladay, raping and sodomising her before killing her. Her body was never recovered. Then on 18 October, another young woman fell victim to his charms. The Midvale police chief's daughter, 17-year-old Melissa Smith, was abducted while walking from home to a girlfriend's house. Nine days later, on 27 October, her bludgeoned and strangled remains were found in Summit Park. Like the other victims, she had been raped and sodomised before her murder. Her skull had been fractured by an instrument similar to a crowbar.

On 31 October, 17-year-old Laura Aime left a Halloween party and went for a wander to a nearby park, where she was abducted by Bundy. She was later found on a riverbank in the Wasatch Mountains on 27 November. Her naked body had been beaten beyond recognition and she had been sexually assaulted.

A little over a week after Laura's murder, on 8 November, 19-year-old Carol DaRonch survived an abduction attempt. At a Waldens Bookstore, she was approached by Bundy, who was posing as a police officer. He asked if she'd parked near Sears, and she said yes, then asked for her license number, which she gave to him. Bundy then told Carol someone had tried to break into her car and she needed to go with him to check if anything was missing. She trustingly followed him out of the building, but felt a sudden apprehension as they headed out into the rainy night. Like the other women before her, she had trusted Bundy quickly; at trial, she described him as 'polite ... well educated'.[57] Nevertheless, she asked him for some ID. He responded by laughing, attempting to make her feel at ease, and showed her a fake identification badge.

When the pair reached Carol's car, she saw that nothing was missing.

He told her they had apprehended a suspect and asked her to go with him to the station in his VW Beetle to see if she knew the suspect. Carol felt that something wasn't right and noticed an aroma of alcohol on the man's breath. Alarm bells sounded, and as they walked toward his VW, she became more worried about the situation she was in. Reluctantly, she got into the car, after he gave her another convincing lie about being undercover. When he told her to put on her seatbelt, she said no and was ready to jump, but he'd already driven off. She realised he was heading away from the local police station.

Bundy suddenly stopped the car and attempted to handcuff her, but in the struggle, he connected both cuffs to the same wrist. He pulled out a small gun and threatened her with it, but she opened the car door and fell out. As she got up, Bundy attacked her with a crowbar he had hidden under the driver's seat. He grabbed her and threw her up against the car, but the diminutive Carol broke free from Bundy's grasp and ran wildly onto the road, where an elderly couple came upon her and took the terrified girl to the police station.

After failing to abduct Carol, Bundy went looking for another victim that same evening. Seventeen-year-old Debby Kent had offered to pick up her brother while her parents stayed behind at her school's drama night. Later, another parent told police he had arrived late at the play and saw a light-coloured VW bug racing away from the school. A quick search by police discovered a small handcuff key in the parking lot. The key fit the cuffs that Carol DaRonch had been wearing when she arrived at the police station. While police investigated the disappearances and the attempted abduction of Carol DaRonch, Laura's body was found on Thanksgiving. Like the others, she had been raped and beaten.

After murdering four young women in a little over a month, Bundy spent the period between Thanksgiving and the New Year without killing. The police had linked many of the disappearances and were searching for a local man in Utah. After the New Year, Bundy headed to Aspen in Colorado for his next murder, where police were not looking for a mass murderer. On 12 January 1975, Caryn Campbell was on a ski trip in Aspen with her fiancée and his kids. After a minor squabble with her partner, she stormed off. When she did not return, he went to their room to see if she was there, but she had not made it to the hotel room Bundy had grabbed the woman as she walked to her room, possibly using the policeman/stolen car ruse once again.[58]

On 18 February 1975, as the weather slowly began to warm, the naked and battered body of Caryn Campbell was found in a snow bank off Owl Creek Road, close to the hotel where she had been holidaying with her fiancée and children. She had been raped before being murdered. Police were quick to compare the injuries that Caryn had sustained with the injuries inflicted on Melissa Smith and Laura Aime. Investigators noted, 'You couldn't look at those photographs and autopsy slides and read those reports without noticing gross similarities.'[59]

Bundy's signature was obvious. He had beaten all of his victims in a frenzied attack, and raped and sodomised them, either before or after their deaths. The victims were all young women with similar features and of good moral standing. Unlike killers who chose prostitutes or victims from low socioeconomic backgrounds, Bundy picked women who would be missed, and who represented the type of woman he wanted to be with. There was even a resemblance to his former girlfriend in the victims, demonstrating that the murders had a retaliatory motivation as well.

On 1 March 1975, the skull of 22-year-old Brenda Ball was found in a thick wooded area on Taylor Mountain. Brenda had been missing since June 1974. The police began a search of the area and soon more gruesome discoveries were made. Parts of the skeletons of Lynda Healy, Susan Rancourt, Donna Manson and Roberta Parks were also found. Lynda Healy's skull had been fractured in the brutal beating she suffered. Susan Rancourt's decapitated skull was also severely fractured.

Again, the discovery of some of his victims did nothing to slow down Bundy's killing spree. On 15 March 1975, 26-year-old Julie Cunningham disappeared while on her way to a nearby tavern, in Vail, Colorado. Her body was never recovered. Then on 6 April, 25-year-old Denise Oliverson decided to go for a bike ride to visit her parents in Grand Junction, after having an argument with her husband. When she didn't return that evening, he assumed she had decided to stay the night at her parents' house, but in fact she had never made it there. Along the way, she'd been abducted by Bundy, and her body remains undiscovered. Nine days later, on 15 April, 18-year-old Melanie Cooley disappeared after walking off from her school, and road workers discovered her body on 23 April at Nederland. She had been bludgeoned to death with a crowbar, like many of the other victims, with her hands fixed behind her back and a pillowcase tied tightly around her neck. On 6 May, 12-year-old Lynette Culver was abducted from her school playground, followed by Susan Curtis from a university campus on 28 June; 24-year-old Shelley Robertson from Golden, Colorado, on 1 July; and Nancy Baird on 4 July, from Layton.

This long and successful killing streak, however, caused Bundy to take more risks. As he searched for another victim on 18 August 1975, stoned, he was arrested in Salt Lake City for evading a police officer. He had seen the police vehicle following him, but knowing that he had marijuana in the car, had chosen to keep driving. Of his arrest, Bundy said, 'I really didn't know what was on my mind or what I wanted to do. I was a little bit fucked up.'[60] When the officer searched the car, he found handcuffs, a crowbar, a ski mask and pantyhose. Bundy was arrested for possessing implements for breaking and entering. While out on bail he murdered another young woman, Debbie Smith, in February 1976.

When the police officer told others about Bundy's car and the handcuffs, an investigating officer quickly suspected a link to the man who had been seen with several of the murdered women before their deaths. Carol DaRonch was brought in to see if she could identify Bundy as her would-be abductor; she did so, and he was placed under arrest.

On 1 March 1976, after a trial in which Bundy represented himself, he was convicted of attempting to kidnap DaRonch in Utah. While in prison, Bundy was also charged with the murder of Caryn Campbell, but on 6 June 1977, he escaped from Pitkin County Courthouse lock-up in Aspen. On 16 June, a very dishevelled Bundy was recaptured, but a jail cell in Glenwood

Springs, Colorado, was again unable to hold him, and on 31 December he escaped once more, and went on the run through Denver, Chicago and Michigan. By 7 January 1978, Bundy had arrived in Tallahassee, Florida, and rented a room in a student boarding house. It had been two years since his last killing. He spent his time roaming nearby campuses, looking for victims.

The Chi Omega sorority house at Florida State University was pretty quiet on the evening of 15 January; the students had no idea that a killer was stalking them. Bundy later recalled that, having been in prison and unable to fulfil his need to kill, the vicious attack at the Chi Omega sorority house was a manifestation of his overdue need to harm.[61]

Sorority house members Karen Chandler, 21, and Kathy Kleiner, 20, went to bed around midnight, 22-year-old Lisa Levy at around 11pm, and Margaret Bowman at around 2.30am, after talking to a girlfriend about a blind date she'd had that evening. Cheryl Thomas returned home around 1.30am. She turned on the TV, made something to eat, and fed her new kitten. Her friend Debbie, who lived in the next room, arrived home soon after and shouted teasingly through the wall for her to turn down the TV.

At 4am, Debbie woke to a strange hammering sound. She slept on a mattress on the floor, so she could feel the whole house vibrating from the thumps. She shook her roommate awake and they listened in fear until there was silence. Then the two women heard Cheryl moaning from the next room. Debbie called Cheryl's room phone – the girls had an agreement to always answer the phone, just to make sure they were safe.

When Cheryl didn't pick up, Debbie called out that she was going to call the police. As the girls were speaking to police, they heard a thunderous crash, as if someone was running and crashing through the kitchen. Debbie and her roommate were shocked to see a dozen police cars arrive at their house within four minutes.

As the sorority sisters headed down the hallway to the dorm-mother's room, Karen staggered out into the hall. She had been savagely beaten and blood was streaming down her face. Seeing Karen, the house-mother hurried to check the other rooms. Kathy was alive, sitting on her bed with her head in her hands and blood was running down her arms from the wounds she had suffered. Her jaw was broken in three places.

Lisa Levy had been beaten, her right nipple almost bitten off, her left collarbone broken, and she had been strangled. A hairspray bottle had been jammed into her vagina and there was a double bite mark on her left buttock, which would later help identify Ted Bundy. Paramedics tried to save her, but she was pronounced dead at hospital.

Margaret Bowman was found lying on her stomach across her bed. She had been beaten across the head with a crowbar, which had shattered her skull instantly. A stocking had been pulled tightly around her throat. She did not survive the attack.

Cheryl was the last of the women to be attacked by Bundy. She was found lying diagonally across her bed, barely conscious, whimpering and writhing in pain. Her face was swollen and turning purple with bruises and she had several serious head wounds. Her skull was fractured in five places (causing permanent hearing loss in her left ear); her left shoulder was dislocated; her jaw was broken; and her cranial nerve was so damaged that she would never have normal equilibrium again. She suffered the worst injuries that night, and was in hospital for a month, but somehow survived the attack. If the girls hadn't shouted out that they were calling the police, Bundy would certainly have killed her. Instead, he fled the scene before police arrived, only escaping by minutes. In his wake, he had left the fullest extent of his brutal homicidal signature.

Less than a month later, Bundy struck again, this time killing his youngest victim. Twelve-year-old Kimberly Leach disappeared on 9 February 1978. She had left class to go and find her wallet, which she had left somewhere in the playground, and was seen by a friend talking to Bundy. It was the last time she was seen alive. On 12 April 1978, after eight weeks of intense searching, her decomposed remains were found hidden in a pigsty. She had been raped before being murdered.

Though Bundy was being sought all over America for the Chi Omega attack, and a string of other murders, it was another traffic stop that brought him to justice. He was arrested by a traffic officer in Pensacola, Florida, on 15 February 1978 for driving a stolen car, and taken into custody, where the officer found that he had arrested American's most wanted killer.

Bundy, representing himself at trial, attempted many different lines of defence during his trial, including insanity, but was sentenced to death, plus 196 years, for the murders of the students at Chi Omega House on 13 July 1979. He was also sentenced to death by electrocution for the murder of Kimberley Leach on 9 February 1980. While in prison, Bundy admitted to the murders of other victims, making the confessions in an attempt to stave off his looming execution date. Often speaking about himself in the third person, he gave details of victims who had not been found, hoping these bargaining chips would save him. But it was too little too late, and on 25 January 1989, Ted Bundy took his final seat in the arms of Old Sparky at Starke Prison, Florida.

When confronted with the question of why he had murdered so many young women, Bundy chuckled to himself and asked, 'Is there really enough time to explain it all?'[62] Reflectively, he explained that he could see how certain feelings that he was experiencing over his lifetime developed to such a point that he needed to act on his destructive fantasies.[63] His killing spree lasted for years and there are still some among his victims who have never been found.

Bundy concealed his earliest murders by hiding his victims' bodies in remote bushland. A similar ruse was used by Australian murderer Ivan Milat in the late 1980s and early 1990s, which allowed him to conceal his crimes for more than five years. The Belanglo State Forest would forever be attached to the family, when another Milat man used the same location to commit murder.

Chapter 4
Ivan and Matthew Milat

Ivan Milat was Australia's worst serial killer, before the crimes of the Snowtown gang took that record from him. Throughout his present incarceration, he has professed his innocence to anyone who will listen, including this author, and sent out hundreds of pages of court transcripts, covered in his own notes, questioning the validity of the arguments raised during his trial. A member of the next generation of Milats, though, would not help his cause. Matthew Milat was Ivan's great-nephew, who admired his great-uncle's notoriety as a famous villain in Australian history. While most children want to grow up to be like their parents, perhaps taking over the family business, Matthew wanted to be a killer like his uncle. He even joked to friends about his homicidal ideas, saying, 'You know what my family does.'[64]

While most of the Milat family chose to distance themselves from their infamous member, Matthew became obsessed. Ivan had been a rapist before he turned to murder, whereas Matthew had grown up listening to the stories and whispers about his uncle, and gone straight to killing.

On 27 December 1944, Ivan Robert Marko Milat was born to his Croatian father, Stephen, and Australian mother, Margaret. He was the fourth child in what would be a large family of 14 children, 10 of whom were boys. The large family lived in a yellow, three-bedroom, weatherboard house in Guildford, on the outskirts of Sydney. Ivan, like most of his brothers, went to Patrician Brothers High School in the south-western Sydney area of Liverpool, while the younger members of the family attended the local schools in Guildford.

At school, Ivan was good at football, but his academic performance was poor. According to him, if you did not achieve to a high standard, 'you would get your butt kicked for not pulling your weight'.[65] Stephen worked seven days a week, yet it was never enough to keep his family from being hungry. Most of the Milat boys left school at a young age and were given the choice to go out and get a job, helping with the bills and boarding at home, or to leave the family and support themselves. Ivan left school at the age of 15 and quickly got a job in road and construction work, but remained in the family home. He would go on to work all over Sydney.

According to Walter, another Milat sibling, Stephen was strict but fair. If any of the children got into strife, he would whack them to the ground, but if they behaved, they were treated well. Ivan, like his brothers, got on well with his father and was described as a devoted son, who always paid his share of the board and kept the house neat and tidy. Ivan also took special care of his younger brother David, who had lost his arm and suffered irreparable brain damage in a car accident as a teen. Wally recalled how other members of the family would get up late on a Sunday and laze around, but that Ivan would get up early and mow the lawn for his father. He was the brother who most strove for his father's praise, and did all he could to support his family, even after he left home.

Set against the backdrop of devoted son and friendly neighbour, there were hints pointing to his later crimes. In 1971, he was brought up on charges of raping two young backpackers and, when released on bail, fled to New Zealand. He remained there for three years. He was rearrested in 1974 when he arrived back in Australia, but the victims refused to testify and the charges were dropped. Prior to the rape charge, Milat had several criminal convictions for car theft, and spent some time in jail and boys' homes for the offences.

Milat returned in the early 1980s when his father, Stephen, was diagnosed with bowel cancer and underwent several operations. During his last operation, Stephen contracted pneumonia, which led to his death at the age of 86. Ivan looked after his mother as much as he could after his father's death and by all accounts was a devoted brother and son. When not helping around the home, Ivan and some of his brothers enjoyed shooting, and were familiar with firearms from an early age. Before strict gun laws were introduced in Australia in the 1980s, a lot of people kept guns, and they were a part of the family's daily life.

Milat began working with the Department of Main Roads at the Central Asphalt at Granville. He was a hard worker and promoted to leading hand. Eventually, he got some of his brothers jobs with the department, too. Milat did the job for about 15 years, when all of the employees in the construction gang were retrenched, following a change of government. With his extensive experience, though, he was quickly hired by Readymix, where he remained until his eventual arrest for murder.

Ivan met his future wife in the late 1970s. They married and bought a house in the western Sydney suburb of Mount Druitt, but divorced in 1989. After the divorce, Milat had a few relationships, though nothing serious, and he met his final girlfriend during the time the murders were being committed. The couple were introduced by Milat's sister Shirley and were still together when he was arrested.

From a very young age, Milat was an impeccably neat person, almost to a compulsive level. His yard was well manicured and he took care of himself physically. Neighbours interviewed after his arrest could not believe he was a wanted killer.[66] They described him as someone who got on well with the children in the street, letting them ride his mini-bike and go-kart along the quiet avenue. He often washed and detailed his car and attended to his perfectly manicured lawn while chatting to his neighbours. But Milat had a dark secret. In the final week of 1989, he turned to murder.

On 29 December 1989, two young people from Victoria, Deborah Everist and James Gibson, told friends they were going to hitchhike together along the Hume Highway to Albury, on the NSW–Victorian border. A few days later, James' camera was found on the side of Galston Road, Galston

Gorge, about 150km in the opposite direction from where the pair had planned to travel. James' backpack was later found in the same location. The two were reported missing two weeks later, but their disappearance provoked little immediate attention, as backpackers would often lose their way for a while or take exciting detours in their attempt to see the world. Before too long, though, their families began to fear the worst.

A little over a year later, on 20 January 1991, 20-year-old German backpacker Simone Schmidl left Sydney. She intended to travel to Melbourne, where she was to meet her mother, Erwinea. Simone, like the other victims, disappeared somewhere along the Hume Highway. When her daughter did not arrive, Erwinea notified police.

On 25 January 1990, five days after Simone was last seen, Englishman Paul Onions got off a train at Casula railway station, a tiny, unmanned station close to the start of the Hume Highway. His intention was to hitchhike from Sydney to Melbourne and the best place to get a lift was at the start of the Hume Highway. He climbed the steep hill from Casula Station and stopped at the little milk bar on the main road, stocking up on drinks for his trip.

While waiting in the milk bar, Paul was approached by a man who introduced himself as Bill. He offered Paul a lift and the tourist readily accepted. He got into the man's 4WD and they were soon heading off down the highway. They made small talk. Paul thought 'Bill' appeared to be a typical Aussie bloke, who wanted to talk about politics, among other things.

Almost two hours later, as the car neared the turn-off to Belanglo State Forest, Bill stopped the car, telling Paul he wanted to get some cassette tapes from under the seat. Paul decided to use the opportunity to stretch his legs and probably saved his own life by doing so.

As he went to hop back in the car, Paul saw that Bill was pointing a gun at him. He told the Englishman, 'This is a robbery ... get back in the car,'[67] as he retrieved some rope from an old bag under the seat. Paul began running away along the highway. Milat gave chase, yelling, 'Stop or I'll shoot! Get back in the car.'[68] He aimed the gun at the hitchhiker and fired. Paul, in fear for his life, zig-zagged across the freeway's two lanes. Milat tackled him to the ground on the grassy median strip but he fought him off and was able to flee once more.

Terrified, Paul ran down the middle of the freeway, attempting to flag a number of cars until one finally screeched to a halt. He jumped into the sliding rear-door of Joanne Berry's van and screamed for her to drive away. Frightened for her children in the backseat, Joanne did as she was told. Paul stared out of the back window, watching the face of his attacker as the car sped away.

Once out of immediate danger, he was able to explain to the woman what had occurred and together they went to Bowral Police Station, where a statement was given. No action was taken on the report, however, and the original record of Paul Onion's statement was lost.

Two German backpackers, 21-year-old Gabor Neugebauer and his girlfriend Anja Habschied, 20, were Milat's next victims. The couple were travelling around Australia when Milat picked them up on 26 December 1991, driving south down the highway from Sydney. The couple were driven to Belanglo State Forest. There, they were sexually assaulted, stabbed and shot. Anja's head was severed in one fatal strike.

A few months later, on 16 April 1992, British backpackers Caroline Clarke and Joanne Walters left a Kings Cross hostel. They were seen several times along their travels, once when getting into a truck at the Caltex service station at Bulli, and again drinking at the Blue Boar Inn in Bowral.[69] The women were last seen at Boxvale Walking Trail picnic area, in the company of a man. Finally, Joanne and Caroline were reported missing, on 27 May 1992 and 5 June 1992, respectively. The two British women were the last to be killed by 'the backpacker killer', but the first to be found.

On 19 September 1992, two men on a map-reading exercise in dense bushland stumbled across the body of Joanne Walters in the north-west area of Belanglo State Forest, an area that the media would incorrectly call 'Executioner's Drop'. The woman had been wedged under a rock ledge, her body only partially covered by a thin layer of leaf matter. She had been gagged with a cloth and two more pieces of her clothing covered her face.

Her body had suffered multiple stab wounds in what could only be called a frenzied attack. The wounds covered the top half of her front and back torso. Forensic evidence later revealed that Joanne had also been sexually assaulted by her killer.

The following day, the body of Caroline Clarke was also discovered by a police search team, just 30 metres from where her friend had been found. Caroline's body was beside a fallen log and covered in leaf debris. Due to this layer of mulch, her body had decomposed faster than that of her travelling companion. Like Joanne, Caroline's head had been covered before her death; this time, the killer appeared to have used a red sweatshirt to dehumanise his victim before killing her. The examination of Caroline's body showed she had been shot 10 times in the head. Of the 10 gunshot wounds, five bullets were recovered from inside the woman's brain, two were found in the red jumper that covered her head, and the remaining three were located under her head on the forest floor. She had also been stabbed in the lower back, rendering her paralysed. Though the evidence was unclear, it is possible Caroline was also sexually assaulted. Ballistics evidence showed, in markings on some of the bullets, that a silencer had been used. Later, during a search of Milat's home, police found a homemade silencer in the garage.

The discovery of the two backpackers' bodies launched an investigation that would not turn up any solid leads for over a year. Though some closure had been achieved for the girls' families, police were still looking for at least five more backpackers who had gone missing in the years prior. Then, at 1.30pm on 5 October 1993, a local man, fossicking along a lonely track with a metal detector in the Belanglo State Forest, stumbled upon a horrific find – what appeared to be a human skeleton. Unlike the bodies of Caroline and Joanne, these remains were completely uncovered and the killer had made no attempt to hide the victim.

Not knowing what to do, the man grabbed the skull and drove to the nearest police station, where he got the full attention of those on shift. With police in tow, he returned to the forest to show them where he had made the discovery. The words 'serial killer' began to be used.

Police began a search of the immediate area around the victim, initially believing the body was that of Anja Habschied, one of the two missing German backpackers. Hours later, as the shadows crept along the forest floor, police discovered a second ghoulish grave, only 25 metres from the body they were investigating, with an old fallen tree as its headstone. When the body was shown to be male, police assumed they had found both the missing Germans. But they were wrong. The bodies were actually those of James Gibson and Deborah Everist, who had gone missing in 1989. Experts said the bodies had been exposed to the elements for between three and five years, disqualifying the Germans, who had last been seen a year earlier. Three days after the bodies were found they were positively identified through dental records as James and Deborah. Their remains were found only 600 metres from Joanne Walters and Caroline Clarke, yet had remained hidden all that time, despite several police searches.

As their bodies had been reduced to bones, finding wounds and a cause of death proved difficult,. There was enough evidence to show that Deborah had suffered many strikes with a knife, with slicing marks found on her bones. She had also been struck with something heavy that fractured her skull. Furthermore, the murderer had broken the young woman's jaw. A knotted pair of pantyhose found near James' body suggested he had been tied up; with James restrained, the murderer knew he would be able to focus on Deborah without being ambushed. This also meant there was no chance of escape, so the attacker could not be identified, leaving him free to kill again. There was no evidence to show if Deborah's killer had raped her.

James' body, though very much decayed, showed evidence that he too had been stabbed, suffering many blows from a knife. A forensic examination revealed he had been stabbed with such ferocity that the murderer had sliced some of his bones clean in half. There were also chip marks on his bones from knife wounds.

The pair's horrific deaths provoked an outcry from the public. The two double murders were clearly the work of a madman, and residents in the nearby towns of Berrima and Moss Vale demanded police work harder to catch the person or persons who had committed the awful crimes. Though many of the townsfolk were sure the murders were the work of the same person, police – though they agreed the locality, killing methods and means of disposal were similar between the four murders – refused to confirm that they were the work of a serial killer. By now the families of Anja Habschied, Gabor Neugebauer and Simone Schmidl, among others, were worried that their children would turn up in the forest.

A month later, as they searched the forest floor for other missing backpackers, police could no longer deny that the murders were the work of a serial killer. Simone's remains were recovered on 1 November, only one-and-a-half kilometres from where the remains of Deborah and James had been found. The sight that greeted police that day was a haunting recurrence of the discovery of the other four victims. Simone's body was lying beside a large fallen log. Like the others, she had been buried in a shallow grave, with leaf mulch as a covering. Her body had suffered horrific stab wounds and the delay between her death and her body being found meant that most of the evidence that would have helped convict her killer had deteriorated.

Three days after the discovery of Simone's body, the remains of Anja Habschied and Gabor Neugebauer were also recovered, taking the death toll to seven. Gabor had been shot six times in the head. Three shots had been fired into the left side of his skull, and a further three to the rear of his skull. Gabor had also been strangled. A piece of cloth was found in the young man's mouth, and another piece of material was found around his face, suggesting it had been tied as a gag. This time, there had been a struggle between the killer and his victim. Gabor had fought back and was shot while he attempted to protect Anja.

Yet Anja had also died, and her death was by far the worst. Her head had been severed from her body in one violent blow – it would have taken great force and a massive, sharp weapon to do such horrific damage in one strike. To date, the young woman's head has not been found; police believe an animal may have carried it away or the killer might have taken it as a souvenir and hidden it. Anja's headless body had probably been raped. The lower half of her body was naked and her clothes were nowhere to be found. Due to the time that had lapsed since her murder, there was not enough evidence to prove conclusively that a sexual assault had occurred.

Police spent months scouring through information from the public. In the mountains of paperwork, there were details about a number of sightings of the missing British backpackers, given to police by a member of the Milat family. The Milats were known to police in the Southern Highlands, and several members of the family were soon put under surveillance.

In the early hours of 22 May 1994, Ivan Milat was arrested on charges of armed robbery and possession of firearms. Though police refused to say whether they had a suspect for 'the backpacker murders', the media knew something was important about Milat, and within a few days he had been charged with the seven brutal murders and one attempted murder of Paul Onions. Meanwhile, heavily armed police swooped on a number of properties in the area, all belonging to the Milat family. Two properties in Hill Top owned by Milat's brother, Walter, were searched – at one, they uncovered enough firearms to outfit a small army, as well as two backpacks, several pieces of clothing, carpet and a leather bag. Walter was arrested for the possession of prohibited weapons. Milat's mother's house in Guildford was searched, as was another home at Mittagong and a property at Bargo, while two hundred police searched a property at Buxton. Richard Milat was arrested at Moss Vale when police descended on yet another house, and a remote property was searched at Wombeyan Caves, as were a further three properties in Ulladulla and Queensland. Police combed through the rugged land mechanically. They dug up acres of bushland surrounding the numerous properties, taking photos and notes at every step. Several cars were meticulously examined for evidence.

While their brother was in jail awaiting trial, Richard and Walter Milat both pleaded guilty to possession of prohibited firearms. Magistrate Peter Ashton convicted Richard on four charges – two for the possession of illegal firearms, including a crossbow, one for the possession of a licence in the name of Paul Miller, and another for the possession of marijuana. Walter was sentenced to seven counts of possession of illegal firearms as well the possession of marijuana in a supply amount. Counsel for the two men was John Marsden, the same lawyer who had represented Ivan Milat many times over the previous decades. Marsden believed the brothers were being treated unfairly, saying, 'Richard obviously likes guns, likes to play with them, and considers them items of pleasure when [the brothers] go and shoot feral animals on his property at Wombeyan Caves … because we find that odd … I don't think we can judge them on that.'[70]

After months of delays, Ivan Milat's trial opened in Sydney in March 1996, with a plea of not guilty. Photographs of the victims' shirts, covered in stab wounds, were splashed across newspapers and television programs. There was a mountain of evidence to consider, each piece just one part of the puzzle. As the case came to its dramatic conclusion, the defence team tried one last tactic, asking the question that many among the public had already raised – was it possible that Ivan had not acted alone? Some who have studied the case are of the opinion that a second, possibly even a third, killer still walked free. Nonetheless, Ivan Milat was found guilty of all seven murders, as well as the attempted murder of Paul Onions. He was sentenced to life imprisonment with the recommendation that he never be released. Since his incarceration, he has gone on several hunger strikes to bring attention to his plight, with little effect.

Police have attempted to connect Milat with the disappearances of other backpackers over the years. At a coronial inquest, he was called to answer questions regarding the disappearances of Deborah Balken and Gillian Jamieson, two 20-year-old nurses who went missing in 1980. During the author's interviews with the killer,[71] there have been many discussions about these unsolved disappearances, but he has emphatically denied any 'involvement'. Pressed for further information, he changed the subject.

Milat wielded extreme power over his victims. Many of the murders exhibited signs of overkill – additional, unnecssary wounds, often being inflicted post-death. He also chose to remove articles of clothing and equipment to keep as trophies. He exhibited a narcissistic attempt to exert power over his girlfriend by having her wear, unbeknownst to her, the clothing of some of the victims. This gave him a pleasurable thrill as he relived the fantasy of the killings.

Having a killer in the family can often produce far-reaching effects in those closest to them. It can be hard to escape the stigma attached to names such as Dahmer, Gacy or Bundy. Recently, the daughter of serial killer Keith Hunter Jesperson spoke out about this. Melissa had grown up being told by her father to be proud of their unusual surname and that who you were was always attached to your name. Yet in April 2013, when speaking with her father in prison (he was arrested when she was 15), he turned to her and said, 'Missy, you need to change your last name.'[72] Killers' family members are often isolated and stigmatised, as the media and society question their culpability in the killer's upbringing, asking, 'How did they raise their child to be like that?' and 'What did they do wrong?'

The scariest question of all, often pointed at the killer's offspring, is: 'Will they turn out like their parents?' Support groups rightly provide assistance to the families of victims, but little is done to help and understand the families of killers. In Australia, the large Milat family found themselves tarred with the same brush as Ivan, which forced many of them to change their distinctive surname.

There is a saying, however, that a tiger cannot change its stripes, and for one member of the Milat family, it rang true. Matthew Milat, the great-nephew of serial killer Ivan, changed his name *from* Meuleman to Milat, telling friends that he wanted to be like his uncle. He would tell people, 'You know me, you know my family. You know the last name Milat.'[73] He was obsessed with his great-uncle and spoke incessantly about him.

In 2010, at the age of 17, Matthew started living with his grandmother and grandfather – Ivan Milat's brother – in Bargo. He had moved in with them following the breakdown of his relationship with his girlfriend, with whom he had a child. Having lived in Bargo when he was younger, he knew many of the local youths, and started hanging out with his old friends Cohen Klein and David Auchterlonie. Matthew had reportedly been an easygoing teenager until he fell in with his old gang of schoolmates again. The gang would often terrorised the neighbourhood, driving their cars down the back streets at great speeds, and were known for smoking marijuana and looking for trouble. One evening, Milat decided he would take their fun further. He convinced his friend, Cohen Klein, to help him kill someone.

David Auchterlonie turned 17 on 20 November 2010. He spent his birthday with those he loved and had a nice meal with his family. Matthew Milat and Cohen Klein, meanwhile, spent their day smoking marijuana and messing about. Milat brought up the subject of killing someone, as he did regularly. He told Klein he wanted to get a group of mates together that night and kill someone at Belanglo State Forest, the dumping ground his great-uncle had used. Milat mentioned his friend David as a possible victim, messaging and telephoning David several times as he tried to plan the night's events. David told his mate, Chase Day, that Milat had rung using Klein's phone, saying they planned to go that evening 'to Belanglo to have a few drinks and a bit of fun'.[74] Milat insisted that David and Chase go with them. He told the boys they were going to smoke marijuana and get drunk in the pitch-black darkness of the forest, but said something very different to Klein: 'We are going to Belanglo and someone's going to die.'[75]

David and Chase waited for Milat and Klein to collect them from a corner near Chase's home. A little after 9.30pm, the group of four boys stopped at the well-known twin petrol stations just near Sutton Forest, a standard place to stop for those travelling between Sydney and Canberra. Milat and David entered the large service centre, looking for a pair of scissors to cut up their marijuana leaves. While David paid for the scissors, the other three decided they wanted some hamburgers, and all four headed to a nearby fast food restaurant. They purchased burgers and hot chips for their short trip into Belanglo.

Matthew and the boys drove out into the middle of the forest, eating their food in the car. Milat and Klein were in the front, David and Chase in the back. When they arrived at an unsealed dusty crossroad, where the forest spread out beyond the pine plantation, Milat pulled the car over, got out and headed towards the rear of the car. The other three boys remained in the car. David climbed into the front seat to start cutting up the marijuana while he played music on his mobile phone.

Klein became unnerved. He got out of the car and joined Milat outside. While the two spoke, he pressed record on his mobile phone, capturing the next horrific 15 minutes. Later, the prosecutor called it a trophy, which the two boys would later use to relive the murder.

In the recording, Milat and Klein can be heard talking. Klein says to Milat, 'Yeah, go for it,' to which Milat replies, 'Can you feel the adrenaline?' Klein agreed that he could and returned to the car. He told David to go to the boot to see if there was a bong. When David got out and went to the rear of the car, he was met by Milat, who was holding a double-bladed axe. Milat swung and struck David in the stomach with one edge of the blades. Hearing his friend cry out, Chase got out of the car to see what had happened, but was told by Klein to get back inside. Klein also got inside the car, but held his mobile phone out the window to record everything that occurred.

Already bleeding from the first wound, David tried to escape by running around the car. During the pursuit, Milat struck the teenager again, causing him to fall to the ground. Though Matthew claimed to be as dangerous as his uncle, the sound recording proved he was not as cold-blooded. The recording provided the evidence that, as David lay crying on the ground, he looked up to his supposed friend and begged for his life. Matthew could not act with his friend looking at him and repeatedly told David to look away. More than half a dozen times, Milat told David to look away: 'Look at the fucking dirt, Auchto. I am going to fucking kill you if you keep fucking moving.'

Milat swung the axe again and struck David in the back of the skull, as his victim looked down at the forest floor. The sound of Milat hitting David can be heard on the recording. Once David was dead, Milat casually walked back to the car, carrying the bloodstained axe. Chase got out to see what had happened and saw his friend lying dead on the forest floor. He dragged his friend's body away from the dirt track and, helping Milat, covered the body with branches from nearby trees. The boys then got into the car and drove back to Bargo. Chase was threatened and told not to tell police what had happened. Klein spent the night sleeping in the car at a friend's home, while Milat watched movies at another friend's house.

The following day, Chase told his parents what had occurred, and Milat and Klein were soon arrested for the murder of David Auchterlonie. The recording by then had been deleted, but computer technicians were able to retrieve it, giving the prosecution the best possible case against the two boys. They were both found guilty and given extensive jail sentences. The judge who presided over Matthew Milat's trial called him a danger to the community, who showed little remorse for what he had done. In prison, Matthew has written many poems about murder and being a killer, with such lines as, 'I am not fazed by blood or screams, nothing I do will haunt my dreams.'[76]

The Milat family had spawned two killers over three generations. Yet that is nothing compared with the Snowtown killings, in which wives, sons, brothers, friends and mates were all involved – as victims, killers or sometimes both – in a dysfunctional environment arising from a hatred of sexual depravity and greed.

Chapter 5
The Snowtown Killers

There is a meme floating around the internet that says, 'Why test products on animals when we have jails full of paedophiles?' Many people 'like' the image and pass it on. Why subject innocent animals to cruelty, their reasoning goes, when there are convicted felons who have inflicted cruelty on others?

In a civilised society, we rely on our protective and custodial services to mete out justice and see that it is done according to the due process of law. On occasion, however, there are individuals who appoint themselves as judge, jury and executioner.

A case in point occurred in Wollongong, on the south coast of New South Wales in Australia, where a serial killer murdered two men he believed were paedophiles. The violent deaths of both victims were horrific, yet this crime paled in comparison to the series of murders that occurred South Australia, where a gang of killers murdered anyone who made it onto their charismatic leader's list. 'Paedophiles were doing terrible things to children and innocent children were being damaged … The authorities did nothing about it, I was very angry … Someone had to do something about it. I decided to take action and I took that action.' At trial, Robert Joe Wagner tried to explain his actions, positioning the 'Snowtown Gang' as a group of vigilantes.[77]

The case of the Snowtown Gang is one of the worst serial murder cases in Australian history. The gang were responsible for the murders of at least 12 people. The reasoning behind many of the killings was greed (they pocketed money from their victims and cashed their welfare cheques), as well as a vigilant stance against gays and paedophiles, all fuelled by an obsession with torture and murder. Many of the bodies were later found in the infamous bank vault in Snowtown, which gave the case its name.

To understand the nature of these murders, it's important to get a grasp on the relationships and family ties among the murderous group and their victims. John Justin Bunting, the leader of the gang, was born in 1966, the only child of Tom and Jan Bunting. He was obsessed with murder and violence from an early age. He wielded great influence over the members of his group, using threats of physical harm, and by ensuring they always had more to lose – including their lives. Bunting was in a relationship with one of the victims, Suzanne Allen, who in turn had been in a relationship with another victim, Ray 'Jimmy' Davies. Bunting also dated then-married Elizabeth Harvey, the mother of killer James Vlassakis and victim Troy Youde. Victim Veronika Tripp was alleged to be another of Bunting's girlfriends.

Bunting had a hatred for paedophiles and those who he believed gave little to society. His disgust was based on his own childhood sexual abuse at the hand of a friend's brother when he was eight. Bunting claimed that he was taken into the bedroom of the teenage perpetrator, where he was beaten and raped.[78] He spent most of his life reliving the abuse he had suffered, and was desperate to exercise power as an adult, in contrast to the helplessness he had felt as a child. He obsessed over revenge and anyone that crossed his path who fitted his criteria would find themselves on Bunting's 'list' of future victims. He ensured that he had complete control over who lived and who died, just as he did with the wild and domestic animals he encountered. He was present at every single murder committed by the gang, manipulating the others to do his bidding.

Growing up, Bunting enjoyed torturing small animals; to the horror of his school friends, he kept a small jar of acid in which to drown insects and small rodents. The animal torture later manifested itself as a keen interest in anatomy. He poured over textbooks on the subject, and soon found work in a crematorium, then an abattoir. He delighted in telling people about the gruesome deaths of animals at the abattoir, saying he enjoyed his work immensely.[79] At the age of 22, he killed his flatmate's dog, as well as other neighbourhood dogs and cats that strayed on to his property.[80]

Mark Ray Haydon was second-in-charge after Bunting and an active member in the gang's murderous campaign. He had been a shy and retiring child who was regularly beaten and abused by his mother, and was a loner until he met Bunting, with whom he shared a passion for revenge. Haydon was married to victim Elizabeth 'Audrey' Haydon and was slightly older than Bunting. Bunting dated Haydon's sister and later his sister-in-law.

Robert Joe Wagner was another of the killers, nicknamed Papa Smurf for his ability to make victims turn blue by strangling them. He, like Bunting, had been sexually abused as a child and took great pleasure in killing his victims, taking his instructions to choke them from Bunting. He was in a sexual relationship with victim Barry Lane, who had introduced Wagner to Bunting. Wagner claimed to be heterosexual, but after leaving home at the age of 14 to escape abuse, had come under the guidance of the much older Lane. He expressed to Bunting his hatred of Lane for supposedly forcing him into the homosexual relationship,[81] and Wagner was the only homosexual whom Bunting accepted. He also acted as an informant for Bunting about gay men in the local community. The two men were best friends. Barry Lane himself would be involved in one of the murders, and was in a relationship with another victim, Thomas Trevilyan.

Nineteen-year-old James Vlassakis was another of the killers. He was the half-brother of two of the victims, Troy Youde and David Johnson, though these two did not share parents. Elizabeth Harvey was another alleged killer and the Vlassakis' mother; she also dated John Bunting. She died of cancer before she was able to stand trial.

Throughout his life, Bunting was preoccupied with murder, and talked often about killing people. He would tell anyone who listened, particularly the transient people who came and went constantly from his house, that he believed gays and paedophiles didn't deserve to live. He talked about how he would torture and bury them, and by August 1992, he was ready to turn his fantasies into reality.

Clinton Trezise was a 22-year-old homosexual who had dated Barry Lane, a transient who spent a lot of time at Bunting's home. Lane, though also homosexual, was welcomed by Bunting, particularly as he was in a relationship with Robert Wagner, one of Bunting's closest friends. Trezise was last seen at Bunting's home on the last day of August 1992. Bunting knew of Clinton's sexual orientation, but wasn't sure if he was 'into kids as well'[82] – regardless, Bunting said he 'didn't deserve to live'.[83] Clinton, nicknamed 'Happy Pants' by Bunting, was set upon by Bunting, Wagner and Lane. He was dragged into the bathroom, where Wagner bashed the young man over the head with a hammer, while Bunting used a shovel to hit him in the face. The brute force of Bunting's blows crushed the man's skull. The other men bashed and choked the dying man. The body was cut into pieces and taken to Lower Light a few days later. The men buried the body in a shallow grave.

Barry Lane was excited by his participation in the murder and told others what had occurred, but when friends of Clinton confronted Bunting with Lane's story, the psychopath dismissed the story as a lie. The eventual discovery of Clinton's remains two years later was reported on television programme *Australia's Most Wanted*. While watching the show, Bunting boasted to a very young James Vlassakis that it was 'his handiwork'. Wagner added, 'We buried someone out there.'[84]

Twenty-six-year-old Ray 'Jimmy' Davies was the next to die at the hands of Bunting and his friends, three years after the murder of Clinton Trezise. Jimmy was a mentally handicapped man who resided in a caravan on Suzanne Allen's property in Salisbury North. Suzanne Allen was dating Bunting at the time. On Christmas Day 1995, the friendship between Suzanne and Davies soured when Suzanne's grandsons told her, and her daughter Annette Cannon, that Jimmy had sexually molested them. Suzanne and her daughter took the boys to the police station that same day and made a formal complaint against Jimmy. They also told Bunting what had allegedly transpired.

When Suzanne and her family returned home, Jimmy had disappeared from the caravan, leaving all his belongings behind. He had been sleeping in a car outside the caravan when Bunting and the others paid him a visit. Bunting and Wagner assaulted the man, and forced him into Bunting's car. The gang then headed with their kidnap victim towards the Adelaide Hills. Wagner spent the trip beating the man as he cowered on the floor in the rear of the car.

When they arrived in remote bushland near Swan Reach, the men spent the next few hours torturing the man. They made Jimmy hand over his bank cards, PIN access codes and welfare payment details. Once they were happy with the information they had received, they drove Jimmy back to Bunting's home, where he was dragged into the bathroom and strangled with car jump-starter cable leads, before being stabbed to death. In his later confession, James Vlassakis stated that Bunting told him his mother Elizabeth Harvey had helped stab the man to death. The man's body was then dumped in a hole Bunting had made for a water tank in his backyard. Bunting hauled Davies' caravan away and sold it. He also cashed the victim's subsequent fortnightly pension payments.

By November 1996, Suzanne Allen shared this makeshift grave. Bunting broke off his relationship with Allen after complaining that she sent him compulsive letters; according to Bunting, she refused to accept the relationship had broken down and continued to try to see him. He said that he and Wagner came home to find 47-year-old Suzanne dead of a heart attack, and at trial, the charge for her murder was dismissed due to lack of evidence. According to Vlassakis' testimony, however, Wagner and Bunting choked the woman to death before dismembering her body and de-fleshing many of her bones. Her remains were put into 11 plastic bags and buried in the same hole as Ray 'Jimmy' Davies, which was later covered in concrete. Again, Bunting continued to receive the woman's welfare payments, and was captured on bank security footage cashing them.

When Suzanne wasn't seen for several days, she was reported missing by her neighbours. Police were called again when Bunting and Wagner were witnessed removing furniture and other items from the dead woman's home. When questioned, they said they were helping her move. Telephone calls to the woman were answered by Elizabeth Harvey, who claimed Suzanne was unable to come to the phone, and Bunting fraudulently signed over Suzanne's car to Elizabeth Harvey.

After Suzanne's death, Bunting, Elizabeth Harvey and her two sons, James Vlassakis and Troy Youde, moved to a new house at Murray Bridge. They kept in contact with Robert Wagner, who lived in Elizabeth Grove, 100 kilometres away. The two men were partners-in-crime and there was no way Bunting was going to release his hold over him. He made regular visits and continued to remind his gang of what he was capable of.

Having got away with multiple murders and taking the victims' welfare payments, Bunting saw no reason to end his killing, and his preoccupation with paedophilia had reached fever pitch. He was aware that one of Elizabeth Harvey's previous partners used to abuse both her sons, James Vlassakis and Troy Youde, and that Troy later sexually abused the younger James. Bunting could not stand the thought of homosexuality or paedophilia, both of which repulsed him; he believed they were one and the same.

Michael Gardiner was the next target for John Bunting. The 19-year-old was last seen in early September 1997 and had discussed with friends his plans to move house. Bunting had shown distaste for the openly homosexual man, who wore women's clothing on occasion, believing he was also a paedophile. The man, whom Bunting called the 'biggest homo',[85] was abducted from a home owned by a cousin of Wagner's de facto wife in Elizabeth Grove. Bunting and Wagner grabbed him and drove him back to Bunting's home. Once inside the home, Michael was systematically abused and tortured. He was burned with live wires and suffered several burns to his scrotum and penis. A small handheld firework was lit and forced down his urethra, causing internal burns. Bunting then crushed each of the man's toes with a pair of pliers, while the other killers burned his face and ears with cigarettes. Then one of the men twisted a rope around the man's throat using a tyre iron until he choked to death. Pathology reports later showed that

Michael had ingested methadone, although he was not a drug-user. After his death, Michael's limbs were removed. The body parts were stuffed into a large blue barrel, which Bunting had purchased only weeks before with plans to store subsequent bodies – just as serial killer Jeffrey Dahmer had done a decade earlier.

Bunting, Wagner and the others returned to the man's rented house and ransacked it, searching for his wallet and bank details, but they left empty-handed. The men then decided to get Michael's landlord, Nicole Zuritta, to find it for them. They made several threatening phone calls to the frightened woman, demanding she hand over the murdered man's wallet and personal items. Michael's voice was included in the phone calls – the killers had made the man record messages as they tortured him. James Vlassakis was finally sent to Nicole's home to collect the items. She reluctantly handed them over once the killer had convinced her Michael was alive and safe elsewhere.

The murders were gaining momentum. So far the gang had killed four people in the space of five years – now eight more people would lose their lives in the next 18 months.

A little over a month after the murder of Michael Gardiner, Barry Lane found himself on Bunting's list of people who deserved to die, after having spent several years as an apparent friend and fellow killer himself. Lane had been in a sexual relationship with Wagner until it soured, with Wagner making it clear to Bunting that the relationship had been conducted through coercion. In October 1997, 42-year-old Barry was forced to call his mother and sister to tell them he was moving to Queensland. The phone calls seemed strange to the women, who could hear other voices in the background, prompting the man through the conversations. Then, once Bunting knew no one would look for the man, he planned his murder. His motive was that he believed Lane had sexually abused Wagner from the age of 14. He was also worried by Lane's confessions to friends that he had assisted in the murder of other victims. He had to be silenced.

Lane was bashed repeatedly by Bunting, Wagner, Vlassakis and Haydon. His lover, 18-year-old Thomas Trevilyan, was convinced to join in the murder. too One of the men took a pair of pliers and crushed Barry's toes as he screamed in pain. He was then put in the bathtub, where the men took turns to hit him in the genitals. He was eventually strangled to death with a tyre iron garrotte. His body was wrapped in carpet and left in the house for several days before being dismembered and put into one of the blue barrels in Bunting's back shed. Over the ensuing months, Wagner withdrew more than $15,000 in welfare payments from Lane's bank accounts.

Thomas Trevilyan knew his days were numbered after the murder of his lover – Bunting was already watching him. That did not stop Thomas, though, from talking about his part in Barry's murder. He moved in with Wagner and his fiancée. She didn't like the idea of the man living with them, but Wagner told her he wouldn't be around for long. He just wanted to keep a close eye on the next victim until it was time to act.

On Tuesday 4 November 1997, Thomas was witnessed terrorising the daughter of one of Bunting's friends, chasing the girl around the yard with a knife. The little girl was holding a puppy and Thomas was determined to kill 'the mutt'. When Bunting heard about the incident, he decided the time had come. While the rest of Australia was watching television coverage of the country's most famous horse race, the Melbourne Cup, Bunting and Wagner grabbed the teenager from Wagner's home and drove him to his death. They stopped the car at a secluded area near Kersbrook, tied a rope around Thomas' throat, then tied the loose end around the branch of a tree. Thomas was hoisted up and forced to stand on a milk crate. As he begged for his life, Bunting kicked the crate out from beneath the man's feet. He dropped to his death, choking at the end of the rope. The young man's body was found hanging at One Tree Hill the following day. Police believed he had chosen the secluded spot himself; Thomas, a diagnosed and medicated schizophrenic, had attempted suicide twice before, once in a similar manner. Police closed the case as a suicide, with no idea that a group of killers in the area were simply becoming more imaginative.

James Vlassakis had looked up to Bunting as a father figure, but seeing him murder six people weighed heavily on the teenager. He became a heavy drug user, turning to heroin to block out the horrors he'd seen. He became friends with another drug user, Gavin Porter, and both teenagers moved in with Bunting. After he was pricked by a needle left lying around the house, Bunting soon added drug addicts to his list of people who should die.

While Vlassakis was out one evening, Bunting and the others set upon Porter, who had passed out in the back of a car on the property. Gavin was brutally beaten before Wagner strangled him to death. Meanwhile, the others ordered takeaway food. The boy's body was placed in another of Bunting's blue acid vats and the gang again impersonated the murder victim to withdraw the government payments he had received.

The next to die was James' half-brother, Troy Youde, who had been on Bunting's list for a long time. In August 1998, in the middle of the night, Troy was handcuffed and dragged into the bathroom, where he was beaten and tortured. Youde, like the others, was forced to record messages to loved ones. Bunting knelt down in front of the frightened man and started reciting the names, with prompts from Wagner, of his victims so far: 'Happy Pants … Jimmy … Barry … Michael … Gavin … Oh, there's too many.'[86] Youde was then gagged and beaten again. A rope was placed around his throat and he was garrotted, with Bunting ordering James to kick his half-brother's dead body.

The next victim was Frederick Brooks, who had been living with his mother Jodie Elliot and his aunt Elizabeth Haydon. Elizabeth was married to Mark Haydon and Jodie was dating Bunting. Bunting had regularly called Brooks a paedophile and the man had made it onto his list. In September 1998, at Bunting's insistence, Brooks was handcuffed by Vlassakis and a pair of thumbcuffs were also applied. Wagner forced him to make recordings and give over his bank account details. Brooks was then gagged and shocked with electricity before being murdered. His body was transferred to Haydon's home a few days later, where he was dumped in a large pit.

Police had no idea a serial killer gang was operating in the outskirts of Adelaide and the men continued to murder with reckless abandon. Their next victim was Gary O'Dwyer, a man who had become disabled in a car accident and was living on welfare payments. He was not known by Bunting, but the men saw him and decided to act. O'Dwyer, after chatting to Bunting and Wagner, invited them into his house. At Bunting's signal, Wagner grabbed the victim by the throat and choked him. The man's dismembered body, like the others, was placed in a barrel in the shed. Mark Haydon's wife, Elizabeth, was next. The decision to kill her was made without Haydon's knowledge – Bunting believed that she had told people about the murders they'd committed, and only Bunting and Wagner knew she was slated to die. Like the others, she was taken to the bathroom, where she was beaten, gagged and had a noose wrapped around her throat. Her body was also placed into a barrel.

The following day Elizabeth's brother reported her missing. Police investigated, and uncovered the shed where the bodies had been kept – by that time, though, Bunting had moved the barrels to the disused bank vault in Snowtown, a small town nearby. Police continued their investigations and found that several missing persons could be linked to the men who had last seen Elizabeth. They set up listening devices on several of the men's homes and recorded conversations that alluded to the bank vault.

Another victim was murdered before police could act. David Johnson, James' step-brother, was killed on 9 May 1999. Pretending to have a cheap computer for sale, James enticed David to the bank vault at Snowtown, where Wagner and Bunting were waiting. Inside the vault, the men beat David, forcing him to reveal his bank details. They again made him record messages to friends and family. Then they drove to a nearby teller machine, leaving David with Bunting at the vault. David, being taller and stronger than the short and dumpy Bunting, tried to fight back – he kicked Bunting in the ribs, breaking several bones – but Bunting overpowered the young man and forced him to the floor. When Wagner and Vlassakis returned empty-handed from the ATM, Wagner went crazy and beat the man to death. His body, like the rest, was placed in a barrel.

On 20 May 1999, police let themselves into the disused bank on the main street of Snowtown, to investigate what they had learned from conversations in the bugged houses. The officers moved through the building, looking for evidence that could link the missing people to Bunting and the others. As they came closer to the vault, they were met with the horrific smell of death and decay. With a video camera at the ready, one of the officers moved into the vault, where they found the eight barrels. An officer took the lid off the closest drum and uncovered mutilated human remains. Many of the officers recoiled in horror at the stench that emanated from the vault.

As more law enforcement and the media descended on the sleepy town of Snowtown, many stayed as far from the vault as possible, as the smell of rotting flesh began to reach the street. Technicians worked in short shifts in the close confines, combing every inch of the vault for clues that might identify the killers. In total, eight bodies were found in the barrels. For ghoulish sightseers, the discovery would put Snowtown on the macabre map.

The barrels and their ghastly contents were eventually removed from the scene and taken away for official identification. The killers had made a critical mistake – rather than filling the barrels with sulphuric acid, they had used hydrochloric acid, expecting that it would destroy the bodies; in fact, the acid had preserved most of the body parts. With the bodies of the missing victims recovered, police swooped on Bunting, Wagner, Vlassakis and Haydon.

Vlassakis was the first to confess, and after his mother's death from cancer in 2001, the young man had little left to hide. The first thing he did was point police towards several plastic bags buried in shallow graves in what had been Bunting's yard. These contained the dismembered bodies of Ray Davies and Suzanne Allen. With the eight bodies in the barrels and two found in the yard, police began looking at other suspicious deaths from the previous years. They added the murder of Clinton Trezise, discovered in a shallow grave in 1994, and the supposed suicide of Thomas Trevilyan.

Following his confession, Vlassakis was charged with four counts of murder, to which he pleaded guilty. He then turned state's witness and testified against his co-accused, Bunting, Haydon and Wagner. Facing 12 counts of murder, the three men denied the charges,[87] but Wagner changed his plea to guilty for three of the later murders. Bunting was found guilty of 11 murders and Wagner of a further seven, on top of the three he had admitted. The two were sentenced to life in prison and no parole period was set. Haydon pleaded guilty to assisting in the murder of Troy and his wife Elizabeth and was given 25 years in prison. In sentencing the men, Justice Brian Martin said, 'If I had the power to make an order for them never to be released, I would unhesitatingly make that order.'[88]

The case was a tangled web of revenge, vigilantism and greed. Bunting and his followers preyed mostly on people they believed or assumed to be paedophiles, namely Trezise, Davies, Gardiner, Lane, Youde, Brooks, O'Dwyer and Johnson,[89] as well as those they called a 'waste',[90] such as Porter, murdered for his drug abuse. Lane, Trevilyan and Elizabeth Haydon were killed because they knew about the other murders, and welfare benefits were stolen from most of the victims.

The gang believed that, by killing those they thought were sexually interfering with children, they were righting the wrongs that had happened to them. Led by Bunting's blood lust, the gang of fractured and damaged killers could do little to reject his plans – otherwise they, like Lane, Haydon and Trevilyan, could have found themselves in a barrel.

Chapter 6
Timothy McVeigh

Bullying and harassment can have long-term, far-reaching effects on the individual. A victim of bullying will often lose the ability to make long-term friendships in adulthood. They may become morose and depressed and a previously outgoing child might start to fail at school. While the media often blames bullying for such cases as the Columbine school shooting, discussed later in this book, it is rare that it will lead directly to murder. Victims of bullying usually internalise their problems and in the most extreme cases, when they feel they have no other option to escape the daily barrage of taunts, abuse and physical violence, will resort to taking their own life in the safety of their home. When bullying becomes murder, as in the case of the hate crimes against both Matthew Sheppard and Brandon Teena, who were both murdered by peers due to their sexual preferences and identity, society must question how another person's differences could provoke someone to kill. But we also need to examine those rare occasions when murder is a retaliatory act by those who have been bullied.

There are many consequences of being bullied, as mentioned earlier – victims learn to internalise their problems, and suffer anxiety and depression.[91] In an attempt to avoid further bullying, they become withdrawn and introverted, trying to prevent further attacks. But it is this reactive nature of a bullying victim, coupled with other indicators, that can see them cause death and destruction.

'It was a beautiful day in Oklahoma City – at least, it started out as a beautiful day. The sun was shining. Flowers were blooming. It was springtime in Oklahoma City.'[92] So said the prosecutor in his opening statement, in the case against 'the Oklahoma bomber'. On 19 April 1995, Timothy McVeigh, a 27-year-old ex-soldier, had parked a rented truck in front of the Alfred P. Murrah Federal Building in Oklahoma City. He got out of the driver's seat, closed the door behind him and casually headed toward the getaway vehicle, driven by his friend and co-conspirator Terry Nichols. He placed tiny protective plugs into his ears and ignited two timing devices as he drove away. Just above the explosive-packed rental truck was a childcare centre, where children of employees in the building spent their days. Moments after the explosives were detonated, 168 people, including 19 children, were killed, as upper floors concertinaed down onto the floors below. Hundreds more were injured and 300 surrounding buildings were damaged in the blast.[93] Until September 11, it was the worst terrorist attack ever carried out on US soil.

As a small boy in Pendleton, NY, Timmy McVeigh was the second of three siblings. He began life as a typical child. Many children would play together in the street or eat at each others' homes in the mostly middle-class and white community. Vicki Hodge, a neighbour, remembers the bomber with fondness as a 'clown, always a happy person'.[94]

All that changed when the boy was 10 and his parents divorced. McVeigh went to live with his mechanic father Bill and his new life was far from idyllic. As a quiet and stable home life was pulled out from under him, the lanky 10-year-old became the victim of bullies at his new school. He was subjected to regular beatings and had his head flushed in the toilet on more than one occasion. His pleas for help from his father and teachers were ignored and he soon learned to hate people in authority, as well as the bullies. This hate would shape the rest of his life.[95]

He knew he had to learn to defend himself and soon fell under the influence of his grandfather (and gun enthusiast) Eddie. He had finally found a connection to someone in his family, which made him feel like he belonged, but it was not enough to bring McVeigh out from the shadows of the bullying he had endured.

A loner in his young life, McVeigh began teaching himself survival skills and trained in marksmanship. He would spend hours away from the bullies' taunts, 'shooting holes in soft-drink cans in a ravine'.[96] The reality of school life slipped away as McVeigh, a boy of average intelligence who did well academically, found little to entice him from his fantasy world of guns. The second Amendment to the Constitution of the United States, which specifies the right to bear and keep arms, was a mantra for the boy. He also became a survivalist, stockpiling food and weaponry as he waited for the overthrow of the government or the outbreak of war. Though he boasted in his high school yearbook about finding 'California girls' after graduation, he was frightened of the opposite sex, and it has been suggested that he never had sexual relations with a female at all during his life.[97]

At the age of 20, after dropping out of computer school and floating between menial jobs, McVeigh joined the army. There, he made new friends: Terry Nichols, his platoon leader in basic training, who shared McVeigh's paranoid ideas about the government;[98] and Michael Fortier. McVeigh's commander, Master Sergeant James David Hardesty, called the cadet a standout and saw a lot of potential in him,[99] but after spending several years serving at Fort Riley in Kansas, McVeigh received a discharge after failing to make it into the Green Berets.

He took a menial job as a security guard, fighting a deep depression, and immersed himself in what he believed to be the decline of America, also the title of a 1992 letter he wrote to *Lockport Union-Sun* newspaper. He also wrote to his local congressman about a woman's rights to carry mace in her purse. In his February 1992 letter, he wrote: 'I strongly believe in a God-given right to self-defence. Should any other person or a governing body be able to tell a person that he/she cannot save their own life, because it would be a violation of the law? In this case, which is more important: faced with a rapist/murderer, would you pick a) die a law-abiding citizen or b) live and go to jail? It is a lie if we tell ourselves that the police can protect us everywhere, at all times.'[100] His anger with and questioning of government officials was nearly at breaking point.

Watching the violent August 1992 standoff between federal agents and Randy Weaver, an alleged white supremacist, was a possible catalyst for the solidification of McVeigh's beliefs and plans. McVeigh saw Weaver as a man who had been protecting his home from intruders, and the standoff, during which Weaver's wife and child were killed, as proof that the government was untrustworthy. Only a few months before this incident, his friend Terry Nichols had renounced his US citizenship, sending a letter to the government asserting that he was 'no longer a citizen of the corrupt political corporate state of Michigan and the United States of America'.[101]

McVeigh left the home he shared with his father and lived sporadically with both Terry Nichols and Michael Fortier between 1993 and 1995. The three men, who shared paranoid political views and opposed gun control laws, would travel to gun shows espousing their views. The Randy Weaver incident had planted the seed that the government was spying on and killing its own people, and the April 1993 siege of a Branch Davidian complex at Waco, Texas, was the final straw for McVeigh. Eighty people died in the standoff, which saw the compound burn to the ground. The event set McVeigh and Nichols to plotting revenge on the United States. They even travelled to the Waco compound to hand out flyers about gun control, and sent letters to many government officials, which discussed the use of violence against federal agents as 'retaliation for the events in Waco'.[102]

While staying with Fortier, Nichols and McVeigh were introduced to marijuana and crystal meth. While high, the men would plan ways to fight against the United States and the United Nations. The pair would head out into the Arizona desert, where McVeigh practised making his own explosive devices, which grew more and more elaborate. Fortier knew what they were plotting, but refused to be part of their plan to 'blow up the Federal Building in Oklahoma City, Oklahoma'.[103]

By 1994, McVeigh and Nichols had started working from McVeigh's new home in Arizona, which he had transformed into a survivalist's bunker, planning to destroy the Alfred P. Murrah Federal Building in Oklahoma. They chose the building for the government agencies it housed, including the Drug Enforcement Agency (DEA), Bureau of Alcohol, Tobacco, Firearms and Explosives (ATF), and military recruitment agencies. Disguising themselves and using fake names, McVeigh and Nichols began purchasing the ingredients they needed to make a 3,000–6,000 pound bomb, large enough to destroy the building and make a global impression.

So it was that, at 9am on 19 April 1995, McVeigh pulled a large, rented Ryder Truck into a vacant parking spot right out front of the building, and casually got out of the driver's seat. According to Prosecutor Joseph Hartzler at McVeigh's trial, he was there to settle a grievance: 'The truck was there to impose the will of Timothy McVeigh on the rest of America and to do so by premeditated violence and terror, by murdering innocent men, women and children, in hopes of seeing blood flow in the streets of America.'[104] Hartzler's impassioned opening speech succinctly explained the characteristics of a man determined to cause destruction for his own reasons. He continued: 'The only reason that [the victims] are no longer with us, no longer with their loved ones, is that they were in a building owned by a government that Timothy McVeigh so hated that with premeditated intent and a well-designed plan he had developed over months and months before the bombing, he chose to take their innocent lives to serve his twisted purpose. In plain, simple language, it was an act of terror, violence, intended to serve selfish political purpose.'[105]

McVeigh's paranoia about the US government's attempts to control people – in itself a delusion of bullying on a grand scale – was his key motive. Since the age of 10, when his life had been turned upside down and he became the victim of bullying, he had felt himself to be persecuted. Hartzler made sure to point out the contradiction between the bomber's total disregard for others' lives and his own need to protect himself by the fact that he wore earplugs during the explosion.

After the bombing, McVeigh avoided detection for only a brief time, and was arrested by Trooper Charles Hanger only 75 minutes after the fact.

The car in which McVeigh and Nichols were travelling, a 1977 Mercury Marquis, had lost its rear licence plate, and after they were pulled over, the two men were found to be carrying loaded concealed weapons. Once in custody, McVeigh and Nichols were charged with the bombings and went to trial. McVeigh was sentenced to death and was executed on 11 June 2001. Nichols was sentenced to life in prison.

Childhood bullying, and the upheaval that followed his parents' divorce, had caused McVeigh to be depressed and lack social skills. He lost confidence in those who were there to protect him and make him feel safe, then acted out these emotions on a larger scale, in which fantasies of cover-ups and conspiracies overrode his rational thought processes. This developed into a deadly obsession to bring down a government department through an 'act of terror and violence',[106] as the bombing was described at McVeigh's trial, and his military and survivalist training allowed him to make that obsession a reality.

Chapter 7
Dylan Klebold and Eric Harris

People have referred to the coming together of the two Columbine killers, Eric Harris and Dylan Klebold, as a perfect storm. The mother of one of the survivors explained that Klebold had befriended the loner Harris; Klebold was friends with lots of people, but in Harris he saw something special. Harris, in turn, saw something in Klebold. He believed he could mould the boy into a killing machine, who would help him act out his final assault on 20 April 1999, as part of his plan to 'kick natural selection up a few notches'.[107]

The Columbine High School massacre, though mostly know as a high school shooting, was meant to be, according to the diaries of the killers, a bombing to rival Timothy McVeigh's act of terrorism. And like the Oklahoma bombing, the attack was orchestrated by two people, one wielding a powerful influence over the other.

A relationship between murderers in which one participant is more powerful than the other or others has occurred since time immemorial. In the case of the Menendez brothers, the dominant older brother forced the younger to participate in the killing of their parents. The murders of members of the Clutter family in 1959, immortalised in Truman Capote's *In Cold Blood*, were committed by two young men – while Richard Hickock planned the murders, the weaker partner, Perry Smith, conducted them at the behest of his dominant friend. The Snowtown killings, already discussed, saw the collusion of a stronger man with other, weaker killers, who helped him commit at least 11 murders. The list goes on, and the Columbine killers were no different. Eric Harris was the mastermind and planner – he bought the weapons, he designed the bombs, and he was the boy with the plan. Klebold was caught up in the fantasy and believed he had nothing left to live for.

In the Boston Marathon bombings of 15 April 2013, we saw a similar scenario. At the time of writing, early reports indicate that Tamerlan, the older brother, was a boxer, who allegedly had charges for domestic assault against his name, and openly claimed he had no American friends and couldn't understand the culture of his adopted homeland.[108] His younger brother, Dzhokhar, who led police on a door-to-door manhunt, was described by friends as a person who 'fit in with everyone',[109] and public opinion holds that the elder brother must have convinced him to participate.

In a chilling similarity to cult leaders like Jim Jones and Charles Manson, the few friends Eric Harris did have said he was 'charismatic, an eloquent speaker, well-read, the kind of guy who could bullshit for hours about anything and be witty and brilliant'.[110] Yet Harris, a young teen who had studied the Oklahoma bombing and was shocked to learn that Timothy McVeigh did not stay to watch his bombs explode, wrote in his journals that his plans were far grander than McVeigh's had been. He wrote about the varying levels of carnage he wanted to see, and hoped the bombs he planned to set off around his high school would kill hundreds.[111]

Both Harris and Klebold kept diaries leading up to the murders, which gave police the best insight into their intentions on that fateful April day. The massacre was not decided on overnight – they had planned it for more than a year. The diaries detailed their collection of weapons and videos showed them practising with high-powered shotguns and rifles. Looking back even further, there were hints of what was to come. Almost 10 years before the massacre, at the age of eight, Eric Harris had already written his first list of people to kill. He would later create a website, which he used to discuss his murderous fantasies.

In January 1998, Harris and Klebold were arrested for breaking into an electronics van and stealing $400 worth of equipment; both boys were on parole at the time of the shooting. Harris later wrote that he thought the owner of the van deserved to die for being so stupid as to leave the van where it could be robbed. Their friends also knew that the boys had a key to the computer rooms at school and had stolen various pieces of equipment.

A year before the massacre, Harris wrote in online chatrooms about what he hoped to achieve. On 29 April 1998, he wrote, 'Sometime in April next year, me and V [Klebold] will get revenge and we'll kick natural selection up a few notches. We've learned the art of making time bombs, we'll set hundreds of them around roads, bridges, buildings and gas stations, anything that can cause damage and chaos. It'll be like the L.A. Riots, the Oklahoma bombing, WWII, Vietnam, Duke and Doom all mixed together ... I want to leave a lasting impression on the world.'[112] He used the codename NBK to talk about the massacre he planned, a reference to the film *Natural Born Killers*, in which a couple find fame by killing their way across America. Harris wrote, 'NBK came quickly. Everything I see and hear, I relate to NBK somehow. It feels like a god-damned movie sometimes.'[113]

Harris also made a new kill list, which included the name of a boy from school. The student, Brooks Brown, had seen a web page entry, written by Harris, which read: 'I will rig up explosives all over town and detonate each one of them at will after I mow down a whole fucking area full of you snotty ass rich mother fucking high strung godlike attitude having worthless pieces of shit whores. I don't care if I live or die in the shootout, all I want to do is kill and injure as many of you pricks as I can, especially a few people like Brooks Brown.'[114] Brooks notified his father, who told the authorities. A formal complaint was made, but police lost the documentation, and it was only after the massacre that they investigated. Brooks, who survived the massacre, later wondered if police could have stopped the spree with early action on his complaint, and saw this oversight as of one many factors that combined to allow the boys to carry out their plans.[115] Brooks had also seen Harris and Klebold experiment with black powders and pipe bombs. He had been a friend prior to the online threats, and filmed them blowing up tree stumps and shooting at trees on the outskirts of town.

Six weeks before the shooting, Harris' parents took him to see a doctor, who prescribed the antidepressant Zoloft. But Harris' condition deteriorated and his outbursts became violent. He was suicidal and expressed thoughts of murder. Once taken off the medication, he was prescribed a similar one, marketed under the name Luvox, which could have made his symptoms worse. A study of the chemical fluvoxamine, the active ingredient in Luvox, by the Institute for Safe Medication Practices, identified the drug as 8.4 times more likely to be associated with violence than other medications.[116] Harris was later found to have had a therapeutic dose of the drug in his system during the shooting.

In the weeks prior to the attack, Brooks also noticed a change in the boys. He later reported to the FBI that he had 'grown somewhat apart' from the pair, saying, 'Harris and Klebold had been acting a little different … cutting classes and sleeping in class … they had been somewhat more secretive in the last couple of weeks.'[117] On the day of the massacre his relationship with the boys, though a strained one, would ultimately save his life.

On 3 April 1999, Harris' feelings of rejection l hit an all-time low, and he once again turned to his diary to mete out his feelings. 'I hate you people for leaving me out of so many fun things. And no don't fucking say, "well that's your fault" because it isn't. You people had my phone # and I asked and all, but no, no no, no don't let the weird looking Eric KID come along. ohh fucking nooo.'[118]

Brooks Brown later speculated that Harris felt even more lonely when he was unable to find a date for the prom, while the shy Klebold attended with a female friend. The pair felt like outsiders at school, which was a typically hierarchical one – at the top were the jocks, noted for wearing white baseball caps, and at the bottom were Harris and Klebold. Klebold wrote about his own rejection by those higher in the pecking order at school: 'You've given us shit for years. You're fucking going to pay for the shit. We don't give a shit, because we're going to die doing it.'[119]

In the late hours of 19 April 1999, the two boys talked to others in an online chatroom, perhaps as a form of cathartic cleansing ahead of the following day. One of them mentioned that 'something bad' was going to happen in Colorado.[120]

The next day, 20 April 1999, was a dark one in American history. For Harris and Klebold, it would usually have commenced with Bowling Club from 6am to 7.15am. They were seen in the bowling alley carpark, but did not attend the class. Harris was meant to sit for his Chinese Philosophy test that day, and Brooks Brown was concerned, but not surprised, when Harris missed the big exam. He knew that the teenager's class attendance had become erratic recently.

At 11.10am, Harris and Klebold arrived at their school, Columbine High in Littleton, Colorado. Harris parked his car in the junior parking lot and Klebold parked his in the senior one, closest to the school buildings. Both cars were positioned near entrances and exits to the cafeteria, their first target. They were wearing black trousers and boots, black trench coats and t-shirts. Harris' t-shirt had NATURAL SELECTION printed on it. Klebold's read WRATH.

Brooks Brown left the school building to have a cigarette and saw Harris getting out of his car. He reminded Harris of the big test they had that day but Harris just looked at him, saying, 'It doesn't matter anymore. Brooks, I like you now. Get out of here. Go home.' Brooks watched as Harris took a duffel bag from the boot of his car, then wandered away. Though Harris had named Brooks as a target, he saved his life by telling him to leave.

By 11.14am, Dylan Klebold and Eric Harris had readied themselves for murder. They were armed with a number of explosive devices, as well as guns and knives. Their bombs ranged from small CO2 containers to 20lb propane gas tank bombs. The smaller devices were designed to detonate via an ignition fuse, while the larger devices were set on timers. The boys planted two 20lb bombs with timers in the cafeteria, known as the Commons. Though surveillance cameras were installed in the area, the planting of the bombs was not recorded. The bombs in the Commons were meant to explode at 11.17am, during the Lunch A period, when more than a quarter of the students would take their lunch break.

The boys returned to their cars to await the explosions.[121] They had planned a three-pronged, terrorist-style bombing attack, set to commence with the bombing of the cafeteria, which they hoped would kill all 448 students inside. They also hoped the explosion would bring down the library on the second floor and trap any survivors. They planned to wait at their cars, shooting survivors who tried to escape, then set off explosives in their cars that would kill arriving ambulances and police. The planned attack, however, 'quickly devolved into a forty-nine minute shooting rampage when the bombs that Harris built fizzled'.[122]

Klebold had written in his diary of his expectations for the attack. 'It will be the most nerve-wracking fifteen minutes of my life after the bombs … seconds will feel like hours.'[123] Already their plan had not gone the way they hoped, although three miles from the school, a diversionary pile of explosives did detonate – a small pipe bomb and aerosol canister caused a large grassfire, which held the attention of the fire brigade.

When they realised the bombs inside the school had failed, Harris and Klebold decided to set off on a shooting spree, armed with two sawn-off shotguns, two 9mm guns and almost 100 small incendiary devices. Harris set the timer bombs in the trunks of both of their cars and they prepared to enter the building, intending to take out as many people as they could.

First, they threw a pipe bomb at a group of students near the school's entrance, but the bomb did very little damage. Then a group of students exited through the doors and were met by the two boys in the black trench coats. Seventeen-year-old students Rachel School and Richard Castaldo were the first to be shot. Richard was shot five times; he survived the attack, but was left paralysed. Rachel was shot four times, including one bullet to the head, and was killed.

The two realised that their trench coats, worn to hide their weapons, were more of a hindrance than a help. Harris removed his coat as he headed towards the entrance stairs. Three teenagers, Daniel Rohrbough, Sean Graves and Lance Kirklin, left through the same doors for a cigarette after their lunch break. They saw Harris and Klebold with guns, but assumed they were playing a trick and ignored them. Sixteen-year-old Lance was shot twice, one bullet striking him in the leg and another in the chest. His friend Daniel was struck in the chest. Lance, along with his friend Sean, tried to flee. Lance was shot again in the leg and Sean was hit in the back and chest. A final shot to his leg stopped him running.

Seeing the carnage, a group of students sitting on the grass near the cafeteria tried to flee, which drew the attention of the shooters. Fifteen-year-old Michael Johnson was shot while running for a nearby lock-up shed. Three other students made it to the sheds uninjured. Mark Taylor, 16, who had been sitting with Michael, was paralysed in the gunfire and remained where he fell, hoping that playing dead would prevent Harris and Klebold from shooting him again.

Seventeen-year-old Anne Marie Hochalter was the next to be wounded. Eating her lunch in the sun with friends, she tried to flee the gunfire, but was shot and paralysed by Harris. The boys threw pipe bombs onto the roof, and fired randomly on students fleeing the scene, without causing any injuries. As they fled, students heard one of the gunmen say, 'This is what we always wanted to do. This is awesome … Today the world is going to come to an end. Today's the day we die.'[124]

Inside the school, having heard or seen the gunfire, most of the students hid in locked classrooms. Coach Dave Sanders ran through the school, telling students and teachers to hide. His bravery saved the lives of hundreds of students. Calls began filtering in to emergency services.

The injured Sean Graves was crawling to safety when he saw the gunmen heading towards him once more. He rubbed blood from his injuries over his face and played dead as they moved past him. Daniel was not so lucky. Klebold walked over to the 15-year-old and shot him dead at point-blank range. Klebold then placed the barrel of his shotgun against Lance's jaw and fired again; the critically injured boy survived his injuries.

The killers stepped on Sean as they headed into the cafeteria, but the wounded teenager did not react to the weight of their boots.

At 11.21am, both boys headed into the cafeteria, which was now empty. They went towards the bombs they had set, wondering why they had not exploded. Meanwhile, a police officer having lunch near the smoking area was the first person to respond to the scene, having received a call saying that someone had fallen and was paralysed in the car park.

Walking along the vacant and smoke-filled corridors, the shooters looked from room to room, shooting randomly at walls and lockers and laughing as they searched for prey. Teacher Patricia 'Patti' Nielson saw the gunfire and assumed it was a prank getting out of hand. Intending to tell them to stop, she went out into the corridor with 17-year-old student Brian Anderson. Stopping at a set of glass doors, she saw Harris raise the gun to chest height. He shot at both of them through the door and their skin was pierced with glass and shrapnel. Patti turned and ran towards the library, where she knew there was a phone. Brian followed.

By then, police had arrived on the scene, but did not enter the building. This decision was later criticised and would eventually see a policy change in how police managed 'live shooters'. They exchanged gunfire with the two gunmen, but remained outside the building. Several students were shot as they tried to flee the school. Seventeen-year-old Stephanie Munson was struck in the ankle, but she continued to run for safety.

Coach Dave Sanders, having locked many students in their classrooms, finally came face to face with Harris and Klebold. He turned away from the shooters and tried to flee, but was shot twice in the neck by Harris. While Harris reloaded his weapon, Klebold dashed past the fallen coach and began shooting down the next corridor towards the cafeteria, before being rejoined by his companion. They spent three minutes shooting along the library corridor and firing off various small explosives into the cafeteria below. Two more bombs were thrown at lockers.

Coach Dave Sanders was able to crawl into a nearby room, where students applied first aid treatment in an attempt to save his life. A call to 911 about the coach's injuries was met with an assurance that help was on its way. As the two boys prowled the corridors, they looked into several of the locked science labs, including the one Dave Sanders had entered. The students who were giving the teacher first aid hid out of view when the gunmen looked in.

At 11.25am, Patti had made it to the library and warned all students she found there to hide. Crouching behind the library loans counter, she dialled 911. She remained on the line during the next seven minutes, which would later be described as hell for those inside the library. Fifty-six students were hiding among the desks and shelving, with no way to escape.

Fifteen-year-old Evan Todd looked around the corner of a column at the entrance to the library and found Harris staring straight back at him. Harris threw a small pipe bomb at the teenager, which did little damage. Evan looked around the column again and Harris fired several shots at him. The bullets splintered the column, injuring Evan.

Patti's 911 call gave an accurate recording of what happened next.[125] When Klebold and Harris entered the library, both shouted for everyone to get up. Harris called out again, threatening, 'Stand up right now or we'll blow your fucking heads off!'

When no one moved, he walked to a desk and yelled, 'Fine. I'll start shooting then.' Klebold shot at 16-year-old special needs student Kyle Velasquez, who was still sitting at one of the computers. He was hit in the back of the head and died instantly. Kleobold excitedly exclaimed, 'Woo hoo!'

The shouting and shooting continued. 'All jocks stand up … white baseball cap,' said Klebold, pointing out those who wore the unspoken uniform of the popular kids. No one stood up. Meanwhile, Harris looked out the library window and counted dozens of police cars outside. He called out to Klebold, telling him, 'The pigs are here,' and fired a volley of shots out the window. Klebold moved from desk to desk, firing shots at Makai Hall, Daniel Steepleton and Patrick Ireland. All three teenagers were injured. Revelling in the harm he was causing at close range, he again shouted, 'Yahoo!'

On the line with emergency services, Patti Nielson was saying the Lord's Prayer. The dispatcher asked her to stop praying and tell her what was happening. Patti said, 'They're killing kids.' She dropped the phone so she could hide, but the line remained open.

Harris pointed his shotgun at 14-year-old Steven Curnow and fired a single shot, killing the boy instantly. He then turned the gun on 17-year-old Kasey Ruegsegger and fired, injuring her. As she moaned in pain, Harris abused the injured girl, saying, 'Stop your bitching, it's merely a flesh wound.'

It was now 11.32am. The press were arriving on the scene. Police remained outside, assisting those who had fled the buildings.

Harris moved to another area of the library and ducked down under one of the desks, where Cassie Bernall, 17, was hiding. 'Peek-a-boo,' he said, firing at point-blank range and killing her instantly. The kickback from the gun pushed Harris back against the desk behind him. The gun's butt hit him in the face and broke his nose, but he seemed to be unaware that it was bleeding.

Klebold turned the gun on Patrick Ireland, who had been shot moments earlier, but was trying to administer first aid to Makai Hall. He shouted, 'Die … down on the floor,' before shooting him three more times, including two shots to the head, causing critical injuries. Harris then pointed the gun at Bree Pasquale, who begged for her life. Harris told her everyone was going to die and that they were going to blow up the school. He then noticed the blood coming from his nose and turned to Klebold, complaining the gun had hurt him. He walked away from Bree, leaving her to survive the slaughter.

Klebold called out to Harris. 'Reb?' he said, using his online name. 'Hey man, there's a nigger over here.'

Harris answered quickly, 'Shoot him.'

Eighteen-year-old Isiah Shoels begged for his life as Klebold tried to pull him out from under the table. When he was unable to get him out, Harris joined Klebold and fired a shot, killing the young man. Hiding beside Isiah was Matthew Kechter. Klebold aimed the gun at him, and fired, killing him too. Then Harris lit several small pipe bombs and threw them around the library, causing damage to the shelving and structures. He threw one at the area where Makai Hall, Patrick Ireland and Daniel Steepleton were. Makai picked up the bomb and threw it away from them before it exploded.

Seventeen-year-old Mark Kintgen was the next to be injured. Harris fired indiscriminate shots at the shelving before turning the gun on the boy, hitting him in the head and shoulder. Several students who tried to flee as Harris turned away were then shot. Lisa Kreutz and Valeen Schnurr were struck by a single bullet, then Harris fired again at a group of students, and Lauren Townsend was killed in the gunfire. He fired under more desks and injured 16-year-olds Nicole Nowlen and John Tomlin. As John crawled from beneath the desk, Klebold fired a shot, killing the teenager instantly. He shot at Kelly Fleming, hitting her in the back and killing her, and Jeanna Park, who was with Kelly, was also injured.

As the two gunmen reloaded, Harris spotted John Savage hiding beneath a table. Harris asked the boy to identify himself as Klebold pointed a gun beneath the desk. John told them his name and peered out from his hiding spot. Klebold was an acquaintance of his.

Unsure what else to say, John asked Klebold what he and Harris were doing. Nonchalantly, Klebold responded, 'Oh, just killing people.'

John asked if Klebold was going to kill him as well. Klebold shook his head and replied, 'No man, just get out of here, just run … run, run.' At 11.35am, John sprinted from the building, not stopping until he had reached the police line outside.

Harris next turned his gun on 15-year-old Daniel Mauser and shot him in the face, killing him instantly. Then both shooters fired on 17-year-olds Corey DePooter, Stephen 'Austin' Eubanks and Jennifer Doyle. All three were injured. Another shot killed Corey. Complaining that he was out of bullets, Harris considered Klebold's suggestion that they start stabbing people instead.

The two killers left the library. They threatened the injured Evan, who was near the door, but did not shoot him. They were heard leaving the library, saying they were heading back to the cafeteria, where they shot at the propane tanks and caused several explosions. At 11.46am, Klebold threw a bomb at the propane tank, causing a fire that forced them to flee.

The two went on firing indiscriminately through several rooms before again returning to the cafeteria to find that the sprinkler system had doused the fire and the larger bombs had still not detonated. They were dejected; their grand plan had failed.

At 12.02am, the two killers headed back to the library and started firing at rescue services outside. Then, at 12.05am, two more shots were heard. Klebold had fired a shot into his left temple and Harris had fired his gun into his mouth. The two had committed suicide after murdering 13 people and maiming 23 students and teachers.

An hour after the attack first began, SWAT teams and police finally entered the building. It would take them more than three hours to find all the injured, dying and dead.

Following the shooting, many questions were raised about the boys' mental states. Both teenage killers were seeing psychologists at the time of the massacre and Harris was taking medication to help him deal with his issues. Some blamed his homicidal breakdown on these medications, while others were quick to point the finger at violent video games and films, particularly after the killers' references to the film *Natural Born Killers* were published. Their parents, meanwhile, had to face the world and try to apologise for the actions of their children.

As friends of Harris and Klebold explained, the two boys were OK on their own, but together brewed up a perfect storm of homicidal rage. They felt they were misunderstood and rejected by an hierarchical school society, and took their anger out on those they believed had wronged them.

Chapter 8
Charles Manson

As the abandoned offspring of a teenage mother, Charles Manson started life on the back foot. Born to Kathleen Maddox in Cincinnati in 1934, and known for the first three weeks of his life as 'No Name Maddox'[126], his alcoholic mother would take off for weeks at a time, leaving the young boy to fend for himself or be passed around the family. His official surname, Manson, was inherited from one of the men she married, but a Colonel Scott was also chased for child support, which was never paid. Kathleen once gave Manson away in exchange for alcohol and spent most of her life in and out of prison.

As a small child, Manson lived with his aunt and uncle, who took pleasure in beating the boy and forcing him to dress as a girl. By the age of 12, he had run away numerous times, and ended up at the Gibault School for Boys. He was tiny and malnourished, smaller that most of the other boys in the home, so at first glance was the perfect victim for a bully, but he was always one step ahead of the others, bullying them before they could attack him. A year after being sent to the home, he ran away to his mother, but she had no time for him and sent him back. He felt completely abandoned and unloved, and though he had an IQ of 109, was illiterate. By the time he hit his teens, his only sexual experiences were homosexual and abusive.[127] Psychiatrists would later call him a 'very emotionally upset youth, slick but extremely sensitive, dangerous, with homosexual and assaultive tendencies'.[128]

He continued to escape from the home and turned to robbery to feed himself. His first conviction was at the age of 13, when he robbed a grocery store, but his criminal activity soon escalated to more violent crimes. He moved from car theft to armed robbery and later to rape, charged in 1952 with the aggravated sodomy of a young boy as he held a blade to his throat.[129] He was sentenced briefly to prison. On his release, Manson began targeting promiscuous young girls, pimping them out to others. He had his first heterosexual experience at the age of 17 and quickly married the girl, Rosalie Jean Willis, in 1955, before he was again sentenced to prison for prostitution procurement charges. While in prison, he told a psychiatrist, 'She is the best wife a guy could want. I didn't realise how good she was until I got in here. I beat her at times. She writes to me all the time. She is going to have a baby.'[130] He was released from prison, but skipped out on a further charge.

At 25 years of age, Manson was sentenced to 10 years prison for parole violations and attempting to cash a forged cheque. His son, Charles Manson Junior, was born while he was in jail. Alone in his prison cell, where he had already spent many years, he began imagining a new world in which he was the beloved leader, finally receiving the love that had always been denied him.

On his release in 1967, having spent most of his life in institutions and 'in need of a great deal of help in the transition from institution to the free world',[131] an older Manson joined in effortlessly with the new hippie and drug culture. He told his parole hearing that he hoped to find a record deal, and spend his time writing and performing music, having been taught how to play guitar in prison by gangster Alvin Karpis.[132] He was even introduced to Terry Melcher, a record producer and the son of Doris Day, by Beach Boy Dennis Wilson, with whom Manson lived for a time, after being picked up hitchhiking with two young girls.[133] Manson surrounded himself with impressionable women, giving them LSD and asking them to follow him. A group of 'followers' had soon grown around him.

In 1968, Manson took his ever-increasing band of misfits to the broken-down Spahn Movie Ranch just outside of Hollywood, where many Westerns had been filmed. At the ranch, the women were given chores and were expected to sexually service the octogenarian ranch owner, as well as male members of the group. They also helped the owner with his horse rental business and rode dune buggies around the vast property. They often ventured into the desert, consuming large amounts of drugs and conducting orgies.

According to his followers, Manson could be benevolent and caring, winning over any sceptic with a smile. He would take followers aside, one on one, preaching to them, taking an interest in their lives, helping them work through their problems or issues, and espousing a message of love and devotion. He would tell them they were smart, intelligent and beautiful, that society had dealt them a raw deal, and that he would help them become a beacon of light and love. He knew what people wanted and needed to hear, because these words were what he had been longing for his entire life. Where Jones, discussed in a later chapter, preached equality, Manson preached love.

Though he never called himself Christ, his followers believed 'he was the Messiah come again'.[134] He was very charismatic, and whatever he told them, they accepted, believing he communicated directly with God. To prove they were under his control, Manson would schedule sessions during which his followers, known as the Family, had to mimic his movements, but he realised that to keep them in his power, he would need to isolate them from the outside world. At the Ranch, newspapers and television were forbidden. Manson told them his word was all they needed, claiming he would rule after the coming Armageddon. He criticised his followers for thinking independently; if they spoke out against his ideas, he said, 'Thinking is stinking.'[135] Others were told to prove their devotion by inflicting violence on those who questioned him. If someone attempted to leave, he threatened to hunt them down, tie them to a car and drag them back. The outwardly peaceful community was certainly not all it seemed.

Manson's followers became restless and bored with the hard work and seclusion. He knew he was losing control of them, and that people would soon leave the commune he had created. He also knew that if they went into town, they would see his stories of the apocalypse were the delusions of a man who believed he had been left behind by the rest of the world. He was having problems with one of his followers in particular, Charles 'Tex' Watson, a young and handsome man who was just as charismatic as the wild-looking, older Manson. Tex was considering usurping Manson as leader of and Manson sensed a struggle for power was coming. Needing to reassert his dominance over his followers, he became more violent and threatening. 'It's all coming down,'[136] he would say repeatedly.

And down it came, to the shock of the entire world.

After being arrested and jailed on vehicle theft charges in mid-August 1969, Susan Atkins, a member of the Family, told her fellow inmate Virgina Graham about the things she'd been up to with Charles Manson. She talked about the love-making sessions, stolen cars and other thefts, and her cellmates were loath to believe her until she told them what had occurred on the night of 8 August 1969. She claimed that she, Charles 'Tex' Watson, Patricia Krenwinkel and Linda Kasabian had all gone to a house at 10050 Cielo Drive around midnight. Their original plan was to kill Terry Melcher, the record producer who had rejected Manson's music. Melcher no longer lived at 10050 Cielo Drive – the house was being rented by filmmaker Roman Polanski and his wife, actress Sharon Tate – Manson said he had seen 'movie types' entering and leaving the mansion, and decided to go ahead with the slaughter. Atkins claimed to have been there before and knew that there was often a lot of money in the house.

When the four pulled up outside the property, Kasabian lost her nerve and remained in the car. Watson, Krenwinkel and Atkins continued on through the wrought-iron gates, cutting the telephone lines before entering the property. They came across teenager Steven Parent outside; he had tried to sell a radio to his friend Garretson earlier that evening and was just leaving when the killers arrived. Watson shot him four times as he begged for his life. Neighbours later remembered hearing gunshots, but did not investigate.[137]

From the front lawn, the trio quickly entered the house, where they found coffee heiress Abigail Folger sitting in the lounge room reading a book. She did not look up as the group entered the room. Susan crept into a bedroom, where Sharon Tate, who was eight-and-a-half months pregnant, was sitting in bed. Her ex-boyfriend and hairdresser Jay Sebring was sitting on the end of the bed. Susan forced the couple into the lounge room. There, she tied them up over the rafter, in such a way that they would strangle each other if they moved. Another guest at the home was Voytek Frykowski, a Polish-born playboy and friend of Roman Polanski (who was not home that night). He made a run for the front door. Susan stabbed him three or four times as he ran out onto the lawn screaming, 'Help, help, somebody please help me.'[138] Susan Atkins and Watson 'finished him off'[139] outside.

Susan laughed as she told the story to Virginia Graham, recalling that Sharon Tate was the last to be slaughtered. Tate pleaded with the murderers to spare her. Susan grabbed her by the arm and Sharon cried, 'Please don't kill me, please don't kill me, I want to live, I want to have my baby.'[140]

Susan stared at Tate glassy-eyed, and told her coldly, 'Look, bitch, I don't care about you. I don't care you are going to have a baby. You had better be ready. You are going to die and I don't feel anything about it.'[141]

Susan stabbed Tate multiple times. She told her shocked cellmate that she'd wanted to remove the baby from Sharon's womb, and take the victims' fingers and eyeballs, but didn't have time. The group headed back to the ranch, all of them in a state of ecstasy.

At 8.30am the following morning, Winnie Chapman, the housekeeper at 10050 Cielo Drive, bashed down the door of the neighbouring house, screaming, 'Murder! Death! Bodies! Blood!' Neighbour Jim Asin rang the Los Angeles Police Department and the savage multiple murders were revealed.

When police arrived, they were greeted with a sight of morbid carnage. The bloodied body of a young man – Steven Parent – marked with four gunshot wounds, was slumped over the steering wheel of a car in the driveway. The bodies of two more victims were close to the mansion's front door. Voytek Frykowski, aged 32, had been shot twice, struck over the head 13 times and stabbed 51 times. The second victim, Frykowski's 25-year-old girlfriend Abigail Folger, was dressed in her nightgown and had received 28 stab wounds. Both lay in pools of blood.

The police entered the mansion, noting that the front door had the word PIG written on it in blood. In the lounge room, Sharon Tate, dressed in her underwear, was lying in a foetal position in front of the fireplace, soaked in her own blood. It was evident that she had been heavily pregnant. She'd been stabbed 16 times. A white nylon rope was tied around her neck in a noose. The rope ran over a rafter and around the neck of the second victim, Jay Sebring, who was lying soaked in blood only two metres away. He had a bloody cloth covering his face and hands. The position of the man's hand showed he had died while trying to defend himself from his attackers. He had been shot once and stabbed seven times.

While police were investigating the carnage inside the mansion, other officers had found themselves a suspect outside. The barking of a dog led them to 19-year-old William Garretson, the caretaker for the property, who had been in the guesthouse all night and claimed to have heard nothing suspicious. When shown the scene of the murders, he collapsed in shock and was arrested. He was detained by police, but released after passing a polygraph test, with the LAPD stating, 'Mr. Garretson was truthful and not criminally involved in the ... murders.'

The press quickly began calling the killings 'ritual slayings'. They also honed in on the fact that Sebring was the ex-lover of Tate, wildly surmising that the night had been a drug-fuelled sex orgy that ended in death. The LAPD, however, looked for more plausible motives. Robbery was unlikely due to the fact that valuables and jewels were lying around in plain view and had not been taken. None of the victims had been sexually assaulted, but drugs were found in the house, including LSD, marijuana, cocaine, MSD, and the hallucinogenic MDA (a combination of LSD, cocaine and heroin). Autopsy reports revealed that there was MDA in the blood of Folger and Frykowski.

With this evidence, police began to wonder if the killings really had been the result of a drug party 'freak out', in which someone had gone crazy and committed murder, or perhaps the result of a drug deal gone wrong. The LAPD even debated whether it could have been a 'hit' killing. But these theories all had problems. The telephone lines had been carefully cut; if the killings were drug-induced, this could only have been done after the spree, which made no sense. The frenzied nature of the attacks also made it unlikely that the murders were the work of professionals, and police were sure they could not have been committed by one person alone. Ultimately, they were left with the theory of a drug deal gone bad.

While the LAPD continued to look into the drugs angle, with information showing a drug delivery had been due to arrive within days of the murders,[142] the Los Angeles Sheriff's Office (LASO) arrested a hippie musician, Bobby Beausoleil, for the murder of school teacher Gary Hinman, who had been stabbed to death. Beausoleil had been caught driving Hinman's Fiat with the murder weapon still in the car. Significantly, the words POLITICAL PIGGY had been written in blood on the wall of Hinman's home.

The LASO told the LAPD that Beausoleil lived with a 'family' of hippies on the Spahn Ranch, an old movie set, in Death Valley. Their leader was a man named Charles who believed he was Jesus Christ. The sergeant in charge of the Tate killings was uninterested, however, and the LAPD told the LASO detectives, 'We know what's behind these murders, they're part of a big dope transaction.'[143]

The evening after the Tate killings, the LAPD were dealing with another heinous double murder. On Sunday 10 August 1969, 15-year-old Frank Struthers returned from a holiday to the home he shared with his mother and stepfather, Rosemary and Leno LaBianca, at 3301 Waverly Drive. He thought it was strange that the blinds were drawn and nobody answered his knocking, so called his sister Susan, and together with her boyfriend, they entered the house. Leno was lying on his back on the living room floor, wearing pyjamas, with a bloodied pillow case over his head and his hands tied behind his back. Around his neck was a cord from a heavy lamp, pulled tight enough to strangle him. He had been stabbed multiple times in the stomach and an ivory-handled bloody fork still protruded from one of the wounds. The word 'WAR' had been roughly carved in his flesh.

On one of the walls, somebody had written 'DEATH TO PIGS' in blood. On the opposite wall, the word 'RISE' had been written. On the refrigerator door, also in blood, were the words 'HEALTER [sic] SKELTER'.

When police arrived, they also found Rosemary LaBianca in the bedroom. She was soaked in blood, with her short pink nightgown and a dress she had put on bunched up around her head. Like Leno, she had a pillow case over her head and a lamp flex tied around her throat. She had been stabbed 41 times in the back and legs.

Though there were striking similarities between these killings and the Tate murders, it was another three months before the LAPD acknowledged that these were the acts of the same killers; the closest they came before that was to suggest that it was the work of a copycat. When the LAPD began to investigate the LaBianca murders, they found that Leno was the president of a chain of LA supermarkets and that he had gambling debts, which led detectives to the theory that it had been a mafia killing.

The following Saturday, the LAPD raided Spahn Ranch. They were not looking for murderers, but an auto-theft gang who had been stealing VWs and converting them into dune buggies. The raid was not a success. A legal loophole was found – the warrants had been misdated – and the 26 followers who had been arrested were released. Thirty-four-year-old Charles Manson was among those taken into custody.

Meanwhile, the LAPD's two separate homicide investigations into the Tate and LaBianca murders were covering little ground. The evidence at the Tate killings had uncovered 25 unknown fingerprints and three pieces of a broken gun grip, found to be part of a Buntline special .22 Longhorn Standard revolver. A description of the unusual gun was circulated, but no information came back. They had also found a buck knife down the back of chair and a pair of spectacles, but none of their clues gave up positive leads. Persisting with their theory of a deal gone wrong had led detectives to four drug dealers, but three provided alibis and the fourth passed a polygraph test. As for the LaBianca investigation, there were no leads whatsoever. Hollywood became increasingly fearful, as friends of Sharon Tate wondered if they would be next. Stars such as Frank Sinatra and Mia Farrow were said to have gone into hiding.

On 10 October, police mounted another raid on the Spahn Ranch. They were investigating an arson attack and a series of car thefts, but also knew that local rumour had it the ranch was home to orgies, drug use and crazed hippies, who called themselves the Family and rode through the desert in dune buggies. The first raid resulted in 10 women and three men being arrested. Two babies were also discovered, suffering from severe sunburn. Police recovered several stolen vehicles and an arsenal of guns, including a sub-machine gun.

On 12 October, they returned, and arrested seven more people. Searching the primitive bathroom at the back of the ranch house, one officer noticed some hair sticking out of the top of a small cupboard under a sink. When he called out, a small man in a buckskin vest came out, cracking a joke about cramped space. On his arresting sheet in Independence, his name was listed as: 'Manson, Charles M. aka Jesus Christ, God'.

Kitty Lutesinger, 17, was among the girls arrested in the Barker raid. She was a girlfriend of Bobby Beausoleil, who was already in custody for the murder of Gary Hinman, and was five months pregnant. Scared and pleading for protection, she told police that it was Manson, their leader and saviour, who had sent Beausoleil to see Hinman, an aquaintance of Manson, with another follower, Sadie Mae Glutz. Manson believed Hinman had inherited $20,000. After keeping the man captive for two days whilst they ransacked the house, to no avail, Beausoleil eventually held Hinman down while Sadie stabbed him to death.

The police had trouble sorting out who was who after the raid, as all the girls gave police a range of aliases. Nevertheless, they established that Sadie Mae Glutz was in fact Susan Atkins. Susan was charged and sent to the Sybil Brand Institute, a county jail for women. There, she began to tell her sordid stories to fellow inmates, who called her 'Crazy Sadie'. She bragged about her sexual exploits and her involvement in the murders to anyone who would listen, telling many of her tales to two ex-prostitutes, Virginia Graham and

Ronnie Howard. She told them she was the one who had stabbed Hinman while Bobby Beausoleil had pinned him down, and also gloated, in great detail, about the Tate and LaBianca murders.

These stories found their way to the ears of the LAPD, as did talk among a local bikie gang, whom Manson had approached to join the Family after several of his members took off following the murders. Manson told a bikie gang that his group had 'got five piggies'[144] and asked them how to dispose of bodies. Police soon descended on the ranch for a final time and arrested all remaining members. Based on Atkins' conversations with her cellmates, police were able to identify the group's main leaders and killers, arresting Patricia Krenwinkel in Mobile, Charles Watson in Texas and Leslie Van Houten in California. Linda Kasabian handed herself in to police in New Hampshire.

Atkins was offered a deal that would spare her the death penalty if she testified at the grand jury hearing. Kasabian was given the same deal, and accepted, making Atkin's deal null and void. It did not stop Atkins from explaining, in great detail, her time with Manson. She told the court she was 'in love with the reflection of Charles Manson and that there was no limit to what she would do for him'.[145] Her testimony was the backbone for the trial that followed, more akin to a media circus, in which all six defendants faced murder charges. It also appeared that Manson, in prison, was still able to control his followers on the outside. When he shaved his head, his Family did too; when he cut a cross in his forehead, they did the same.

After nine months at trial, during which most of the killers, including Manson, testified, the gang were all found guilty of first-degree murder and sentenced to death. In 1972, a Supreme Court ruling overturned the death penalty and the sentences were commuted to life. Manson, Watson, Van Houten and Krenwinkel remain in prison, while Atkins died from cancer in 2009. Manson's next parole hearing is set for 2027. Should he live that long, he will be 93. Summarising the case, prosecutor Vincent Bugliosi described Manson as having sent out 'from the fires of hell at Spahn Ranch three heartless, bloodthirsty robots' to do his bidding.[146]

Interviewing Manson in prison, FBI behavioural expert John Douglas saw a different side to the man, and his experience would form the basis of the behavioural analysis process made famous in films like *Silence of the Lambs* and the television programme *Criminal Minds*. Manson would begin their interviews by trying to enforce an obvious change in power,[147] the 5ft 2in 'guru' sitting on the back of his chair to appear taller than the statuesque, seated agent. He had done the same when preaching to his followers, sitting on a large boulder. Douglas described Manson as having 'wild, alert eyes and an unsettling kinetic quality about him'.[148] It was this kinetic energy that drew young followers to him. Douglas surmised that 'once he had these lost souls in his sway, he instituted a highly structured delusional system that left him in complete control of their minds and bodies … [he used] sleep deprivation, sexual congress, food control and drugs'[149] to ensure their submission and assert his dominance.

In the 1970s, Jim Jones used similar techniques to control the parishioners of the Peoples Temple at Jonestown. Many have spoken of getting as little as one hour's sleep per night as they worked to please their leader.

Chapter 9
Jim Jones

He called it 'revolutionary suicide'.[150] To the rest of the world, it was a massacre. Jim Jones, a man who began his ministry in 1953, was responsible for one of the largest mass suicides in history and the single greatest peacetime loss of American citizens' lives until the terrorist attacks of 11 September 2001. On 18 November 1978, more than 900 men, women and children, including Jones and his inner circle, were found dead in the compound they had set up in Guyana, known as the Peoples Temple Agricultural Project, or Jonestown. The mass suicide came after Congressman Leo J. Ryan and four other people visited the settlement. The visit had been arranged to check on the welfare of the parishioners, but ended with mass suicide and murder.

Jones was born to a poor family in Indiana in 1931. His mother worked several jobs to feed her children, while his unemployed father spent most of his time in a drunken stupor. As a small child in this dysfunctional family, Jones felt neglected, his mother being mostly absent and his father mostly unconscious. He yearned for something more than what life had dealt him and felt as though he had been 'born on the wrong side of the tracks'.[151]

Childhood friends recalled that, even at five years of age, Jones was obsessed with death and religion. He would often kill small animals and conduct funerals for them, preaching about death and God, and making his few friends attend as mourners. Children mainly stayed away from the odd boy. As a teenager, he found a kinship with African-American people, believing his childhood experiences as an outcast were akin to how they felt in American society. One day he tried to bring a homeless man to his house to feed. When his father refused the man entry, Jones left with the vagrant, and would not speak to his father for years to come.[152]

Jones found himself drawn to the Pentecostal church. One of its preachers became a father figure to the impressionable Jones, who quickly made up his mind to become a pastor himself. He believed in equality and preached that everyone should feel welcome in his chapel; there would be no segregation. It was a radical and unpopular idea. As an advocate for racial equality, Jones was seen as an inspirationalleader. He soon created his own church, which he called the Peoples Temple. His church events saw attendance in the thousands and politicians would turn up to take photos with the influential reverend. His ministry focused on helping those in need, particularly people of African-American descent. According to one of his followers, 'The Prophet is supremely and totally dedicated to building an ideal society where mankind is united, life (human and animal and plant) is cherished, and the joys of nature and simplicity are esteemed.'[153]

At mass, people would tell their stories of being saved by Pastor Jim Jones. Through the Peoples Temple, they claimed to have found direction and guidance in their lives. Services were scenes of joy and delirium as people danced in the aisles and raised their hands to the roof, hundreds of members working themselves into a frenzy before Jones even appeared. He would run healing sessions in which people in the audience stood up to have their ailments cured; once, he was said to have made a woman in a wheelchair stand up and walk. Later, those who survived the massacre discovered that those who had been 'healed' were close friends of Jim, whom he had convinced to feign ill health.

Demonstrating his belief in racial equality, Jones adopted children of different ethnic backgrounds. By the end of his life, he had an adopted African-American son, two adopted Asian-American children and a biological son. While growing his flock in San Francisco and Indianapolis, Jim Jones created two more churches in California that would become the Peoples Temple. He chose the small town of Ukiah for the main site, as an article in *Esquire* magazine had named it among one of nine places in the world that would survive a nuclear attack. One hundred and forty-one parishioners followed their charismatic leader from Indianapolis to Ukiah, believing they had found their paradise.

Jones' message to his parishioners was to sell their possessions and share all things in common. His mantra was 'to feed the hungry and clothe the naked, take in the stranger'.[154] The members went on cross-country recruitment drives in silver buses and within five years the congregation had gone from a little more than 100 people to many thousands. Older persons were encouraged to sell their homes and give their entire savings to the church, with Jones promising to look after them in return. They were allocated rooms in his senior centre home, attached to the Ukiah Peoples Temple church, where they were looked after by the younger members. Many parishioners worked up to 20 hours a day doing Jones' bidding. He slowly turned his followers into subservient, malleable robots, just as Manson had done before him, and they gradually gave up their free will.

Every one of his parishioners had a job to do. Anyone working in a job outside the Temple would surrender their payslips to Jones, who would give them $5 in return for sundries not provided by the Temple. The church had its own medical and dental staff and all basic needs were met by other members. Those without skills were put to work in the church's fields or tending animals. Jones also told his followers that everyone in the world was homosexual and that he was the only heterosexual person on earth. He said that sexual relationships took away from the church's plans for helping others and convinced everyone that he kept celibate to ensure his messages from God were pure. Later, many young men claimed they were propositioned by Jones, and confessed to having sex with him.[155]

In an ominous incident in 1979, Jones tested his followers' loyalty. He passed out punch and asked everyone to drink, which they did without question. He then told them they had all consumed poison. There were screams and hysteria, but Jones calmed everyone down, explaining that it had only been a test – the punch was not poisoned and he was pleased to see that everyone was committed to his cause. In hindsight, survivors believed this was a trial run for his later 'suicide drills'.[156]

During the 1960s, members of the Peoples Temple would often attend protests. Busloads of enthusiastic worshippers would turn up to fight for equal rights and freedom. Jones gained more power, meeting with congressmen and political leaders, and even First Lady Rosalynn Carter in 1976. Yet he was increasingly paranoid and believed people were trying to kill him. He trained close personnel to protect him, hoping they would stand in front of a bullet should someone try to assassinate him, and by the 1970s he was taking a range of barbiturates and other drugs, claiming he had kidney disease. When the San Franciscio temple burnt down and needed to be rebuilt, he used it as evidence that people were trying to destroy him and the Peoples Temple. These claims helped to convince the congregation that it was time to move somewhere where they would be safe.

Lester Kinsolving, an investigative journalist for the *San Francisco Examiner*, began looking into the local branch of Jim Jones' Peoples Temple. In September 1972, he published a series of articles that exposed the man who called himself a prophet, and after many members began to leave, Jones was forced to move his flock. When the articles made national news, he arranged to lease a large pocket of land, approximately 3,800 acres in size, in northern Guyana, South America. This site would become known as Jonestown.

He quickly began shipping worshippers and supplies to the compound so that they could construct a new church and homes there. By the time of the massacre in 1978, more than 1,000 parishioners were based at the Guyana location. Jones himself moved to the new commune in August 1977, as further criticism of his ministry was surfacing in the press.

People who lived at the new compound likened it to a prison camp.[157] Isolation from family and friends was the first difficulty. They also worked from dawn until dusk, looking after the elderly and the children and tending to animals and crops. When not working, the members would attend mass several times a day. Tapes would be played, praising the progress of the Guyana development and brainwashing members into believing they were creating a new Eden. The tapes were also played to congregations in America to recruit more members for the Guyana compound. At mass, people would be made to stand up in front of the congregation and confess their secrets, after which Jones would ask those assembled to decide on and mete out the appropriate punishment. Young men and women were often summoned to Jones' room, where he would have sex with them.[158]

People who wanted to leave Jonestown lived in fear, knowing that others would rat them out, including their own family. Though some thought what was happening was wrong, no one knew how to speak out, and they were all deeply brainwashed.

Jones compulsively taped his own voice. His voice played repeatedly over loudspeakers at Jonestown, so he was echoing in people's heads 24 hours a day. He talked regularly about a possible attack by the US and brainwashed his followers into believing they could never go home. By 1978, he was quite sick, and his recordings were slurred and manic. He made followers practise how to prevent others from leaving and people reported each other for any type of suspicious behaviour. The worst crime was to try to leave. Jones, a lonely man who had felt abandoned as a child, expressed this fear of abandonment in the treatment of his followers.

Deborah Layton, a Temple member who had been allowed to leave the Guyana compound, complained to officials about the conditions of the new camp. Deborah's letter explained that most of the parishioners were sick with diarrhoea and working extremely long hours at the direction of their leader. She said that most were forced to work 11 hours a day to get fields ready for planting, exhausted and with little food. She went so far as to raise concerns about Jones' religious delusions; her letter spoke of his claim to 'divine powers'.[159]

California congressman Leo Ryan received numerous letters from constituents complaining about the treatment of family members who had followed Jones from Californian ministries to Guyana. On 1 November 1978, Ryan sent a telegram to Jones, announcing his intention to visit as part of a congressional inquiry into the activities of the Peoples Temple. He was called a few days later by Jones' lawyer, Mark Lane, who explained that Ryan would be allowed to visit, but only under strict guidelines, including that no family members of Peoples Temple members or media would be allowed. Ryan ignored the guidelines. On 14 November 1978, he arrived in Guyana with several concerned family members, as well as a band of journalists, photographers and other staff, for a fact-finding mission into complaints of human rights abuses. A few days later, the group made their way to Jonestown via light aircraft.

Many of the people Ryan met in Jonestown told him they were having the time of their lives, and the rapture that greeted him was enthusiastic and exciting. But then several people secretly tried to pass notes to the congressman and his group. One man tried to pass a note that was dropped, and when a little boy saw the failed exchange, he began shouting that people were trying to escape. As darkness fell, questions were being asked, and people were telling Ryan that they were being held prisoner.

When some of his followers tried to leave with the party who came to visit, Jones realised he was about to lose control. Everyone was ordered into the communal hall, even as a storm hit Jonestown, turning the sky black. Jones was interviewed on camera and told the journalists that his people had lied to them. He gave the group permission to leave and told them not to come back. As the team tried to go, accompanied by 15 fleeing members of the Temple, Congressman Ryan was attacked by Temple member Ron Sly. Sly attempted to cut Ryan's throat with a knife, but was subdued, and Ryan survived the attack. The group hastily departed the compound, heading to the nearby airstrip.

On Jones' orders, three armed followers arrived at the airstrip in a tractor, pulling a trailer that held more armed followers, as the Ryan group were boarding their plane. They commenced shooting at Ryan's party, most of whom dropped to the ground under the plane's fuselage. One of the 15 escaping followers, Larry Layton, who was already inside one of the two planes, withdrew a concealed gun and shot at those onboard. Five people, including Ryan, were killed on the airstrip, and others were injured. Some were able to flee into the dense jungle that surrounded the field.

Soon afterwards, at Jonestown, everyone was directed to return to the communal hall where Jones began his final speech. 'The congressmen is dead,' he said. 'You think they're going to allow us to get away with this? You must be insane. They'll torture our children here. They'll torture our people. We cannot have this.' Fear was the only emotion left in Jonestown. 'If we can't live in peace, we'll die in peace,' Jones announced.[160]

Jones was prepared with enough poison for everyone, a combination of cyanide and sedatives, mixed into a large vat of Flavor Aid (not Kool-Aid, as has been reported). Small children had poison squirted into their mouths. There were screams of pain and agony throughout the enclave, as hundreds drank the poison, and others watched as their loved ones slowly died in front of them. People were holding their dead children to their bosoms as they themselves died, the cyanide killing them quickly. Christine Miller, one of Jones' inner circle, spoke up, stating that by dying they would be defeated. She asked Jones if it was too late to try to go to Russia, the place that Jones often spoke about as the perfect socialist environment. Miller was discredited and admonished by Jones, and followers soon realised they were surrounded by armed church members. Jones appealed for calm. Those who were not hysterical were in a daze, accepting of the horror happening around them. The hysteria that can be heard on sound recordings is haunting and terrifying.

During the mass suicide, Jones is heard saying, 'For God's sake, let's get on with it. We've lived as no other people have lived. We've loved like no other people have loved. We've had as much of this world as we are gonna get. Let's be done with it.' In the background, people are screaming as they die, or wait to die. A survivor of the mass suicide said people looked like they felt trapped; they knew they had no choice but to abide by their prophet's words.[161] 'Die with a degree of dignity,' Jones demands on the recording. 'Don't lay down with tears and agony. Death is just a stepping over into another plane. Don't be this way.'[162] All the while, the agonised cries continue on the tape.

In hindsight, the survivors said there were many red flags about Jim Jones, but they chose to ignore them and rationalise their leader's delusions. Nine hundred and nine people, 276 of them children, died of cyanide poisoning that night. Tim Carter, one of the five members who survived by fleeing into the jungle and hiding from the Peoples Temple militia, lost his wife and baby son in the mass suicide. 'It was a slaughter … senseless waste,' he said.[163] Jones' own life ended with a single self-inflicted gunshot wound to the head, after he had taken a lethal dose of Pentobarbital.

He had demanded that his faithful prove their complete devotion and they had done so. He maintained his control over those who followed him by making them repeatedly prove their loyalty, and when he became concerned that people were defecting, he moved his entire ministry to a foreign country. The remoteness of Jonestown, and his people's inability to contact the outside world, was his final step in gaining complete control over their lives. Jones' suicide recording ends with: 'We didn't commit suicide, we committed an act of revolutionary suicide, protesting the conditions of an inhumane world.'

Larry Layton, who had ambushed Ryan's delegation, was arrested by the survivors and stood trial for the murders on the airstrip, but was found not guilty by a Guyanese court. His defence was that he had been brainwashed by Jones.[164] He was returned to US soil, where he was convicted of aiding and abetting in the murder of Leo Ryan, the attempted murder of Richard Dwyer, and conspiracy. Those who fled the massacre and hid in the thick jungles were eventually found by the Guyanese army.

After the events of Jonestown became widely known, politicians who'd had their photo taken with Jim Jones distanced themselves from the man. State Assemblyman Willie Brown said, 'If we knew then he was mad, clearly we wouldn't have appeared with him.'[165]

The State Department was criticised for its inaction on the complaints they'd received in the years prior to the massacre, and an inquest was eventually held, which blamed the deaths at Jonestown on the Guyanese prime minister.

The site of the Jonestown massacre is now a deserted, broken-down shell. It was used briefly as a Laotian refugee camp, but was often looted, and then largely destroyed by fire during the 1980s. Today it is slowly being swallowed by the encroaching jungle.

Chapter 10
Marc Dutroux

One of the world's worst predators, Marc Dutroux, was born in Brussels on 6 November 1956. He was the eldest of five children born to school teachers Jeannine and Victor Dutroux. The family travelled to the Belgian Congo for work before returning to Ixelles in 1960. His parents' marriage was an extremely unhappy one, peppered with many episodes of violence and rage. His parents would often blame their eldest son for their unhappiness and took out their anger on the small boy. He claimed that he suffered beatings at the hands of both parents through most his childhood. According to his father, he was a 'difficult child'. Dutroux developed a deep resentment of both his parents and would later, in court, blame his mother for the direction his life took.

When his parents divorced in 1971, Dutroux stayed with his mother for a short period before moving in his grandmother. He particularly resented his mother for his schooling, claiming she had forced him to go to an agricultural school and doomed him to the life of a stable hand, rather than sending him to an academic secondary school. Dutroux left his grandmother's home at the age of 15 and spent most of his time living on the streets, eventually turning to male prostitution to survive. By the age of 20, he had married his first wife, and they had two sons before divorcing. The reasons for the dissolution of the marriage were spousal violence and the sexual abuse of the children at the hands of Dutroux.

He was also accused of having an affair with numerous women, including teacher Michelle Martin.

Dutroux moved in with his lover Michelle, and the two were married soon after his first divorce. They would go on to have three children. Dutroux and Martin, just like the Wests' and Homolka and Bernardo, were a dangerous combination. The pair engaged in a number of criminal activities, including robbery, to furnish the lifestyle they wished to live. In addition, they purchased several dilapidated and squalid houses with the proceeds from stolen cars and other schemes, and commenced large-scale renovations.

In 1979, Dutroux was sent to prison for the first time, for a variety of offences, including car theft, drugs and robberies. There, he made several new acquaintances, including Jean Michel Nihoul. The pair spent their days in the exercise yard, fuelling each other's sexual fantasies about what they would do on their release. Dutroux's incarceration did little to deter him from continuing his life of crime, and soon after his release, he was stealing cars and committing robbery once again.

On 13 February 1984, emergency services were called to a blaze at an abandoned mansion at Auderghem Champignonniere, just metres from a local police station. Once the flames had been extinguished, firefighters were shocked to discover the naked and mutilated remains of a teenage female. The young woman's hands and feet had been tied together with wire, which was also looped around her throat. Several days later, the charred remains were identified as belonging to missing 15-year-old Christine Van Hees.[166]

The case unfolded slowly. When the investigating judge, Michel Eloy, suffered a heart attack, he passed the file to Magistrate Jean-Claude Van Espen. The new judge identified another local criminal as the killer, which moved the case away from a suspected paedophile ring, said to include influential people among the Belgian establishment, as well as Dutroux and Nihoul.[167] The gang's sex parties, later exposed by victims who were abused during the festivities, were just a glimpse of what was to come.

During the 1980s, Dutroux fed his desire for the sexual abuse of young girls, spending a lot of time stalking children at local swimming centres in the suburbs of Belgium. In the company of Nihoul, Michelle Martin and their accomplice Michel Lelièvre, Dutroux would watch out for the perfect victim, one that fit his precise taste of a girl that looked young for her age and was under-developed. Once a girl was found, Dutroux or one of his gang would grab the girl and bundle her into a white van he owned. The victim would be raped before being released.

According to his criminal record, his first official victim was an 11-year-old girl. As she walked away from a local pool, the child was grabbed from behind by Dutroux and Lelièvre. Dutroux covered the frightened girl's eyes, mouth and nose with his hand, so she could neither see nor scream for help as she was bundled into the back of his van. Her eyes and mouth were taped shut and she was viciously raped by her abductor. Later, when the girl retold her story to police, she claimed that Dutroux made jokes during the entire ordeal in a bad American accent, presumably in an attempt to confuse her and hide his identity. The little girl was able to remember many aspects of the attack in great detail and provide police with a description of her attackers.

Before police could find the girl's attackers, Dutroux stuck again. His second victim was a 15-year-old student, who was riding her bike to school when she was grabbed by Dutroux and forced into the back of his car. Like the 11-year-old, Dutroux taped the girl's mouth and eyes closed, then savagely raped her and told her that she was being attacked because her father was a bad man.

By 1989, police had closed in, and Dutroux was arrested for the rapes of five girls. He was sentenced to 13 years for the attacks, while his wife's sentence as an accessory was suspended, as she had young children. During another term of imprisonment, Dutroux was charged with a number of further infractions, including violence towards other inmates and dealing in stolen goods. He also began planning his next move. He knew that raping girls and setting them free would see him imprisoned repeatedly, so he decided his victims could not live. Later, he claimed to have heard one of the other inmates talking about a plan to build a bunker in which to keep sex slaves, and the idea appealed to Dutroux. He began to make detailed plans for the construction of a series of bunkers beneath the various dilapidated homes he owned, envisioning a catacomb of dungeons, each housing chosen victims who would be ready to serve his every whim.

While Dutroux was in jail, his mother wrote to prison officials, concerned about the path her son was treading and believing he was a threat to society. She told authorities, 'What I do not know, and what all the people who know him fear, it's what he has in mind for the future …'[168] Dutroux's mother said her son should remain in prison or at the very least be watched closely on his release. These were harrowing words from a desperate mother, yet her fears went unheeded; no one responded to her letter or bothered to follow it up.

Psychiatrists who interviewed Dutroux during his imprisonment claimed the man was not a 'classic' paedophile. The age of the victim did not arouse any specific response 'beyond allowing him to kidnap them … manipulate them … [and] … confine them'. The report assisted Dutroux's campaign for release and he left prison in 1992, only three years into his 13-year sentence. According to the parole board, Dutroux was no longer a danger to society, so there were no restrictions on the conditions of his release. Local officials were not told that a serial child rapist had been released into their midst and Dutroux was allowed to move freely around Belgium. He even convinced a psychiatrist that his incarceration had left him unable to work, resulting in him gaining a considerable monthly disability pension. Dutroux and Martin divorced on his release, though they continued to live together.

In April 1992, only weeks after his release from prison, Dutroux abducted his next victim. The young girl was grabbed as she walked along a road in Jambes, but was fortunate enough to fight off her attacker and escape. In hindsight, this attempted abduction appears to have been a practice run for a more sinister plan, as Dutroux did not fight the girl and allowed her to get away. The rapist returned to his poisonous fantasies and began the excavation of large amounts of dirt from beneath several of the homes he owned. He stole earth-moving equipment to manage the job without alerting police. The bunkers were built in a labyrinth of tunnels connecting several of his criminally obtained homes, which were situated along the railway tracks through the rundown suburb of Chaleroi.

A vital piece of evidence was brought to the attention of police. Informant and career criminal Claude Thirault told police he had been approached by Dutroux with an offer of $9,000 for every young girl he could procure. Thirault told police of the man's plan to construct several concrete, sound-proofed bunkers, where he would incarcerate captured girls as sex slaves. According to Thirault, he had a very distinct list of requirements. He wanted girls who appeared young for their age, underdeveloped, and with shoulder-length or longer hair. Police investigated Thirrault's claim, though they initially did not take him seriously. When officers visited one of Dutroux's homes in November 1993, they found a series of underground tunnels that warranted further investigation and officers began surveillance that lasted for several weeks. It was not a full-time operation, however; the known child abuser was watched only during daylight hours, which left his nocturnal activities, and those of his criminal associates, unchecked.

As his prison cells neared completion, Dutroux attempted to abduct a number of girls. In July 1994, a young girl named Eva was taken, had her mouth and eyes taped before being raped by Dutroux, and released following the attack. In mid-1995, several others were grabbed across a vast area – a young girl, Aurelie, managed to escape his clutches in Gerpinnes in May 1995; in Slovakia, in June 1995, he raped another girl, Henriata, who was lucky to get away with her life; and in Kortrijk in the north-west of Belgium, another little girl, Sylvia, managed to escape his clutches. Thyfene escaped him when he tried to abduct her in June in Spy, a city north of Dutroux's Charleroi home, and when he tried to capture two more girls in June in Jupile, both Lindsay and Stephanie were thankfully able to get away.

On 24 June 1995, his final plan to abduct children for his torture chambers was ready. Dutroux headed to Ougree, near the border of Belgium and Germany, and attempted to grab two young girls, but Dikana and Vanessa managed to escape. The next two little girls weren't as lucky and it only took a few seconds for them to disappear. Julie Lejeune and Melissa Russo, two eight-year-old school friends, disappeared a little after five in the evening while standing on the Autoroute de Wallonie Overpass at Grâce-Hollogne on the outskirts of Liège. They had wandered away from the park where they'd been playing, and many people travelling along the road that evening remembered seeing the little girls hanging over the bridge railings, waving to cars passing beneath them. The girls were last seen alive in the company of a blonde-haired woman, resembling Martin, who was talking to them near the bridge.

The girls were abducted and rendered unconscious with sleeping pills. They were then taken to a property at Avenue de Philippevillle 128 at Sars La Buissiere, owned by Marc Dutroux. They were brought to the kitchen of the Dutroux home, where they were raped by Nihoul, Lelièvre, Bernard Weinstein and Michelle Martin. After the initial assault, they were imprisoned in the incomplete bunker in the bowels on Dutroux's property, and were repeatedly raped in the first few weeks of their imprisonment.

An investigation into the disappearance of the two eight-year-olds began slowly. The lead investigator went on a six-week holiday and there was no replacement to continue the enquiry. Police were uninterested in the possibility of a double-abduction theory, preferring to believe the two had simply run away. Meanwhile, day after day, the two little girls were brought out of the dark, dank bunkers to the main house, where they were raped and beaten by Dutroux and the others. Some of the attacks may have been filmed and sold to underground paedophile rings.[169] When not being tortured, the girls spent their time in tiny cells, chained to the walls. They attempted to hold on to their innocence by drawing on the walls or making jokes together.

Police finally realised that the girls could have been abducted and began a search in earnest. One area of investigation was to make sure they interviewed all known paedophiles. Dutroux was on that list and police visited the convicted child-rapist's home to question him. While inside the man's home, investigators could hear two young children calling for help, but Dutroux claimed the voices were those of his own children playing upstairs.

Police searched the home in an attempt to locate the source of the voices, but were unable to find the secret door that would have led to the girls. Another entirely separate team, investigating stolen property, had found the secret door but were unaware of the incarcerated girls. The two teams did not share their information, a mistake that would cost the little girls their lives. This second team also confiscated several videos and films that depicted child rape scenes, which were returned to Dutroux unwatched.[170] Police did continue to run surveillance on Dutroux's home, though with little success, as he was still able to abduct his next two victims.

Almost two months after the disappearance of Julie and Melissa, another pair of girls disappeared. An Marchal, 17, and Eefje Lambrecks, 19, were holidaying at the coastal town of Ostend on 22 August 1995, when they were abducted by Dutroux and his friend Michel Lelièvre. Though the girls were older than those usually desired by Dutroux, they were added to his harem of sex slaves. They were given sleeping pills and driven back to Dutroux's home, where they were each chained to a bed and raped for the next several weeks. This time the teenagers were kept in an upstairs room, away from Julie and Melissa, so they would not talk.

Eefje attempted to escape early in her incarceration but was quickly captured by Dutroux in the front yard. The man removed all of the teen's clothing to stop her trying to escape again. Eefje again tried to flee; naked and screaming for help, she fled the dilapidated home, but was caught once more. Following the second escape attempt, he drugged the two teenagers and buried them alive in the yard of his house in Sars-la-Buissière, leaving only Melissa and Julie to continue being tortured and raped.

Dutroux was arrested and charged with the theft of several luxury cars on 5 December 1995. He was sentenced to another three-month term in jail for the crimes. While in prison, Dutroux instructed Martin to make sure his two little captives were kept alive, as he planned to use them as part of his welcome home celebrations, but she was too scared to go near the girls. She entered the cell once after Dutroux's sentencing, and gave them food, but the sight of the abused and tortured children was too much for her to bear. She slammed the 200kg door to the cellar closed and blocked it with other heavy items. The girls slowly starved to death, their tortured and beaten bodies too weak to attempt any escape from the dirty pit that had been their home for almost six months.

When Dutroux was released from prison in April 1995, he immediately returned to the bunker where Julie and Melissa were imprisoned. When he found that the girls had starved to death, he became enraged, savagely beating and raping Martin before burying the eight-year-olds in the yard at Sars-la-Buissière.

On 4 November 1995, Dutroux and Bernard Weinstein abducted two men, Philippe Divers and Pierre Rochow, from Jumet. Weinstein believed the two men had stolen one of his trucks and threatened to kill them. They drove their two captives to the Waterloo home of Rochow to look for clues, and there found Rochow's girlfriend, Benedicte Jadot. She, too, was abducted. The men drugged their three captives and tortured them, but Benedicte managed to escape, and alerted neighbours to their plight. In the meantime, Dutroux freed the two men, who immediately went to police. After an unexplainable delay, officers turned up months later to investigate, but by then Dutroux had drugged his friend Bernard Weinstein and buried him alive next to the bodies of An and Eefje, as retribution for the botched abduction of the three young people.

With the torture bunkers below Dutroux's home empty, and police surveillance no longer in effect, he set about planning his next abduction. On 28 May 1996, he found 13-year-old Sabine Dardenne wandering home from school. She was grabbed off the streets of Kain, Belgium, by Dutroux and his accomplice Michel Lelièvre. They wedged her tiny body into a small metal trunk for the trip to the dungeon under Dutroux's Chaleroi home. When the schoolgirl failed to arrive home, her parents reported her disappearance to the local constabulary. Sabine's disappearance was reported in the local news and when it was linked to several other attacks and disappearances, the case became national news. Like Julie and Melissa before her, 13-year-old Sabine's image was plastered on telegraph poles and across television news reports. Someone had to have seen something, it was felt, and public concern about the string of disappearances became a national outrage. For the next 80 days, as Sabine's parents searched for her, she remained hidden in a rubbish-filled dungeon, only removed to satisfy Dutroux's lust. The young girl documented her captivity, rape and torture, using little symbols in her schoolbooks to note down the brutality her captor had inflicted upon her. She also wrote heartbreaking letters to her parents.

Dutroux decided to abduct another girl in the last week of July 1996. Yancka, 16, was grabbed by Dutroux and raped; her sister had been an assault victim of Dutroux's two years earlier. Yancka escaped shortly after her abduction, and though she reported the attack to police, no investigation was ever made into her complaint. Then on 9 August 1996, Dutroux, Michelle Martin and Michel Nihoul headed to a swimming complex in Bertix, Belgium, where Dutroux had previously abducted and raped several of his victims. Standing outside the centre was Laetitia Delhez. With her cropped blonde hair, the girl looked a lot younger than her 14 years. Dutroux dawdled past the girl, then turned and asked her a question. She ignored him. He asked her the question again and this time, as she began to answer, he grabbed her by the throat, pushed her into the open door of his white van, and drove away from the scene.

With recent press having described similar attacks, Dutroux's daylight abduction was extremely risky. His mental stability was waning and he was becoming complacent and over-confident. Several people witnessed the abduction and a police investigation was quickly mobilised. One man recalled the number plate of the white van, giving police their best lead – it took them straight to Marc Dutroux.

On 13 August 1996, Dutroux and Michel Nihoul were arrested for the abduction of Laetitia Delhez. Both men denied any knowledge of the girl's whereabouts, but after two days of questioning, Dutroux finally revealed the hidden location of Laetitia's prison cell. He also confessed to holding Sabine Dardenne in the dungeons. With the press in tow, ready for a live-to-air reunion with their parents, police brought the two frightened girls to the surface, ending their horrific ordeal of rape and torture. Both girls were filthy and cried hysterically as they hugged their parents, still unable to believe that they had been rescued, leaving behind, at least physically, the dungeons where they had been chained by their necks to their beds and half-starved, while being forced to service their captor.

Dutroux also led police to the graves of four of his victims, as well as that of accomplice Bernard Weinstein, whom he had drugged and buried alive. Carine Russo, Melissa's mother, pleaded with investigators to let her see her daughter's body, even taking a lawyer with her, but her request was refused. Police said that it was against the law for her to see her daughter's remains, and when she asked who had identified her daughter, she was told that Dutroux had made the formal identification of the victims.[171] Hair, semen samples and various other pieces of evidence were collected, but nothing was done to further establish the identity of anyone else who might have had access to the victims prior to their deaths.

The two young survivors were interviewed at length about the attacks they had endured. They recalled their captor trying to convince them that he was hiding them from someone who was trying to extort money from their parents. He tried to explain that he was in fact doing them a favour by keeping them chained up and raping them continuously. Dutroux told police he was only a pawn in a larger organised child sex ring, stating that many of those involved were people of importance in Belgium.

The enormity of the case was beginning to surface. Jean Marc Connerotte, the judge in charge of the Dutroux investigation, 'broke down in tears as he described the bullet-proof vehicles and armed guards needed to protect him against "shadowy figures" determined to stop the full truth coming out'.[172] The judge called for any victims of the paedophile network to come forward and 27-year-old Regina Louf was the first brave person to do so. Following her courageous action, 11 more victims spoke up about the horrors they had endured. Louf told investigators of the harrowing abuse she had suffered and was able to give specific details of what had happened to her, where and when. The young woman also named important people in the case, including judges, influential businessmen and even royalty. She identified Jean Michel Nihoul, one of Dutroux's associates, as a ring-leader in her abuse and spoke of a number of murders she had witnessed, including that of Christine Van Hees.

Justice Connerotte began a thorough investigation into the victims' testimony (known as the X Dossiers). Several officers were sent to interview the victims, who in turn identified other victims, as well as their abusers, the killers and the homes where the crimes had taken place.[173] Regina and others finally felt safer, knowing they were one step closer to shutting down the paedophile rings. Then, in a dramatic twist, Justice Connerotte was sacked due to a conflict of interest; he had attended a fundraising function for the girls who had survived Dutroux's clutches, so officials believed he had lost his impartiality. Many Belgians believe that Connerotte was coming close to identifying the paedophile network and could have named high-ranking officials among the suspects.

Following his sacking, the investigation into victims' testimony was halted indefinitely and a new judge, Van Espen, was appointed to take over. Although Van Espen reportedly had familial links with some involved in the case,[174] it was decided that there was no conflict of interest and he continued as investigating judge for the duration of Dutroux's trial. Many Belgians could not believe the media circus the trial had become and took to the streets in protest against the judicial system. In the 'White March' protest, demonstrators dressed in white and carried white balloons and banners.

In April 1998, Justice Minister Stefaan De Clerck and Interior Minister Vande Lanotte resigned over the Dutroux affair. Shortly thereafter, Dutroux escaped from police custody for a period of three hours. The man had apparently convinced prison guards to undo his handcuffs while he sat in a library reading up on his own case evidence. This breach of protocol resulted in the Chief of Police's resignation and the officers being disciplined. One detective, Georges Zicot, was arrested for theft, insurance fraud and document forgery, and it was eventually clarified that he had connections with Marc Dutroux, the seventh police officer to be linked with the man.[175]

At his trial, Dutroux admitted to charges of kidnap and rape, but said he was not responsible for the deaths of the two eight-year-old girls and the two 18-year-old women whose bodies had been found in the gardens of his home. The letters Sabine wrote during her captivity, documenting the sexual abuse she endured, were read out at the insistence of the brave young girl and her mother. When asked why he had not handed Sabine over to the paedophile ring he claimed had been controlling him, Dutroux said he had grown attached to the pretty pre-teen, and knew that if she had become property of the 'ring', she would have been killed.

Sabine appeared at the trial on April 20. When Dutroux attempted to reply to statements she made, Sabine asked the judge to 'make him be quiet'. The contempt the now 20-year-old felt for the man was obvious to every person in the courtroom and members of the gallery cheered her comments. The young woman continued her testimony, documenting her time in the basement torture room where she was kept when not being raped, with Dutroux attempting to reassure her that she was being protected from a wider network of sinister predators.

Psychiatrist Walter Denys appeared as a witness at trial. He had interviewed Dutroux at length and was adamant in his diagnosis of the Beast of Belgium. 'He is the perfect psychopath,' Denys stated. According to the doctor, Dutroux displayed no remorse for the demise of his victims, nor the ritualistic abuse they suffered. The psychiatrist believed Dutroux felt he was not to blame for what occurred.

In the final stages of the explosive trial, Dutroux made an impassioned speech. He said that he felt sincere regret for what had happened, yet claimed the part he had played was only a small element in a larger, organised paedophile ring. In a hushed courtroom, Dutroux continued, 'I am not a murderer … I am not asking for forgiveness. I can't do much to change the irreversible.'

In June 2004, eight years after his arrest, millions of Belgians watched the sentencing of Marc Dutroux on live television. He was found guilty of the abduction and rape of six of his victims in 1995 and 1996, as well as the murders of An and Eefje, and Bernard Weinstein. He was also found guilty of imprisoning and raping the two surviving girls. He was sentenced to life imprisonment without the possibility of parole and the judge called him a danger to society. Dutroux's wife Michelle Martin was sentenced to 30 years imprisonment and Michel Lelièvre received a 25-year sentence. Michel Nihoul was acquitted, but sentenced to five years for drug charges.

Regardless of whether a network of high-powered paedophiles was involved, Dutroux himself was a classic sexual predator. According to psychiatrists who interviewed the killer in prison, he was 'less a paedophile than an icy-hearted predator with a murderous desire to control his victims … the age of the victims did not seem to arouse in him any given effect or to play a particular role, beyond allowing him to kidnap them, to manipulate them, to confine them'.[176] This chilling analysis sums up the character of one of the world's worst sexual predators.

Chapter 11
Jeffrey Dahmer

From the day of their wedding on 22 August 1959, the marriage of Lionel Herbert Dahmer and Annette Joyce Flint was not a happy one. The two fought and bickered all the way from the altar to their divorce. Joyce would often walk out, leaving Lionel to go and find her and try to patch things up. He was the quieter and more reserved one of the couple, and always tried his best for the family. He studied hard for his chemistry degree at Marquette University and strove for better things. He was logical, and often thought hard before giving an answer, whereas Joyce, or 'Rocky' as her friends called her, would jump to conclusions and argue a point to the very end. She was defiant and troublesome, and always made sure that Lionel was aware of her needs and wants.

On the evening of New Year's Day 1960, in the dead of winter, Joyce walked out of the house and went to a local park to sit and cry. She had no shoes on and no warm clothes. She was quite emotional and her pregnancy was a further burden; it had been a stressful one for Joyce, and she had suffered bouts of unexplained partial paralysis during the pregnancy, with doctors unable to find the cause of the problem. Lionel went looking for her and coaxed her back to the warmth of the house. For the entirety of February and March 1960, Joyce was forced to give up work and was bedridden with nausea and pain. She was given 'injections of barbiturates and morphine, which would finally relax her',[177] as well as Phenobarbital.

Lionel later believed that these drugs, filtered through in utero to his son, were to blame for Jeffrey's later life as a cannibalistic serial killer. Any noise from the surrounding apartments would send Joyce into a frenzy of anger, so Lionel decided they should move for the sake of her health. When Joyce was seven months pregnant, the couple moved into a house in West Allis, which was owned by Lionel's family.

On 21 May 1960, at 4.34pm, Jeffrey Lionel Dahmer was born at Evangelical Deaconess Hospital in Milwaukee. He weighed 6lbs 15oz and was 18-and-a-half inches long, with light red hair and bright blue eyes. For a brief moment, with the birth of such a beautiful child, the couple were extremely happy. They named the baby Jeffrey Lionel and loved him dearly. Joyce recorded every part of the baby's early life in a scrapbook, including her own thoughts and emotions.

Newborn Jeffrey was almost perfect, except for a problem with his hips, which required a cast for four months, then lifts until the age of six. At first, the problems scared Lionel and Joyce, but they were only mild. At the early age of six-and-a-half months, he stood alone, and crawled two months later. He had his first haircut two weeks after that. Dahmer had a pet turtle and goldfish at 18 months and an intense interest in animals, even at a young age. He was so gentle with the turtle, according to his mother. He also helped his father nurse an injured baby bird back to health. When Dahmer was two, the family moved again, this time to Ames, Iowa, so Lionel could work on his PhD.

At the age of four Jeffrey began to complain about severe pain in his groin and was diagnosed with a double hernia in his scrotum. He was admitted to hospital and had surgery to correct the fault. Looking back, Lionel said that it was after this operation when Jeffrey began to be more introverted and quiet. The child was embarrassed and traumatised about the procedure; when he woke from the operation he thought they had cut his penis off.[178] Nearly 30 years later, he said he still remembered the pain.

In November 1966, the family moved again. This time they travelled to Doylestown, Ohio, but they did not settle there long, moving again and again as they searched for the right place to bring up a family. On 18 December that year, Jeffrey's younger brother David was born. With Joyce going through another difficult pregnancy and birth, Jeffrey felt even more neglected and introverted. At school, teachers said he was extremely shy and kept to himself. His mother was heartbroken, sending him to school when she knew he would spend his time there alone. Though he was intelligent, he did not live up to his potential, preferring to be disruptive in class rather than pay attention to his work. He did fancy one of his teachers and later recalled giving her a bowl of tadpoles. The teacher gave the tadpoles to another student, who killed them.[179]

In 1968, Jeffrey was sexually molested by a neighbourhood boy in rural Bath Township. Unreported at the time, the childhood incident may have played a pivotal role in explaining his subsequent crimes. At 10, he began 'experimenting' with dead animals using the chemistry set his father had given him. He would decapitate rodents and bleach chicken bones with acid. He famously nailed a dog's carcass to a tree and mounted its severed head on a stake.

By the age of 13, Dahmer had started drinking alcohol, and by 14, he was drinking heavily. 'He was a gentle person, but when he got drunk it would take four policemen to hold him down,' said his future stepmother, Shari Dahmer.[180] A year later, he had his first homosexual experience, but would later reflect that he had already started to fantasise about sex with corpses. Though he still maintained decent grades at school, his alcoholism had reached a point where he would even drink in class. Other students saw him as a weird loner who did stupid things just for attention.

At the age of 18, Jeffrey witnessed the bitter divorce of his parents, who fought over the custody of his younger brother. In the end, his mother took off with David, leaving Jeffrey to fend for himself. He moved in with his grandmother.

His first killing happened in 1978, shortly after his mother had left. Steven Hicks had planned to meet friends after a rock concert, but Dahmer enticed the young man back to his grandmother's home, where they had sex.

When Steven tried to leave, Dahmer struck him with a dumbbell, killing him instantly. He then took the body into the crawlspace beneath the house, where he dismembered it and put the pieces into plastic bags.

In the nine years that followed, Dahmer claimed he was able to keep control of his urges to commit murder. During this hiatus, he was charged with many other offences, including assault of a young boy, indecent exposure, disorderly conduct and drunken behaviour. He also tried a stint in the army, but was discharged due to his alcoholism. During his time in the military he was stationed in Baumholder, West Germany, where five unsolved murders involving mutilated bodies occurred.[181]

Once discharged, Dahmer began working at a chocolate factory in Milwaukee. His homosexuality was difficult for him to accept; he began frequenting local gay bars, but kept pretty much to himself. On the rare occasions when he could manage a conversation with fellow drinkers, he would often spike their drinks, merely for the purpose of experimenting.[182]

By 1987, Dahmer was unable to control himself any longer, and began the killing spree that would make him famous. On 15 September 1987, Dahmer met Steven Tuomi at a gay bar called Club 219 in West Allis. After some chit-chat, the two retired to a nearby hotel for sex.

Dahmer later could not recall much of that evening, but woke the next morning to find Steven strangled, with blood coming from his mouth. Knowing he had to get rid of the body, he went out and bought a large suitcase and shoved the dead body inside it. He took it home to his grandmother's basement, where he dismembered the corpse and put it out in plastic bags for the garbage collectors. The mystery of Tuomi's disappearance remained unsolved until Dahmer confessed to his murder in 1991.

In January 1988, Dahmer picked up 14-year-old James E. Doxtator outside Club 219. James was enticed by Jeffrey's offer to pose for nude photographs in exchange for money. After drugging the teenager, Dahmer strangled James, then dismembered his corpse and put the remains out in the trash once again. Only two months later, in March 1988, he met 25-year-old

Richard Guerrero at the same club. Richard went back to Dahmer's home, where he was murdered, raped, photographed and dismembered.

By September 1988, Jeffrey's odd hours had become too much for his grandmother, and he was asked to move out. On 25 September, he found an apartment on Milwaukee's North 25th Street. The next day, he met a 13-year-old boy by the surname of Sinthasomphone. Dahmer lured him to his new apartment and drugged him, but the boy escaped and Dahmer was charged with indecent assault for enticing a child for immoral purposes. He was released on bail.

On 29 March 1989, Jeffrey visited gay bar La Cage. At closing time outside the bar, he was approached by a man called Anthony Sears. Anthony's friend Jeffrey Connor offered to drive the two men to Dahmer's house. He dropped them off at the corner of 56th Street in Lincoln, West Allis, and Anthony Sears was never seen alive again. His skull, scalp and penis were later found in Jeffrey Dahmer's apartment.

In May 1989, Dahmer was sentenced to eight years for the attack on the young Sinthasomphone. In prison, he told other inmates of his desire to kill thousands of black men because he hated them so much.[183] He was released after serving only 10 months of his sentence and moved to a new home on 25th Street. In June 1990, he was on the prowl again, and victim number six was Edward Smith. He drugged the man and strangled him, later raping the corpse and dismembering the body. A painted skull, discovered two years later in Dahmer's apartment, was found to belong to Edward. Later that month, Raymond Smith met Dahmer in the Phoenix Bar; the pair retired to the 25th Street apartment, where Raymond was murdered and raped.

On 3 September 1990, after not killing for three months, Dahmer picked up Ernest Miller, a young black man, from outside a bookstore. Back at Dahmer's apartment, the men had sex before having a drink, Ernest's laced with a sedative. Dahmer's urge to kill boiled over into a frenzied attack – instead of the usual strangulation, he slit the man's throat. He wanted to keep the skeleton, so he cut most of the flesh from the bones, and dissolved the rest in acid vats, before bleaching the skeleton. He also kept the biceps in the freezer.

On 27 May 1991, police responded to a neighbour's concerned call – they had discovered a bleeding and naked 14-year-old boy, Konerak Sinthasomphone, who had escaped from Dahmer's apartment. Konerak was the brother of the other young boy who had escaped. The police called it 'a homosexual lovers' spat' and returned the boy to Dahmer, who quickly dispensed with him.

Three weeks later, Dahmer met David Thomas, who was enticed to the apartment. Dahmer killed him and photographed the body in different states of dismemberment; Thomas' sister later identified him from the photographs that were taken. Then a month later, on 30 June, Dahmer went to a gay pride parade in Chicago, where he met Matt Turner. He invited Matt to come with him to Milwaukee; once home, they had sex, and Matt was strangled after being drugged. His head and internal organs were later found in Jeffrey's freezer and his headless torso was also found in the apartment.

One week later, on 7 July, Dahmer met Jeremiah Weinberger in a bar called Carol's Gay Bar. From there, both men travelled back to Milwaukee. For a few days, they lived together as a couple, until Dahmer decided to kill him on the fourth day. At the time of Dahmer's arrest, Jeremiah's head was in his freezer, and his body was found next to Turner's.

In February 1991, another victim, Curtis Straughter, met Jeffrey Dahmer. Curtis was murdered with Dahmer's leather belt, and Dahmer kept his skull, hands and genitals. He was later identified by dental records. On 7 April, he met Errol Lindsey outside the same bookstore where he'd met Ernest Miller. Dahmer invited him to his apartment, where he was drugged, raped and dismembered, and Errol's skin was kept. Tony Hughes was the next victim; the pair met at his old haunt, Club 219. Tony was deaf and dumb, but communicated by writing with and lip reading. At Dahmer's apartment, he was drugged and strangled to death. Dahmer raped the body for three days before dismembering it. The smell in the apartment was becoming unbearable; tenants in the other units began to complain.

On 15 July 1991, Dahmer picked up Oliver Lacy. The 24-year-old was drugged and strangled and Dahmer had sex with the corpse. Four days later, he picked up out-of-work Joseph Bradeholt, who posed for photographs for money and joined Dahmer in consensual oral sex in the apartment. Dahmer then drugged his victim before strangling him. Bradeholt was dismembered, his head joining the three already occupying the freezer, and the rest of his body added to putrefying vats of acid.

The time between killings, which had once been years, had come down to a few days. Dahmer was out of control and the killing compulsion drove his every move. His final intended victim was Tracy Edwards, but through the haze of drugs he'd been fed, the man was able to escape. Upon encountering police, Edwards was relieved, yet incoherent. Naked, with a handcuff dangling from his wrist, he tried to explain to the officers that a man was trying to kill him.

The Milwaukee police went to the apartment to investigate and found the unimaginable. Blue, 55-gallon acid vats in the bedroom were filled with rotting torsos, and a heart was stashed in the freezer 'to eat later'. Skulls, stripped of hair and skin, were displayed on shelves, and there was a bucket full of hacked-off hands in the fridge. A torso in the kitchen sink had been ripped open from neck to groin. A jar contained a pickled penis, while another severed penis was lying on the sink and another was in a lobster pot in the fridge. Officers also found Polaroid photographs of men engaging in homosexual activity, some of them dead. In many of the photographs, the corpses had been dismembered and mutilated. As police looked around, they realised the pictures had been taken in that very room.

Dahmer's time was up. An insanity plea was rejected by the court and on 27 January 1992, he was found guilty and sentenced to 15 life sentences. He would serve a little less than three years, however, as he was beaten to death in prison by Christopher Scarver, a convicted killer on antipsychotic medication, on 28 November 1994. Scarver – who claimed to be Christ, because he was a carpenter and his mother's name was Mary – killed the cannibal, along with convicted wife-killer Jesse Anderson, with a bar from a piece of exercise equipment. It was only the second time during Dahmer's incarceration that he had associated with other inmates; the previous excursion had resulted in his being seriously injured.

Hearing of her son's death, Dahmer's mother exclaimed, 'Now is everybody happy? Now that he's bludgeoned to death, is that good enough for everyone?'[184]

Chapter 12
Colin Pitchfork

As the husband of a social worker, Colin Pitchfork attempted to understand his own mania, which led him to rape and murder two teenagers. This understanding did little to comfort him, however – he still suffered from his compulsions to expose himself and rape young girls.

Pitchfork was the second of three children, born to parents who had little time for their middle child. He grew up in the village of Newbold Verdon in Leicestershire, England, and felt deprived of parental affection for most of his childhood, his parents preferring to devote their attentions to his older sister and young brother. He attended local schools, where he achieved average results, and was bullied in his mid-schooling years because he had entered puberty early.[185] Leaving school at the age of 16, he gained an apprenticeship as a baker at Hampshires Bakery in Leicester, where he was employed until his arrest at the age of 23.

The first signs of Pitchfork's sexual perversions emerged during his teenage years. He liked to expose himself to fellow students, and by the age of 17, had exposed himself several times to teenage girls. Then in February 1979, at the age of 19, he crept up behind a 16-year-old girl and forced her into a nearby field, where he 'undid her clothing, and put his hand down the front of her jeans'.[186] When he thought he heard someone coming, he fled, leaving the girl to hurry home and call police. Pitchfork was arrested for the attack and ordered to attend a Woodlands outpatient treatment program. Having suffered little punishment or deterrent, he was encouraged to continue exposing himself to young girls, until his flashing finally turned to murder.

Two years after his arrest, he married his wife Carole, and the couple had their first son by 1983. Babysitting his son on the evening of 21 November 1983, while his wife attended a course, Pitchfork decided to go for a drive to help put the baby to sleep. Travelling through Narborough, he spotted 15-year-old Lynda Mann walking along the Black Pad footpath, traversing the short distance between the homes of two friends. Black Pad was a tree-lined back street that locals used often. It was unusual that no one else was walking their dog or using the laneway that evening.

A little after 7.15pm, Pitchfork drove past the girl, and parked his car near the footpath where she was heading. He left his baby sleeping in the back seat and headed out into the evening. According to Pitchfork, the attack he launched was an opportunistic crime; he saw her and wanted her. In the dark, he doubled back towards the unsuspecting teenager. From a distance, he asked her for directions, pretending to be lost. Obligingly, she tried to explain how to get back to the main road, but as she got closer to him Pitchfork exposed his genitalia. The girl screamed in shock and ran away. In her panicked state, she ran towards a footpath that led across a large field, rather than towards nearby houses.

Pitchfork grabbed her as she tried to flee. He dragged Lynda towards the vacant block and away from the footpath, and stripped her of her clothing from the waist down.[187] He then raped her as she struggled against him. She tried to fight him off, even telling him that she had noticed his wedding ring and asking how his wife would feel, knowing that she was married to a rapist. Later, Pitchfork himself explained what happened: 'Her two big mistakes were running into the footpath and saying "What about your wife?" She'd seen my wedding ring.'[188]

He tried to explain himself to the girl before realising he had given her a lot of information that could prove helpful in identifying him later. He admitted during his police interview that Lynda had been terrified as

142

he stripped her clothes from her body. She had done most of the undressing herself, as she was too scared to try and fight him. Eventually, as he continued to rape her, Pitchfork strangled her with her own scarf.

Lynda's body was found the following morning, but police had little to go on. The hours after her murder turned into weeks, then months, without an arrest.

Criminal psychologist Paul Britton created a profile of the killer for police.[189] He believed the killer was a local man who knew the terrain of the Black Pad path, was in a stable, heterosexual, long-term relationship, but was driven by a sexual fantasy that saw him target younger girls. The profile was partially accurate – Pitchfork was not a local, but had been to the area many times, as he and his social worker wife were planning a move to the borough. As a baker in nearby Leicester, he also made birthday and celebratory cakes for many of the town's people.

A month after the murder, Pitchfork and his wife and baby moved to Littlethorpe, a town within the constabulary's net. In a door-to-door investigation, police arrived at the Pitchforks' home. Police officers waited in the living room while Colin took his time in the attic to calm himself before emerging to face the officers. Though he did not have an alibi, he was not suspected as the killer. Police assumed that a man caring for his baby at home would not have ventured far, and certainly would not have left his son alone.

Pitchfork realised that he had got away with the murder and again began exposing himself to teenagers. In October 1985, he sexually assaulted a teenage girl, threatening her with a screwdriver and telling her he would hunt her down if she reported the assault. He had grabbed her from behind and pulled her into a dark corner near a row of lock-up garages. He was arrested for indecent exposure and again avoided incarceration, instead being given a probationary term. Shortly after his non-custodial sentencing, in January 1986, his wife gave birth to their second son. Pitchfork doted on his two small children, lavishing the love on them that he had longed for as a child, and lost the desire to expose himself for a time. But that feeling would last only a few months.

Pitchfork struck again on 31 July 1986, and this time, he was careless. He attacked his next teenage victim in broad daylight. Dawn Ashworth has collected her wages from her newsagency job and made plans with a girlfriend to go out that evening. When she arrived home, however, Dawn's parents asked her to babysit her younger sibling for the evening. Dawn obliged, letting her mother know that she would walk to her friend's home to cancel their plans. After being unable to find her girlfriend, Dawn headed home, taking a short cut via the Black Pad that sliced a significant distance off her trip. Her father had begged her not to take that route, particularly after the murder of Lynda Mann only two years earlier.

As he had done with Lynda, Pitchfork spotted the girl as she walked along the Black Pad pathway, stopped his car nearby and got out. He doubled back to where he knew the teenager would cross his path. Once she was near him, he exposed himself to her before dragging her into the scrub. She tried to fight him off and was punched several times in the face during the attack. Pitchfork left significant bruises over the girl's body where he had grabbed her violently and her perineum and anus were torn during the attack. He strangled her while he raped her, before covering her dead body with fallen foliage. Her body was found two days later where he had left it.

With no leads after weeks of investigation, police turned to the new technique of DNA testing. In a British first, more than 5,000 men were tested, in the hop that police would find a match for the killer's semen. While laboratories worked tirelessly to run every DNA sample that came in, police arrested a possible suspect. The teenager confessed to the murder of Dawn Ashworth, but was quickly discredited when his sample did not match that found at the two crime scenes. Police were still no closer to catching Pitchfork and he attempted to attack another girl in June 1987. Fortunately she was able to escape.

By August 1987, as a majority of men had had their blood samples done, Pitchfork began to falter. Several letters arrived requesting that he visit his local police station to give a blood sample. He convinced a friend – his co-worker at the bakery – to go in his place, telling him that he had given a sample himself for another friend, and that if he gave blood he would be arrested for a different crime. His naïve friend believed the story, taking the test in his place. Pitchfork thought his plan was foolproof, but the friend boasted about how he had taken the sample for Pitchfork while having drinks with bakery co-workers. One of them, who had always thought Pitchfork was a little strange, called police. They checked the man's background and found that he had been arrested several times for indecent exposure.

On 19 August 1987, police waited for Pitchfork to arrive home from work. He was arrested, and submitted a blood sample that proved he had murdered both Lynda and Dawn. When asked by his wife why he had attacked the girls, his answer was honest and brutal: 'Opportunity. She was there and I was there.'[190] Paul Britton, in his book *The Jigsaw Man*, would call Pitchfork's interview and confession 'cold'.[191]

Pitchfork pleaded guilty to both murders and was sentenced to two life sentences. He was also found guilty of the other rapes and assaults he had committed. The psychological report submitted at trial suggested that he had a 'personality disorder of psychopathic type accompanied by serious psychosexual pathology ... [and that he] ... will obviously continue to be an extremely dangerous individual while the psychopathology continues'.[192]

At sentencing, Justice Otten said 'the rapes and murders were of a particularly sadistic kind'[193] and recommended no minimum sentence. There was no doubt that Colin Pitchfork would have continued to rape and murder had he not been imprisoned. Even at his sentence re-determination in 2009, when a reduction of two years was made, the judge declared that the reduction did not mean Pitchfork would go free. He was not to be released until it could be proven he no longer posed a risk.

Compared with other sexual killers, Pitchfork was unusual in some respects. He was all too aware of his responsibilities to his wife and child, in addition to the need to satisfy his deviant urges. He timed the attacks so that he would be home in time to spend the evenings with his wife and child, and even committed one of the murders while his baby son slept in the car nearby. The two sides of his personality mingled together almost seamlessly.

When police arrived to arrest him for the rapes and murders of the two teenage girls, his wife asked him outright if he was responsible. Pitchfork confessed to her that he was. Criminal psychologist David Canter explained that it was hard for her to absorb the sudden news that the husband she loved and had children with could be a wanted killer.[194] She slapped him hard across the face, the only reaction she could muster under the circumstances.

Chapter 13
Melinda Loveless

Sixteen-year-old Melinda Loveless was a person who did not care at all for other people's happiness. She was self-centred and hedonistic, and only concerned with her own emotional wellbeing, to the detriment of those who came into her life.

Her personality had been moulded as a teenager, as a result of the lack of love in her own childhood. She was the third of three daughters born to Larry and Marjorie Loveless, and even before the children were born, her father's sexual exploits and violent temper had seen him in trouble. He had molested his wife's younger sister, as well as other family members, and eventually turned his attentions to his own daughters. At Melinda's later trial, her sisters told the court how Larry had raped and beaten them repeatedly throughout their childhood.[195] Melinda had shared a bed with her father for most of her young life, and when he abruptly left, she felt rejected and unloved, possessing as she did a warped idea of familial love.

In 1991, Shanda Sharer was a pretty 12-year-old girl on the verge of womanhood. It was a year of new starts and changes for the girl, who had blonde, permed hair. After being bullied at her previous school, she had enrolled in a new high school and met many new people.

Amanda Heavrin, 14, was among the first of Shanda's new friends, and the two of them became more than friends when they entered into a lesbian relationship. Amanda had previously been in a relationship with Melinda

Loveless, a pretty teenager with long, dark, wavy hair and a violent jealous streak. When Amanda started seeing Shanda, she unceremoniously dumped Melinda, who refused to accept that the relationship was over. When she discovered that her ex-girlfriend was seeing 12-year-old Shanda, she was relentless in her pursuit of the young girl and her attempts to win Amanda back.

Loveless would later describe her 16-year-old self as a 'monster … [a] bad person'[196] and Shanda's mother Jacque believed Melinda was a 'person who had absolutely nothing inside of her … Look into her eyes, there is nothing there.'[197] Shanda's mother was describing a psychopath, someone devoid of empathy, and her assessment was accurate. Loveless simply saw Shanda as someone who was in her way, keeping her from her own happiness. The rejection she felt when Amanda left her for Shanda was further exacerbated by her emotional frailty, and would eventually explode in a jealous and murderous rage.[198]

Melinda's threats of violence became so extreme that six months later Shanda's parents moved her to a new school. By Christmas 1991, Shanda had broken all ties with Amanda, yet Melinda still maintained her violent thoughts. While Shanda commenced at her new school and made new friends, Melinda Loveless also made friends with someone new. Normally she would have had little time for someone like Mary Laurine 'Laurie' Tackett, a flighty 17-year-old who found it hard to concentrate for extended periods, but when Loveless heard Tackett voice her desire to kill someone, she set plans in motion to arrange for Tackett to murder Shanda. She told Laurie terrible things about the 12-year-old, expressing her hatred of the girl and planting the seed. From there, it only took a few weeks for a plan to come to fruition. Soon it had gone beyond talking, and Loveless was ready to kill her rival.

Loveless asked Tackett to sleep over on 10 January 1992. A rock concert was on that night and Loveless hoped Tackett would go, providing an alibi for what she really had planned, but Tackett was not keen to go just with Loveless. They both considered the other a friend, but in reality found each other slightly odd. Loveless mocked Tackett's interest in the occult, while Tackett believed Loveless was more talk than action.

On the way to Loveless' home, Tackett collected two more friends. Fifteen-year-old Hope Rippey was happy to spend the evening with Tackett. Though she had never met Loveless, she wanted to attend the concert. Fifteen-year-old Toni Lawrence tagged along. She had met Loveless before, albeit briefly, and had nothing better to do. Heading to Loveless' home, each girl told their parents a lie about what they planned to do that night and who they were going to be with.

The three turned up at 16-year-old Loveless' home, where the teenager was already riled up. She grabbed a knife from the kitchen and told the others she wanted to go and threaten Shanda with it, explaining to the two newcomers why she felt wronged by the 12-year-old. She tried calling Shanda, without success, so the quartet decided to drive to the girl's home in Tackett's car. With Loveless hiding in the back seat, Rippey and Tackett turned up at Shanda's house and explained that they were friends with Amanda, who had asked them to pick her up. Shanda believed them, but that they should return later to pick her up.

To pass the time, Loveless, Rippey, Lawrence and Tackett went to the rock concert in nearby Louisville as planned. At the concert, Rippey and Lawrence met up with two guys and went back to Tackett's car. When Tackett and Loveless came back to the car and saw the two couples making out, they tried to call Shanda again, only to find that all calls went to the answering machine.

A little after midnight, the group left the rock concert. Loveless' talk of scaring Shanda had turned more violent and she was adamant they go and collect the girl. With Loveless once again hiding in the car, Tackett and Rippey called on Shanda, who agreed to go with them to see Amanda.

Sitting in the front of the car, Shanda spoke about Amanda, claiming that they were back together. The girls continued to goad her, knowing that her words were inciting Loveless. She suddenly appeared from under a blanket in the back seat and pulled Shanda's head back, holding the knife to her throat. Loveless demanded to know the extent of Shanda's relationship with Amanda, asking if the two of them had had sex. When Shanda, terrified for her life, replied that they had, Loveless exploded. She screamed in Shanda's ear, 'You're a liar and Amanda knows I am going to kill you ... Amanda said she wants you dead just as much as I do.'[199]

They group drove to Witches Castle at Utica, a dilapidated ruin of a building that had once housed a bed and breakfast, and that local children believed was haunted. There, they tied Shanda's hands together, while Lawrence took a black t-shirt from the boot of the car. She poured whiskey on it before setting it on fire, then returned to the car with Rippey.

Outside the car, Loveless demanded that Shanda strip naked. She punched her hard in the stomach, making Shanda crumple over in pain, then pulled her head down as she brought her knee up and connected with Shanda's face. Tackett helped Loveless hold Shanda down on the dirty ground as blood flowed from the blow to her face. Loveless tried to cut the girl's throat with the dull kitchen knife she had played with earlier. When it failed to slice into Shanda's skin, Loveless stood on the knife hoping it would pierce the 12-year-old's throat. When that did not work, Loveless and Tackett took turns stabbing at Shanda's chest with the dull knife, causing superficial wounds.

One of the girls retrieved a rope from the car. Tackett and Loveless took an end each and wrapped it tightly around Shanda's throat, choking her until she passed out. Believing she was dead, they dragged Shanda back to the car and threw her into the trunk. The girls drove home to Tackett's house, leaving Shanda's naked body in the boot. During the night, a loud scream from the car sent Tackett out to 'take care of it'.[200] Tackett took a sharp knife with her. When she opened the car's boot, she stabbed Shanda repeatedly until she stopped screaming. The teenager then returned to the room where the other girls were, covered in blood. Knowing something horrific had happened, Rippey and Lawrence said they were tired and wanted to sleep.

Loveless and Tackett decided to go for a drive. As they drove along the quiet early morning streets, Shanda again started to scream. Tackett pulled the car over and said she would make sure Shanda was dead, hitting the injured girl several times across the head with a tyre iron. As they drove on, Tackett recounted to Loveless how good it felt to hit Shanda. She went into explicit detail about feeling the 12-year-old's skull cave in and even made Loveless smell the blood and brain tissue stuck to the tyre iron.

They pulled over again and opened the trunk, only for Shanda to sit up and moan in agony. They struck her again in the head, closing the trunk, and drove towards a bridge where they thought they would be able to toss her body over the side, but when a car went past, the girls lost their nerve and kept driving. They stopped the car several times, only to hear Shanda moaning and attempting to kick her way out of the trunk. The girls would take turns going to the boot to hit her with the tyre iron or slice at her skin with the knife.

As dawn broke, they drove back to Tackett's home. Rippey and Lawrence woke as the other two arrived. Loveless and Tackett encouraged the other two to go and look at the girl's blood-covered body in the boot. Lawrence refused to look at what they had done, but Rippey did. Instead of feeling guilty about her own involvement, Rippey grabbed a bottle of window cleaner from the trunk and sprayed the acidic liquid into Shanda's wounds. Shanda still tried to fight, life clinging to her tortured body. With the girls standing around Shanda, one of them, though none has admitted to being the culprit, sodomised Shanda with the bloodied tyre iron before Tackett slammed the trunk down on her head once more.

The four girls decided they should burn the body. They headed to a local petrol station, where they bought a bottle of drink to use as a container for gasoline. Tackett tipped the liquid out of the bottle and filled it with petrol. Rippey told the girls that she knew a perfect place to burn the body at Lemon Road, a deserted stretch of road used by locals as a dumping ground for rubbish and old whitegoods. When they arrived, Rippey suggested the four of them pick up Shanda's body using a blanket, and place it on the ground. Tackett told Rippey to pour gasoline over the 12-year-old's beaten body. According to conflicting testimony, Tackett set her on fire.

The four girls got into the car and drove a short distance, before Loveless decided to go back and make sure Shanda was dead. When they returned, the fire was almost out. Shanda had suffered severe burns to the top portion of her body, had curled up in a foetal position and was shuddering in her final death throes. Loveless found the scene funny and told the others, who joked along. She grabbed the bottle of remaining gasoline and poured the rest over the lower half of Shanda's body, again setting her on fire. The four girls drove away and went to a local fast food place for breakfast. They joked that the burnt sausage patties looked like Shanda's body after the fire.

Lawrence was the first to confess to her parents, followed by Hope Rippey. Both of them arrived at the police station soon after the murder to tell authorities what they had witnessed. By the following morning, as Shanda's parents continued to search for their missing daughter, Melinda Loveless and Laurie Tackett were under arrest for murder. Both were found guilty and sentenced to 60 years imprisonment. Rippey was given a 60-year sentence also, but later received two 10-year reductions. She was released in 2006. Lawrence was sentenced to 20 years for her part in the killing and was released in 2000. At the time, the media called it a 'crime of passion and peer pressure'.[201]

After spending half her life behind bars, Melinda Loveless sought freedom following the release of Hope Rippey and Toni Lawrence. In an interview she gave to a news program, she said she had finally begun to understand the implications of her selfish and violent actions. As a woman of almost forty years of age, she explained her actions with brutal honesty, holding back the tears many had hoped to see earlier: 'I was the monster. I get it. I was the bad person.'[202]

Finally, as a mature woman, herself a victim of childhood abuse, she had begun to understand the violence and hatred that had welled up inside her. While incarcerated, she has become a proficient trainer of assistant animals, with many being adopted as companions for abused and sick children.

Chapter 14
Robert Thompson and Jon Venables

To kill a child is one of the most heinous crimes imaginable. For human beings, one of the only species to murder its own without cause, it is unconscionable that we would want to cause harm to children. What is even more incomprehensible is that a killer might be a small child himself. Since the murder of James Bulger hit the media, it has remained in the minds of Britons, more than 20 years after the crime. Barely a month goes by without an article about the case or the killers.

A child killing another child, though rare, was not entirely without precedence, and Jon Venables and Robert Thompson, the killers of two-year-old James, were not the first children in England to do so. Mary Bell's crimes, for example, predated James' murder by more than 25 years. The case roused public shock and revulsion in much the same way as the Bulger murder, as experts and families tried to comprehend how a child could torture and kill another.

Bell was the daughter of a prostitute, who was forced to service her mother's clients. Having become disassociated from the abuse she'd suffered, she reacted to those who tried to get close to her with pure rage. Unable to understand the trauma she herself had endured, she inflicted harm on those around her, and strangled four-year-old Martin Brown on the day before her 11th birthday. She then mutilated and murdered three-year-old Brian Howe two months later. Like James Bulger's killers, Mary Bell would be granted anonymity for life following a sentence of penal servitude at Her Majesty's pleasure.

In the case of Thompson and Venables, both children came from broken homes and suffered 'great social and emotional deprivation. They grew up in an atmosphere of matrimonial breakdown, where they were exposed to, saw, heard or suffered abuse, drunkeness and violence … [there was] no doubt that both boys saw video films frequently showing violent and aberrant activities.'[203]

Jon Venables was born on 13 August 1982 to Susan and Neil Venables. The boy was the second of three children and lived in Walton, near Liverpool – not the poorest suburb, but far from privileged. His older brother had disabilities including a cleft palate and anger issues, while his younger sister had learning and developmental problems.[204] His parents separated just after the birth of his sister, but continued to share the responsibility for raising the children. Jon spent half the week with his father and half the week with his mother. It was not an ideal arrangement, but worked for the family, for the most part.

At his father's home, Venables was allowed to watch adult horror films.[205] A piece of evidence not shown at trial was a graphic picture drawn by Jon Venables after he had watched the film *Halloween*. He wrote a description to go with the picture that described how the man was killing his victims in the film. The picture alone is chilling, with a knife-wielding, large-breasted killer standing amid his victims, who are splayed around him with blood gushing from their many stab wounds. Though it is not unusual for small boys to enjoy playing with guns and pretending to shoot each other in the playground, the drawing was the work of a child who had been exposed to violent ideas and images. He wrote that the killer in his drawing was a man, but then feminised the figure by giving it large breasts.

Venables had no fear of teachers or school principals, or even his father. The only person he feared was his mother, who would subject him to regular beatings.[206] The possibility that Venables was connecting his mother with the main character in *Halloween* in his drawing was later raised by author Blake Morrison, who stated that 'the drawing suggests how seeing *Halloween* deeply disturbed an already deeply disturbed little boy'.[207] Was Venables demonising his mother in the picture? Juxtaposing the monster with the physical punishment he suffered at his mother's hands?

His mother was often worse the wear for drink, and police were called when Venables and his siblings were left home alone during her binges at the local pub. Venables was known to kick other children in the shins if he did not get his way, but when other parents called his mother to complain, she would hurl abuse back at them. Dr Susan Bailey described him at trial as a boy of average intelligence, who could distinguish right from wrong.[208]

Robert Thompson was born on 23 August 1982. Most children at school knew him as an unfeeling thug. Later, while Venables often cried during the court trial, Thompson rarely showed interest. He was the fifth of seven boys in the home, and survived by acting the way his older siblings did – beatings were applied by the older children to the younger ones, all the way down to the youngest. Early in his childhood, Thompson was often punished by his father, who would use a belt to beat the boys while he shouted obscenities at them. Once he left, Ann Thompson was unable to cope with the boisterous children and turned to drink, spending her days at the pub. She had also been severely beaten by her husband and suffered a miscarriage during one horrific row.

A report into the family unit likened it to *Lord of the Flies*. The boys all picked on the sibling that was next youngest to them, from the 20-year-old to the eight-year-old, and Thompson was bullied by his brothers for sucking his thumb. They were in and out of state care after bite marks and brutal beatings were reported to welfare agencies, and most of the time the rag-tag siblings had to fend for themselves. Thompson was often seen wandering the streets in the early hours of the morning. Like Venables, his psychological assessment at trial described him as a boy of good or at least average intelligence who knew the difference between right in wrong, and he has since displayed signs of post-traumatic stress when revisiting the crime in therapy. Venables is said to be inconsolable when someone mentions the murder.[209]

During their trial, Venables and Thompson, then aged 11, sat with lawyers and social workers.[210] The days ran shorter than a school day and regular breaks were offered to the young offenders, who sat playing with the ties they had been told to wear in court. Venables would often cry during the testimony of witnesses and experts, looking to his parents for comfort. Thompson's parents were not there. While Venables mother tried to explain that her son followed another bad egg, his father, others would tell a different story. A teacher who testified at trial stated that Venables had once tried to choke a fellow classmate with a ruler pressed against the child's throat, his violence striking without warning. Venables had also changed schools to escape bullying.[211]

Thompson and Venables, though forever linked due to the murder they committed, did not start out friends. Thompson picked on the 'cry-baby' Venables and pushed him around. It was only when the two of them, both suffering from learning difficulties, were kept back a year and placed in the same class that they became friends, and quickly began truanting together.

On 12 February 1993, the two 10-year-olds were truanting for the fourth time that year. On a previous occasion, Venables' father had caught them and managed to grab his son, but Thompson escaped and taunted his friend's father as he ran off. This time, the two boys headed to the local Strand Shopping Centre in Bootle, Merseyside. It was a Friday and the centre was full of mothers, busily running errands before their children came home from school, as well as many local unemployed people who had little else to do. With a hundred shops in the small centre, there were plenty of places for kids to get into trouble.

The boys had gone to the centre with the idea that it would be fun to steal a young child away from his mother, take the child to the nearest busy road and throw him out into the traffic, a chilling prospect on its own for two children to come up with. While waiting for the right child to come along, the two boys caused mischief in every store they visited. They spent their day stealing an odd assortment of items, including batteries, model paint and a few toys, but soon even stealing bored them.

They chose a first victim and managed to get the little toddler's attention, luring him away from his mother by showing him the toys they had stolen. Their elation turned to disappointment, however, as the toddler's mother sprinted to the entrance of the store and grabbed her little boy, shocked that he had managed to get so far from her so quickly.

A pregnant Denise Bulger was also shopping at the centre, with her two-year-old son James, her brother's fiancée Nicolas and her little girl. They had a few errands to run, including getting meat and groceries for the evening meal. Little James was restless. By the time they'd been to Marks and Spencer, the supermarket and the butchers, he'd had enough of shopping. For a Friday, A. R. Tyrns Butchers was quite busy, and Denise had to wait in a queue to be served, while blond-haired, blue-eyed James, wearing a thick overcoat to protect him from the elements, played at her feet. He complained that he wanted to go home to Kirkby, and Denise promised her little boy that after they bought some lamb chops for their dinner, they would go home.

Standing on the upper level of the shopping centre, Jon Venables and Robert Thompson looked out over the lower level and spotted their next target, James. The toddler had taken a few steps away from his mother and was occupied with something else, leaning against the entrance to the butcher's, and unaware that two predators had fixed their gaze on him. At the same time James had taken those few steps from his mother's side, Denise was paying for their supper. She had moved attention from her son for only a moment, explaining to the cashier that they'd given her the wrong order, but it was enough time for the two 10-year-olds to pounce.

The time was 3.43pm. Denise turned and looked down, expecting her son to be at her feet. He was not there. She looked around at those waiting to be served and then at her future sister-in-law and niece, who were waiting outside. James was not with them. That panic that only a parent can know quickly set in. The expectation of seeing her son, who must only have wandered a few steps away, soon dissipated. James was nowhere to be seen.

The customers around Denise quickly realised her little boy had wandered off. People started looking for the toddler as Denise made her way to the centre management's office to get them to make an announcement. It had only taken a minute for the two boys to take James to the upper level and out an exit door. Thirty-nine seconds later, they had left the centre altogether, whilst Denise and others searched for James.

The toddler's journey to his death at the hands of the two children lasted two-and-a-half miles over two hours. Several witnesses saw James with the two boys, but when questioned, they would say they had found him and were taking him to the local police station. No one confronted them when they headed in the opposite direction. One witness claimed to have seen the two boys dragging James, who was extremely distressed and calling for his mother, part of the way. Another saw the two boys drag James towards the railway bridge and heard one of them say that they hated having a little brother. A 14-year-old girl saw one of the boys run up the hill that led to the railway line and thought, at the time, that the toddler was laughing.

Over the centre's intercom system, a disjointed voice asked all customers to look for the little boy. For the next few hours, customers and employees of the Strand searched every corner, looking for a lost, possibly sleeping little boy. With stores closing, police were now on the scene, and several store-owners were asked to return and look again in the hopes that the boy might be locked inside.

If they had looked at the security footage, which was not reviewed until later, they would have seen James being led from the centre holding one of the 10-year-olds' hands, while the other boy dawdled in front of the pair. The boys did not run and did not look worried or concerned. To passersby, they would have looked like they were with their younger brother. But as James' father wrote in his book, *My James*, 'they knew what they were doing was wicked …'[212]

No one had any idea of the horror James was enduring while they searched the shopping centre. Even as police, employees and family members continued the hunt, darkness having fallen over the suburbs, James lay dead more than two kilometres away, having suffered 42 separate injuries in a period of prolonged torture. The toddler had received 22 injuries to his head and a further 20 to his body. The boys had used an iron rod and 27 bricks to beat and stone him, before leaving his body on train tracks to be run over by a train and cut in two.[213]

The 'baby', as the two child killers called him in their statements, had suffered a horrendous ordeal. He had his nappy removed during the final assault and his foreskin had been violently retracted, exposing the glans of his penis. James had had batteries forced into his mouth and injuries to his rectum, suggesting that they had attempted to insert the batteries into his anus as well. The little boy's left eye had been rubbed with blue model paint the boys had stolen earlier and he had several large gashes to his forehead and skull. He had been hit in the face and mouth and a large wound to his cheek was consistent with being kicked; James' blood was on the shoes Thompson wore that day. When the severed body was found, it was surrounded by several bricks that had been thrown at the toddler, all of them covered in blood. Finally, he was struck with a 10kg iron bar, which killed him.

On the afternoon of the murder, Venables' mother had gone to school to pick him up, as she sometimes would, and found he had missed school that day. She went looking for him along the railway line where she knew the boys had made a cubby house, but stopped looking after a few hours, knowing he would turn up at home when he was hungry. She was not worried about her son, but was angry he had missed another day of school. When he did turn up, she took him to the local constabulary to shake some sense into him for truanting.

The weekend after the murder, Venables was quiet and subdued as the family watched the local news, which showed grainy images of two young boys leading the toddler away. It wasn't long before police knocked on the doors of both families.

When interviewed, the two boys exhibited disturbing behaviour. Venables cried hysterically, lashing out at family who were there to support him. He refused to admit what he had done with his mother in the room, knowing such an admission would provoke her wrath, and it was only once she told him she would still love him that he admitted his involvement.

Thompson, during his initial interview, remained stoic and showed little emotion.

The subsequent trial made international news, as the two boys faced a backlash of public hatred. Questions were asked of the parents regarding how they could raise such 'evil' children. The world mourned the death of the toddler with the big blue eyes, demonising the two who had committed the crimes – calling the two boys 'evil' was a way for people to distance themselves from what they didn't understand. The idea of two bad seeds or rotten apples was easier to contemplate than the possibility that a person could commit such atrocities without being inherently bad or mad.

In Britain, with 10 being the age of criminal responsibility, both boys were accountable for the murder and were found to understand that what they had done was wrong. During their lengthy journey with James, as he fought them and begged to go back to his mother, there was not a moment in which the two killers thought to abandon him. They had committed themselves not only to the kidnapping, but to the murder as well.

On 24 November 1993, Thompson and Venables were convicted for the murder and abduction of James Bulger. They were detained at Her Majesty's pleasure and the trial judge recommended that a period of no less than eight years be served. He stated that 'very great care will have to be taken before either defendant is allowed out into the general community. Much psychotherapeutic, psychological and educational investigation and assistance will be required.'[214]

Jon Venables had been released and was living under a new identity when, in July 2010, he was arrested and sent back to prison for breaching the good behaviour clause that governed his life. Police had found pornographic images of children on his home computer. At the time, police were investigating reports of an online child porn ring, and Venables, living under his new identity, was arrested. To date, co-offender Robert Thompson has slotted into his new anonymous life without incident.

Chapter 15
Martin Bryant

The massacre at Port Arthur remains the worst mass murder to be committed by a single person in modern history.[215] The events that unfolded over the weekend of 28 and 29 April 1996, in the historic grounds of the Port Arthur ruins in the state of Tasmania in Australia, were perpetrated by 28-year-old Martin Bryant, who was born to Carleen and Maurice Bryant on 7 May 1967. He was the first child for the young couple and was delivered only two hours after labour commenced. His mother recalls him as a happy-go-lucky baby and toddler, but that he rejected physical closeness, even with his her.[216] He was walking by the time he was 16 months old and was a notorious escape artist, which his mother found exhausting. During his early school years, he was diagnosed with learning difficulties, hyperactivity and behavioural issues. He found school unpleasant and often refused to go. He was noted to be 'aggressive, destructive and very difficult with other children … stealing, violent outbursts and … tormenting vulnerable children'.[217] He was enrolled in, and suspended from, several special education schools. There is also evidence that he tormented his sister and tortured animals.[218]

At the age of 10, Bryant was briefly hospitalised, having been burned playing with firecrackers. In 1984, he was assessed for a disability pension, and a psychiatrist diagnosed him as being intellectually handicapped and suffering from a personality disorder. Queries were raised about the possible development of a schizophrenic illness.[219]

After leaving school Bryant took several odd jobs to earn money and met Miss Helen Harvey, a spinster, who welcomed the young man into the home she shared with her elderly mother. The two women lived like recluses in the kitchen, with their 40 cats. Bryant would later call her his only friend; the odd couple were often seen wandering the local shopping centres, or enjoying leisurely lunches together. When an ambulance was once called to the home to treat Helen's mother, the stench and decay of the home brought authorities to the door, and the RSCPA removed many of the animals. Bryant and his father Maurice spend weeks helping Helen clean the home.

On 20 October 1992, Bryant and Helen were heading to a shopping centre, with several of the women's dogs in the back of the car, when they were involved in a car accident. Bryant claimed they were distracted by two of the pets fighting, and their car plunged head-first into oncoming traffic. Helen suffered a fractured neck in the accident and died instantly. Bryant's injuries were extensive; he fractured his cervical vertebrae and ribs and suffered a head injury. In her will, Helen Harvey left Bryant a substantial amount of money, property and possessions, which were put into trust for him. For months after the accident, he continued to suffer from severe headaches and was prescribed tranquillisers to help him with sleeping problems and anxiety.[220] He tried to make new friends to fill the void left by Helen, but was rejected by neighbours, who viewed the blond-haired 'surfer-looking' man as odd.

On 13 August 1993, Bryant's father Maurice, who had been his main carer and kept the young man's violent temper under control, headed to a farm house the family owned at Copping. The following morning, a man arrived at the house and found a note on the door stating that he should call police. Maurice had drowned himself in the property's dam after taking an overdose of anti-anxiety medication.

Bryant had lost his best friend and his father. His dad had kept his behaviour under control, and without that guidance, he was a powder keg waiting to explode. He accessed most of the funds left to him by Helen and his father, and began a three-year spending spree that included property, cars and international travel. By the fatal weekend of 1993, Bryant was 'left to his mounting frustrations, his angers, his resentment of rejection and social misunderstanding'.[221]

Bryant spent the evening before the massacre having dinner with his mother and girlfriend. The next day, Sunday 28 April 1996, was a gloriously sunny day after a miserable few weeks of rain and wind. Bryant headed out for the day in his distinctive yellow Volvo, with a surfboard on top. He had many errands to attend to before the day's events, which he would later call 'the accident', could unfold.

The first place he went was Mid Point Newsagents. He went inside and asked if they sold cigarette lighters, and when told that they did, returned to his car to get his wallet. He paid for a lighter and left the store without waiting for his change.[222] From there, he drove to the local supermarket, where he purchased tomato sauce, and then he bought a cup of coffee from a local petrol station. It was an unlikely start to a day of mass murder.

Bryant told the service station attendant that he was on his way to Roaring Beach to surf for the rest of the morning. When he finished his coffee, he drove to another petrol station, where he purchased petrol and again told the salesperson he was heading to the beach for a surf.

Instead of heading to the beach, however, Bryant went to the Seascape Guest House, a quaint bed-and-breakfast he had tried to purchase several times. Bryant knocked on the door and, seeing who it was, the couple who owned the place, David and Noelene Martin, opened the door. Bryant was carrying an arsenal of weapons in a sports bag. With a gun in his hand, he fired several shots above the heads of the frightened owners. He made the couple get down on the floor, and bound and gagged them. He then retrieved a knife from the bag and stabbed David and Noelene to death. Taking the keys to the property with him, he left the Seascape and headed towards the historic Port Arthur tourist attraction.

Many tourists had already arrived at the historic ruins; there were about 1,500 people there, enjoying the long weekend. At lunch-time, the Broad Arrow Café was doing a brisk trade, as it normally did. The café was built from bricks that convicts had made 150 years earlier, and had an outdoor

163

eating area, where people could sit and look out over the ruins as they enjoyed their lunch. Others sat inside, looking out through the big glass doors. Broad Arrow was a popular place to visit and many thousands of people had eaten at the café over the years. Tragically, its last day of trade was the day Martin Bryant came in for lunch. He entered the café just after 1.00pm and ordered his food. He was holding a large sports bag. The staff member behind the counter said hello to him, recognising him as a local.

Bryant sat down and quickly ate his lunch. He attempted to strike up a conversation with a woman sitting near him by saying, 'Great day, isn't it? Hey, there's not a lot of Japs out today. What do you think about that? There are a lot of WASPs, though, a lot of yuppies.'[223] The woman moved away from him.

At 1.27pm, Bryant took an automatic rifle from the sports bag at his feet. He stood up and aimed the gun at the closest person.

Malaysian couple Moh Yee Ng and Sou Leng Chung had come to Australia to visit the beautiful countryside. Instead, they found themselves in the firing line of a mass murderer. Bryant shot Moh Yee, who was sitting at the table closest to him, in the neck. His companion Sou Leng had little time to react before she, too, was shot. Both victims remained in their seats, slumped over their meals.

In the next 15 seconds, a further 10 victims were slain, and many others were injured. The killer fired a shot at Mick Sargent. The bullet hit its target and Mick fell to the ground. Bryant's fourth shot struck the head of Kate Elizabeth Scott and killed her instantly. Seeing the carnage unfolding in front of him, Anthony Nightingale stood up. He had been seated directly in front of Bryant and called out in horror, 'No, not here.'[224] These words were the man's last, as Bryant aimed the rifle at Anthony and fired. A bullet penetrated the man's throat and he was killed instantly.

Walter Bennett and his friends, Ray and Kevin Sharp, were sitting with their wives, whom they instinctively covered as Bryant turned the gun towards the group. Walter and Ray were killed with a single bullet and Kevin was struck in the arm. A second bullet struck Kevin in the head, killing him. Bryant aimed and fired with precision. He did not waste bullets by shooting indiscriminately. His movements were purposeful and deliberate as he took aim and shot each victim with a calm that belied the horror that was unfolding.

Though only ten seconds had elapsed since the first gunshots, those people who were still alive began searching for a way out of the café. Bryant stood in front of one of the doors and fired at those who were trying to hide.

Andrew Mills and Tony Kistan attempted to flee with their friends and loved ones. Tony pushed his wife out the front doors of the café as Bryant took aim and she was the only person to escape through the front doors. She ran screaming from the horrific scene, too scared to look back. In those fleeting moments, she hoped Tony and Andrew Mills were behind her, but the men had been killed by single gunshots.

The next shot hit Graham Colyer, who was injured but survived. Mervyn and Mary Howard were not so lucky. The couple, along with many other diners, tried to flee through the kitchen. As people scrambled to hide in cupboards or behind doors, Mervyn was shot in the head, and then Mary was also shot dead.

Sarah Loughton was the next person in Bryant's firing line. As Sarah's mother, Carolyn, tried to shield her from the gunfire, Bryant aimed the gun at Sarah and fired, killing her with a single shot to the head. Her mother survived. Next, Bryant wounded Robert Elliot with a shot to the head before heading to the rear of the café.

When the gunfire began, Winifred Aplin had been cemented to her seat in fear. Soon after Bryant murdered Sarah Loughton, he turned the gun on Winifred and fired another shot. The bullet killed the mother of four instantly.

The entire episode lasted only 15 seconds. A dozen people lay dead in the café, with 10 more wounded from gunshots and shrapnel.

Nicole Burgess was serving in the gift shop area in the café when she heard gunfire. Confused by what she thought sounded like someone hitting a cardboard box, she hid behind the counter with her cousin Elizabeth

Howard. Bryant came into the shop and aimed the rifle at Nicole, killing her with a single shot. He then took aim and killed Elizabeth. Shooting from such close range, the man's clothing was splattered with the blood of his victims and his shoes were soaked.

Leslie Lever stood in shock as he watched the murderous campaign unfold. Many customers from the café had attempted to flee through the souvenir shop and were now being pursued. Leslie was gunned down as the killer walked past him. Bryant then turned again towards the café and fired at Peter Crosswell, injuring him.

Jason Winter was the next to die. The 28-year-old was crouching under a table with his wife and baby son. The baby cried, terrified and confused by the noise of gunfire and people screaming. Jason tried to console the baby when Bryant took aim. The man was killed instantly by a shot to the head.

Bryant then turned his attention back to the souvenir shop. Ronald Jary, along with Peter Nash and Pauline Masters, attempted to flee through a door, only to find it locked. The trio looked into the eyes of the gunman as he took aim and fired a single shot into each of their heads. -

Ron Neander, 66, and his wife Gwen, 67, were on their first holiday from South Australia in many years. The elderly couple were separated as people attempted to flee. Ron called out to Gwen as the woman came face to face with Bryant. The man aimed the gun at her and fired, and when Ron found her, she was lying in a pool of her own blood. He went into shock. Around him, so many people were dead and injured, yet the killer had only used 29 bullets.

Bryant changed the magazine in his rifle and prepared for the next part of the carnage. What seemed like hours had been only 90 seconds.

Broad Arrow Café worker Brigid Cook ran out of the back door, screaming for people to get away. Her bravery saved countless people from the horror playing out inside the cafe. She ran towards the car park, where people were milling around, waiting to head to their next destination. As the killer followed her towards the tourist transport buses, she screamed hysterically that they should seek cover. Bryant gunned her down, shooting her in the legs. As people hid behind buses, a witness recorded a video of Bryant walking calmly and purposefully around, looking for people to kill. The footage was eerie and terrifying.

Coach driver Royce Thompson heard Brigid screaming and came around the side of one of the buses, only to find himself staring down the barrel of Bryant's rifle. The man tried to flee as the gunman fired, the bullet striking Royce in the back. Though horrifically injured, he rolled under a parked bus to prevent the killer firing any further shots. He survived the initial gunshot, but later died in hospital from his injuries.

Wendy Scurr then made the first telephone call to police about what was happening at Port Arthur. The time was 1.32pm, only five minutes after Bryant fired his first shot.

Neville Quin, 53, and his wife Janette, 50, had come to Port Arthur on a bus trip and were standing near the buses when they heard Brigid Cook screaming for everyone to hide. Bryant took aim and shot Janette in the back as she tried to take cover in the car park. Bryant then looked at Neville, who was frozen in shock. He raised his gun as Neville ran onto the bus, and fired a shot, which missed its target. Bryant hissed, 'No one gets away from me.'[225] He chased Neville and shot him again, hitting him in the neck. Neville survived his injuries.

Bryant decided to leave the area. He jumped into his yellow Volvo, which was parked near the exit, but then changed his mind and continued to shoot at people who were scrambling to safety. When he noticed Janette Quinn was still alive and attempting to crawl along the ground, he walked up to her and fired another shot into her head. Elva Gaylard watched in horror as Bryant murdered Janette and was even more fearful once she could no longer hear or see the killer, not realising that Bryant had come up behind her. She turned to see him raise the gun to her chest and fire, and fell back with a wound to her chest and arm. She would later die in hospital.

On the Port Arthur peninsula, Bryant had killed 22 people in a matter of minutes. But he wasn't finished yet. Back in his car, he headed towards the front gates of the historic tourist attraction, and there continued the carnage.

Nanette Mikac and her two daughters, six-year-old Alannah and three-year-old Madeline, had heard the gunfire and were fleeing the scene when Martin Bryant drove up beside them. Thinking the man was also fleeing and was going to offer them a lift to safety, Nanette turned to Alannah and said, 'We're safe now, pumpkin.'[226] She held their hands as she walked towards Bryant's car. Someone further down screamed at Nannette to run, trying to warn her that she was heading towards the killer, but it was too late.

Bryant laughed and demanded that Nannette get down on her knees. Nannette pulled her two young daughters close to her and begged Bryant to spare them. 'Please don't hurt my babies,' she pleaded, as Bryant aimed the gun at the woman's head and fired a single shot. Madeline, still in her mother's arms, was shot in the arm and then in the chest, and died. Alannah, having witnessed her mother's and sister's murders, fled towards a tree. Bryant gave chase and fired two shots at the girl, but missed. Alannah, terrified and sobbing, tried to shelter behind the tree, but Bryant was soon upon her. He put the muzzle of the gun to the little girl's neck and fired, killing her.

People continued to flee, telling anyone coming into the site to leave. They hid along tracks and behind bushes in an attempt to escape the gunman's purposeful shots. Tourists who had been entering the tollgates abandoned their cars. When Bryant arrived at the tollbooth in his own car, he argued with Robert Salzmann, whose car, along with many other abandoned vehicles, was inadvertently blocking the man's escape route. Unaware of what had occurred at Port Arthur, Salzmann kept up a heated exchange with Bryant until the killer reached into his car and grabbed another gun. He took aim and killed Robert with a single shot, followed by Robert's wife, Helene.

Russell Pollard had seen the exchange between Salzmann and Bryant from his BMW, which was parked in the queue leading into Port Arthur. The man rushed from his car, but was also killed by a shot to the chest. The gunman then dragged Mary Nixon from the BMW's passenger seat and shot her dead. He got into Russell's BMW and headed to a nearby petrol station.

On the way, he pulled over beside Glenn Pears' white Toyota Corolla. Bryant tried to pull Zoe Hall from the passenger seat of the Corolla, threatening her with his gun. Glenn got out of the car and ran at Bryant in an attempt to protect his girlfriend from the gunman. Bryant pointed the gun at Glenn and forced him into the boot of the BMW, then returned to the Corolla, where he shot Zoe dead. She was the 32nd victim.

Bryant drove off in the BMW, with Glenn still in the boot, and returned to the Seascape Guest House, shooting at passing cars on the way. Once at the cottage, he took Glenn out of the boot and tethered him to a railing inside the house. He then doused the car in petrol and set it on fire.

By now, emergency services had been alerted to the massacre at Port Arthur and had started to arrive at the scene, with police guards attempting to help the injured and the dying. At the guest house, the burning BMW was a beacon for police, showing them where to find the murderer.

Inside the house, the phone was ringing. A reporter was trying to find out what was going on by calling local businesses, and when she called the Seascape, Bryant answered the phone. Relieved to finally get an answer, she asked him if he was aware of what was happening at Port Arthur. Bryant, introducing himself as Jamie, said he'd had lots of fun at Port Arthur, giggling hysterically. The reporter knew instantly that she was speaking with the killer. He told her not to call back or he would kill his final victim.

The woman called police immediately, but officers were already on the scene, having followed the carnage left in Bryant's wake. As police surrounded the house, he began to fire at them, and a stand-off ensued. The time was 3.00pm, a mere two hours since the killing had first begun. At 9.00pm, police negotiators arrived on the scene and attempted to talk 'Jamie' into giving himself up peacefully. He demanded that police bring him a helicopter and told them that to show good faith, he would release Glenn Pears.[227]

The siege continued into the night, with Bryant maintaining telephone contact. The police tried to keep him talking as much as they could. When asked if he knew anything about the events at Port Arthur, he was eager to find out how many had been killed. The negotiator told Bryant there were many injuries, and there was silence before he asked, 'They weren't killed?'[228] He seemed disappointed by the possibility that his victims had all survived.

Police tried to get close to the house, but were told to get back, and the situation worsened. The cordless phone Bryant was using went flat, so the lines of communication were severed. Hours of silence followed, only broken by occasional gunfire from inside the house. The killer knew he was cornered.

At daybreak, police noticed smoke and fire inside the guesthouse. The fire roared out of control, detonating much of Bryant's cache of weapons. Police rushed inside the house, where they found the bodies of Glenn Pears, and David and Noelene Martin; Bryant had shot Pears during the stand-off. The killer fled the burning guest house, his clothes and then his flesh on fire. The flames on the man's body were extinguished and he was arrested, and rushed to hospital for treatment. Questioning would have to wait.

Later that evening in Royal Hobart Hospital, Detective Inspector John Warren interviewed Bryant for the first time. The man was sedated due to the burns he had sustained in the Seascape fire. He told the police officer that he was not responsible for the massacre, as he had been surfing all day. Warren noted what the killer said before formally charging him with the murder of Kate Scott, one of the first victims at the Broad Arrow Café. The other charges were added shortly afterwards, once the man was deemed mentally competent to stand trial.

In court, Bryant would answer to 35 charges of murder, 20 charges of attempted murder, three charges of grievous bodily harm and eight charges of infliction of wounds. He was also charged with four counts of aggravated assault, one count of unlawfully setting fire to property (Glenn Pears' vehicle) and one charge of arson for the setting ablaze of the Seascape Guest House. When the charges were read out in court, the man covered his mouth, laughing. His demeanour incensed the victims' families attending court.

At first, Bryant pleaded not guilty to all charges, claiming he had been surfing on the day of the murders. Yet many locals who had survived the carnage were able to identify him. The trial began in November 1996, and the main focus of the case was Bryant's intellectual disabilities. According to the experts at trial, the man's IQ was borderline intellectually disabled.[229] The families and victims were concerned that the man was going to walk free from the charges. Then, in a sudden turn of events, Bryant changed his plea. He pleaded guilty to all charges, again giggling as he did so. The judge passed sentence on 22 November 1996 and Bryant was given 35 life terms. Justice Cox told the young man he should never be eligible for parole. For the remaining charges, he was sentenced to an additional 21 years.

Bryant remains in protective custody in prison and very little is reported about him. The cache of weapons he had amassed was nothing short of shocking, and following the massacre, each state in Australia toughened its gun laws in an attempt to prevent such a tragedy from ever happening again.

Chapter 16
The Krays

'Born to hang' – this was what one of the Kray boys was told at a tender age. To most, such a sentiment would be terrifying; but to this boy, it was something to boast about for the rest of his life.

London's East End in 1933 was a far cry from the area it is today. In the period between the two world wars, the city saw expansion like never before, and in this time of growth, attempts were made to clean up what was left of the industrial revolution, and to look toward a future of electrical lighting and motor cars. The city was soon peppered with high-density housing for those who moved from the inner city. European Jews, fleeing the Nazis, came to settle in the region, with whole communities filling up the long and narrow streets.

Amid all this activity, Reginald and Ronald Kray were born in Bethnal Green. From a mix of Jewish, Irish and Romany heritage, they were the offspring of Charlie, a man who found his talent in pestering local residents to sell him their gold and silver and unwanted clothing to on-sell at a profit, and Violet, the prettiest of three sisters. The twin boys were extremely different from their four-year-old brother Charlie Junior. The older brother's carefree and quiet nature was in stark contrast to the demanding, dark-haired twins, who occupied all of their mother's time from the moment they were born.

In the East End of London, the promise of wealth and opportunity was quickly replaced with malnourishment, poverty and slums. To survive in such conditions, one had to fight for everything. Charlie Kray Senior raised his boys to be fighters. The family also rallied around their matriarch, who was a staunch protector of the family. Violet was the centre of the family unit; Reggie later recalled that she was always 'busy and a very warm person.'[230] Associates of the Kray twins called her the 'Cockney Queen Mother,'[231] referring to the way in which she reigned over her boys, whom she genuinely believed could do no harm. Their father, on the other hand, was a strict disciplinarian who did not like his boys always getting into trouble. He even spoke to the local constabulary about what to do.

As twins, the two boys were inseparable for most of their lives. They had very different personalities, though both exhibited the violence that would become pivotal in their criminal lives.

When gold prices surged, transient workers like Charlie Kray could no longer be a constant presence in their children's lives, often travelling great distances from home to pawn gold or clothing. With their father away, a new influence found its way into the boys' lives – their grandfather, known as Cannonball Lee. A champion boxer, he assisted Violet in attempts to discipline the boys, and soon taught them how to box. It was a talent that would spawn their criminal network.

The twins were often in trouble and soon their boxing prowess left the ring and flowed out onto the streets of East London. The twins' aunt claimed Ronald was 'a born devil … you know what those eyebrows mean, meeting in the middle of your forehead? … They mean you're born to hang.'[232] Ronnie relished in the thought that he would be bad enough to swing from the hangman's noose.

A defining moment in the boys' life came when Ronnie was punched in the back of the head by a local police officer. According to both boys, the officer struck out without provocation, but the boys retaliated with brute force and injured the policeman. From that moment, Ronnie never trusted those in authority. He argued that if they could strike out like that against a teenager, who knew what they would do to a grown man? According to his twin brother Reggie, 'That moment changed Ronnie's attitude of police.'[233]

Before they became the gangsters who ruled the East End, they were sent to do national service. Their associates later recalled many of the boys' shenanigans, such as high-tailing it out of barracks after lockdown, and heading home to their mother for a decent meal. They once threw a bucket of urine over a senior officer, and generally caused havoc, challenging authority at every moment. This behaviour would subsequently lead to both of them being court-martialled and dishonourably discharged. They were removed from service and sent to the Tower of London to do hard time, but according to Reggie, 'they were happy to be kicked out'.[234]

On their return to civilian life, the twins took over The Regal, a billiard hall in Bethnal Green. An associate, Albert Donaghue, referred to the pool hall as a 'labour exchange for thieves',[235] where everyone was trying to sell off their recently (and illegally) acquired merchandise. After the war, the twins surrounded themselves with a gang, though they still preferred to do the beating up themselves. Referred to as 'the Firm', their crew was still small in comparison with the likes of William 'Billy' Hill, Jack Spot and their groups, but Spot's power was declining, and the West End of London was up for grabs. With Billy Hill acting as a mentor for the twins, the young up-and-comers took over everything they could. With their newfound power came fame and fortune; they fed off the notoriety and enjoyed being photographed with the celebrities of the day.

The two Kray boys were very different in the way they managed their new status as gangsters. Ronnie was the brains behind the network of informants and protection racketeers; 'the Firm' was led by Ronnie, 'the Colonel'.[236] Reggie, on the other hand, was the gentler of the two. He preferred to back away from a fight and could forgive and forget in an instant. Ronnie's way of life was to kill, even just to brighten up an otherwise dull afternoon. According to his brother, Ronnie was a paranoid schizophrenic, who suffered extremely unpredictable mood swings. His erratic behaviour caused friction between the brothers.

In 1956, Ronnie shot a man in the face and assaulted another, which resulted in him going to prison for three years. With his violent and irrational brother behind bars, Reggie turned the Firm's properties into profitable businesses, which invited the famous to rub shoulders with the influential. When Ronnie was released, having spent time in a secure mental facility, Reggie was subsequently sentenced to two years in prison.

Ronnie played the role of 'gay playboy gangster',[237] which included an alleged love affair with Lord Boothby, which saw the Conservative politician sue local media. From then on, the media largely ignored the goings-on of the Firm, but new Scotland Yard Chief Inspector Leonard 'Nipper' Read was not so easily deterred. He set out to bring down the twins and his determination resulted in distrust circulating among the Krays and their informants.

On Reggie's release, Ronnie told his brother about a prisoner he had spent time with in Dartmoor Prison. Frank 'the Mad Axeman' Mitchell was incensed that prison officials would not give him an official release date and Ronnie had come up with an idea to spring the man from prison, hoping it would generate enough publicity that Mitchell would be able to negotiate a release date and return peacefully to prison until that time.

The twins went ahead with the plan, but Ronnie had not counted on Mitchell's unpredictable behaviour. The two brothers quickly realised that he was a liability and had to go. Ronnie murdered the man and his body was taken out to sea and dumped, never to be recovered. The Kray brothers were arrested for the murder, but were acquitted. It seemed they were untouchable.

The Krays knew they had to keep control of their large organisation and eradicate the competition, namely the Richardson gang. When the Richardsons got into a scuffle with another organised criminal group, they were almost entirely disbanded, and no longer posed a threat to the Firm. Those of the Richardsons who remained, however, knew that their days were numbered. Ronnie set his sights on George Cornell. According to the owners of the Blind Beggar pub, Cornell had made derogatory remarks about Ronnie's sexual preferences, calling him a 'fat poof' on 9 March 1966. Hearing about the Cornell's remarks, Ronnie drove to the Blind Beggar and shot and killed him, though he later claimed he had killed the man in retribution for the murder of his friend Richard Hart. No charges were laid against the Krays, as no witnesses dared come forward and claim they had seen the shooting.

Lesley Payne was the next victim. Jimmy 'the Hat' McVitie was issued with an order to kill the informant. McVitie instead warned Payne that he had been sent to kill him and allowed the man to flee. In turn, Ronnie coerced Reggie to kill McVitie, saying to his twin, 'I've done mine, about time you did yours.'[238] Reggie stabbed the man to death and left his associates to get rid of the body.

Payne, knowing that he had a target on his back, went to police and confessed all he knew. His statement filled 200 pages and the police finally had evidence on the twins, as well as more than a dozen members of the Firm. The gang was arrested by Chief Inspector Read and his men, and with the Krays behind bars, witnesses and informants came forward, no longer fearing retribution. On 8 March 1969, the two Kray brothers were sentenced to life imprisonment for murder. They were to serve no less than 30 years of their sentence before becoming eligible for parole.

Ronnie was later declared insane and transferred to Broadmoor Hospital, where he suffered a heart attack and died on 17 March 1995. Reggie served his sentence and was released on compassionate grounds, suffering from bladder cancer. He passed away on 1 October 2000. The twin's older brother, Charlie, was sentenced to 10 years in prison for his part in the Firm's killings, and was released in 1975, only to return on drug charges 22 years later.

Ronnie's paranoid schizophrenia was largely controlled by medication, given to him by the family doctor, but his moods remained, for the most part, erratic. His brother Reggie had helped him channel his rage into organised crime, using his inability to fear authority or retribution to scare opponents and keep his associates under control. Had Ronnie not been a twin, with a brother whose personality was his opposite and had a calming and controlling effect, Ronnie might have become a violent serial murder beyond the organised realm of the Firm.

Chapter 17
Josef Fritzl

Austrian psychiatrist Dr Adelheid Kastner, who interviewed Josef Fritzl, described him as an emotional volcano, born to rape.[239] She said, 'he has a malicious vein, an almost unstoppable flood of destructive lava. He feels torn apart. He wants to do everything positive, and then suddenly the evil side of him breaks out.'[240] He acted on that evil with little regard for how it might affect anyone else.

Josef Fritzl kept his daughter, Elizabeth, locked in an underground dungeon for 8,642 days.[241] She was raped at the hands of her father more than 3,000 times and gave birth in the underground prison at least seven times. In 24 years, Elizabeth and some of her children remained completely unseen by the outside world, locked away by her father, who saw his daughter as his wife and partner, rather than his offspring.

Fritzl was born to a mother who fell pregnant only to prove that she was not barren.[242] After being deserted by her husband in 1927, Maria Fritzl fathered Josef with one her cousins, who would share his son's name and with whom she lived with for many years. The couple married, but she later divorced him due to his drinking. She had no desire to raise a child and often beat and abused her son.

Living through the war, Fritzl was often sent to hide in the basement of the home in Amsetten, Austria, that he shared with his mother, as air raids went on overhead. He later claimed that, at the end of the sirens, he was always afraid he would return to the house to find his mother dead. Yet the Nazi invasions were also one of the few joyous times he had with his father. He recalled, as a small boy, listening to Josef Senior talking about the Germans, who he said were arriving to save Austria. He remembered he 'liked his father talking to him, something that didn't happen too often, unless he was being chastised'.[243] The Nazi invasion had a lasting effect on him, as he grew up desiring the restraint and obedience evident around him in occupied Austria. As a small boy in March 1938, often beaten and scolded by those closest to him, he felt betrayed and powerless, but the Nazi invasion showed him what a powerful Austrian could accomplish.

With the Nazis having firmly entrenched themselves in Amsetten, Josef's father spent a lot of time at the local bars, drinking with Nazi soldiers who represented, to Josef, everything that was powerful. As a small boy, he watched his father, a lazy and unreliable man, drink most of his life away. Like his son later in life, the man also had a voracious appetite for sex. Fritzl would leave his father at the local watering holes, extremely drunk, and return home to his mother, who was no longer enamoured with her drunkard husband, preferring to focus her attentions on her son. Fritzl later admitted that 'he adored her with a passion, which he would later confess bordered on the obsessive'.[244]

In 1959, with his father long gone, Fritzl took over the Amstetten house that had until then been owned by his mother. He told neighbours that she had passed away and that he had assumed ownership. The truth was far more sinister, and a historical echo of what he would later do to his own daughter; Fritzl had moved his mother into an attic room in her own house, slowly depriving her of freedom and natural light as he bricked in the room's only windows. She lingered in the locked bedroom until she died in 1980, 21 years after he first forced her into the room. It was the same house in which Elizabeth and three of her seven children would live, hidden in an underground bunker.

Fritzl later told Dr Adelheid Kastner that he 'wanted to punish his mother for his loveless and brutal childhood'.[245] He claimed that she had been a violent woman, who left him battered and bruised, and made him feel weak. The loss of power he had experienced was part of what later spurred him to commit atrocities against his daughter and her (and his) children. He was determined to be dominant.

In 1956, after completing his education, Fritzl married Rosemarie, a naïve 17-year-old who never questioned her husband's actions. Together, the couple had five daughters and two sons. But while his wife tended to the children and his mother – before he bricked her away in her bedroom – Fritzl set about satisfying his extreme sexual desires. In 1967, he was sentenced to prison for rape, after breaking into the home of a married nurse and attacking her while her husband was away. He was then convicted of a second attempted rape and indecent exposure. Rosemarie stood by him through the charges, and after he was released from prison, she allowed her husband back into the house. Elizabeth, their daughter, would later question why her mother let the man re-enter their lives, particularly when he began to abuse her at the age of 11.

Fritzl initiated the diabolical plan to imprison his daughter in 1981, when he commenced the planning and digging out of the basement. Then in 1984, when Elizabeth Fritzl was 18, she was kidnapped by her father. He had been raping and abusing her for seven years by that time, and had finally decided to hide her from the world and make her his plaything. He would later claim that he was concerned his daughter would start taking drugs or become promiscuous.

To lure Elizabeth into the basement, he asked her to help him fix the door to the cellar he had been building. As she leaned forward to help him, he clamped an ether-soaked cloth over her mouth, rendering her unconscious. When she awoke, she was in the sound-proofed prison where she would spend the next quarter of a century. This original cell was only 18 square metres in size, a tiny hole in the ground below the family home. She was told that should she try to escape, she would be electrocuted by traps he had set.

On the second day of her imprisonment, Fritzl appeared in the dark cellar. He chained his daughter to the wall and raped her. He would repeat the routine over and over, appearing in the dark cellar to rape his daughter. He later said, 'I just didn't think about … her being my daughter. I saw her as my wife and as my partner.' [246] Even before he had enslaved her, he was jealous about Elizabeth. He would later say that he planned to continually impregnate her, to make her unattractive to other men and ensure that, should she ever escape, she would not be worthy of other man.

Fritzl would bring piles of video cassette tapes filled with explicit sex scenes to the dungeon. He would force his daughter to watch them with him, to give her tips on how to moan or look at him while he raped her, coaching her on the sounds she should make to make him more aroused. Fritzl would also make her dress in provocative and skimpy outfits, and his daughter would spend nights in agony, brutalised by oversized sexual toys, and. For almost half of her imprisonment, she was chained up, limiting her movement in the tiny prison cell.

With his daughter hidden away, Fritzl constructed a false story, claiming that she had run off. He forced her to write letters to the rest of the family confirming the lie, and continued to maintain a normal life during the years of her incarceration, working as an electrical engineer. He also worked in real estate and was an investment partner in a restaurant. He believed that his success in these areas further cemented his power and his narcissism was a vein that ran through most of his life. Away from the sexual depravity Fritzl inflicted on his daughter, he was known to frequent brothels, where staff described his appetite as sadistic and deviant, going so far as to call the man 'mentally deranged'.[247]

Following a miscarriage in 1986, Elizabeth gave birth to her first child, Kerstin, in 1988, and over the next 14 years, Elizabeth would give birth to another six children. Of the seven, Kerstin, Stefan (born in 1990) and Felix (born in 2002) were kept in the cellar with Elizabeth. Lisa (born in 1992), Monika (born in 1994) and Alexander (born in 1996) were removed from the cellar as toddlers and taken upstairs to live with the rest of the Fritzl family. Josef claimed that his 'wayward' daughter had abandoned them on the doorstep. Elizabeth never knew what happened to those who left the cellar, until her escape. Alexander had been born a twin, but his brother Michael suffered breathing difficulties and died days after birth, as Fritzl refused to seek medical attention.

Over the ensuing years, Fritzl became more and more cruel. If Elizabeth or the children upset him, he would turn off the power, leaving them to huddle together on a mattress in complete darkness. The freezer he had provided would slowly defrost, leaving them without anything to eat, and the smell of rotting food would bring rats. Elizabeth would try and quieten her children. To keep his secret family alive, Fritzl would buy them food and supplies while in other suburbs, under the ruse of looking at property to buy and sell.

More than a decade later, in April 2008, Kerstin, Elizabeth's eldest, became deathly ill. Fritzl made the decision to take the 20-year-old Kerstin to the hospital, unaware that Elizabeth had hidden a letter in her pocket, hoping that someone would find it and discover the true horror of what she and her children were enduring. In the days that followed, Fritzl allowed the others to leave their underground prison and visit Kerstin in hospital. Doctors quickly noticed that all four of them – Elizabeth, Kerstin, Stefan and Felix – were sallow and malnourished. They displayed several trauma symptoms and were distrustful of everyone around them. Police and social services were called and the story began to unfold.

Police arrived at the doorstep of Fritzl's home in the early hours of 27 April 2008 and demanded to be taken to the cellar. There were eight locked doors between the front door and the room where Fritzl had kept Elizabeth and her children.[248] He paused momentarily at the cellar door, which was concealed behind a purpose-built shelving unit. Then he punched the secret code into the electronic panel on the door. The large concrete door that had hidden Elizabeth and her children from the world opened for the final time.

The smell that emanated from the room made the officers reel in disgust. Twenty years of damp, as well as waste and vermin, swelled around the opening. Fritzl did not notice the smell. During the trial, items including clothing and children's toys were brought into the courtroom for the jury to smell. Most recoiled as a soft toy taken from a plastic bag filled the courtroom with the same stench.

The rest of the family were unaware of the secret Fritzl had kept in the basement. The stories he told of the toddlers being dumped on the doorstep by his runaway daughter were believed, as Fritzl painted himself as a caring father. No one, not even his wife, imagined the truth.

In March 2009, Elizabeth slipped into the courtroom to watch her father's trial, avoiding the media by coming in a separate entrance. Still emaciated after her years of abuse, she watched the video screen at the front of the room as it played her victim impact statement, which recounted the torture and abuse she and her children had suffered. When her father saw her sitting with two minders, he realised at that moment that he had lost – she was stronger than he could have imagined. For the first time, he wept.

That moment changed the direction of the trial as well. After 11 hours of videotaped testimony, Fritzl was asked if he had anything to say. He had begun the trial in an arrogant and self-righteous manner, believing in his own innocence, but at that final moment, with Elizabeth watching on, he confessed to all charges of what he referred to as his sick behaviour.

Elizabeth and her two eldest children, Kerstin and Stefan – aged 20 and 19 on their release from the cellar – had spent their entire lives locked in hell and will need a lifetime of treatment to work through the trauma they endured. A third child, Felix, who was only five when released, may in time forget the horrors he witnessed. The three children who had been allowed to leave the basement and live upstairs – Monika, Alexander and Lisa – have been reunited with their mother and other siblings, and the family is left to pick up the pieces of their lives together.

Dr Kastner stated at trial that Fritzl compartmentalised his actions with a 'cellar of his soul'. He suffered from the suppressed trauma of being beaten by his mother, and that caused him to seek ultimate control over his family, whom he believed he owned.

She said, 'He wanted somebody who only belonged to him, somebody who could not be taken from him and whom he had no fear of losing.'[249]

He also compartmentalised the brutality he inflicted on Elizabeth and her children. He claimed that when he left the cellar, he dropped it from his mind; he would go about his daily business and only remember the horror when he returned.

Chapter 18
John List

In 1965, the List family – John Emil; his wife Helen; their daughter Patricia, aged 10; sons John Junior, 8, and Frederick, 7; and John's mother Alma – moved into the 19-room mansion called 'Breezy Knoll' on Hillside Avenue, Westfield, New Jersey. Though the neighbours tried to get to know the new occupants of the house, the Lists were far from friendly, almost to the point of rudeness. John in particular was aloof. He was also a man who keenly felt the overbearing presence of his mother.

'I was always obedient and well behaved,'[250] List would later reflect. He was an extremely reserved child, standing in the background, waiting for permission from his mother to move. Alma instilled the virtues of a strict Christian upbringing in her son, teaching him about the damnation awaiting those who sinned, and encouraging him to do well at school and lead a wholesome life. List and his mother were devout Lutherans who attended church service regularly and would pray together at night. His father had little direct interaction with his son, referring to him as 'the boy'. While his father ignored him, his mother smothered him, keeping the boy indoors when he was not at school, in fear that he would get sick. John was raised to see his father as the 'keeper of their family's salvation and their souls'.[251]

As a young adult, List taught Sunday school and served in the US Army, leaving as a second lieutenant. Following his service, he attended the University of Michigan and obtained a business administration degree, followed by a Masters in accounting, yet he was never good with money and even worse at keeping a job. After completing his degrees, he enlisted in the army against his mother's wishes, and learned that his father had died while he was posted overseas in 1944.

List met Helen at a bowling alley one evening in September 1951. Helen had gone out with her sister following the death of her first husband; with a young daughter in tow, her sister thought she needed cheering up. List introduced Helen to his mother, who didn't think the woman (who had a previous marriage and a child behind her) was wife material, but when Helen fell pregnant after a brief two-month courtship, they married on 1 December 1951. The marriage quickly soured. Helen discovered she was not pregnant after all, and realised that her new husband was strongly influenced by his ever-present mother, with whom she often clashed.

The couple, along with List's mother, moved to Detroit, and in 1955 Helen gave birth to the couple's first child, Patricia. The baby went some way toward healing the rift between the List women. When List moved from his accounting job with the army to a new job in Kalamazoo, the family were happy to welcome a second baby, John Junior, in 1956, followed by Frederick in 1958.

With many new mouths to feed, List was terrified to hear that his company was going through a merger. His worst fears were realised in the reshuffle and he was retrenched. Rather than tell anyone about the firing, he spent his days looking for a new job, and was hired by Xerox. The family moved to Rochester to be nearer to List's new employment, but again, his job was short-lived. He was lucky to find a new job quickly, as comptroller at the First National Bank, and was soon looking to buy a palatial home in Westfield to match his new position. To finance his new home, he arranged for his mother to sell her house.

In the years when the family lived at Breezy Knoll, List lost three jobs. Making payments on the home and living the lifestyle they had become accustomed to was becoming more and more difficult. List's wife and children also grew tired of the Lutheran faith, and the family's attendance at church dwindled until it was almost non-existent. Between jobs, the proud man refused to accept welfare, wandering the streets looking for work. Each day he was out of work, he would continue the pretence of getting ready for the office and leaving at the same time. He would also steal money from his mother's bank account. By the time of the murders, List owed $11,000 on the home loan (about $80,000 in today's money).

List's wife's health was also failing. She had caught syphilis from her first husband, Marvin Taylor, who had died during the war, and with whom she had a daughter, Brenda. She hid the disease from List for most of their marriage, but eventually became more and more of a financial burden, as the dementia she suffered, a by-product of the disease, slowly destroyed her.

At 9am on 9 November 1971, List committed murder after weeks of careful and methodical planning; he had arranged for milk, newspaper and mail deliveries to stop from that day, and informed the children's schools that they were being taken to North Carolina the next day to see his wife's sick mother, to prevent teachers from questioning their non-attendance.

After the children had gone to school, List loaded his father's 9mm Steyr 1912 automatic handgun, and his own .22 calibre revolver. He shot his wife Helen in the back of the head as she sat at the kitchen table eating her breakfast. List then moved to the third floor apartment of his mother, Alma, who was preparing her own breakfast in the kitchenette, and shot her once in the back of the head, killing her instantly. He went to the basement and pulled out the sleeping bags they used for family camping trips. He placed his wife's body in one of the sleeping bags and dragged it into the middle of the empty ballroom.

List busied himself cleaning up the blood while he waited for his three children to finish school. He collected 16-year-old Patricia from school and took her home, where she was the next to die, from a gunshot to the jaw. Next was 13-year-old Frederick, who was shot after being collected by his father from his part-time after school job.

List left the house to watch 15-year-old John Junior play in a soccer match, before driving his son home. Seeing the carnage, John Junior tried to fight his father, but was shot once in the head. When his body continued to twitch, List shot his son a further 10 times. The three children's bodies were dragged into the ballroom with their mother. There, he prayed that they were already in heaven and had forgiven him.

List continued with his usual evening rituals. He ate his dinner at the kitchen table, then spent the evening removing his face from every family photograph in the house, so police would not be able to provide the media with his identity. Following his meticulous plan, he went to bed. In the morning, he turned on every light in the house, put music on the intercom system and turned down the heating system. Then he fled.

Before he fled, he left his pastor a letter explaining his actions, as well as contact details for relatives and instructions about his belongings. His letter explained that his children had abandoned their Lutheran teachings, and that he was concerned about his wife's alcoholism and ailing health.

Dear Pastor Rehwinkel,

I am sorry to add this additional burden to your work. I know that what has been done is wrong from all that I have been taught and that any reasons that I might give will not make it right. But you are the one person that I know that while not condoning this will at least possibly understand why I felt that I had to do this. 1. I wasn't earning anywhere near enough to support us. Everything I tried seemed to fall to pieces. True, we could have gone bankrupt and maybe gone on welfare. 2. But that brings me to my next point. Knowing the type of location that one would have to live in, plus the environment for the children, plus the effect on them knowing they were on welfare was just more than I thought they could and should endure. I know they were willing to cut back, but this involved a lot more than that. 3. With Pat being so determined to get into acting I was also fearful as to what that might do to her continuing to be Christian. I'm sure it wouldn't have helped. 4. Also, with Helen not going to church I knew that this would harm the children eventually in their attendance. I had continued to hope that she would begin to come to church soon. But when I mentioned to her that Mr. Jutze wanted to pay her an elder's call, she just blew up and said she wanted her name taken off the church rolls. Again this could only have an adverse result for the children's continued attendance.

So that is the sum of it. If any one of these had been the condition, we might have pulled through but this was just too much. At least I'm certain that all have gone to heaven now. If things had gone on who knows if this would be the case.

Of course, Mother got involved because doing what I did to my family would have been a tremendous shock to her at this age. Therefore, knowing that she is also a Christian I felt it best that she be relieved of the troubles of this world that would have hit her.

After it was all over I said some prayers for them all – from the hymn book. That was the least that I could do. Now for the final arrangements: Helen and the children have all agreed that they would prefer to be cremated. Please see to it that the costs are kept low.

For Mother, she has a plot at the Frankenmuth Church cemetery. Please contact Mr. Herman Schellkas, Route 4, Vassar, Mich. 41768.

He's married to a niece of Mother's and knows what arrangements are to be made. (She always wanted Rev. Herman Zehnder of Bay City to preach the sermon. But he's not well.) Also I'm leaving some letters in your care. Please send them on and add whatever comments you think appropriate. The relationships are as follows: Mrs. Lydia Meyer – Mother's sister. Mrs. Eva Meyer – Helen's mother. Jean Syfert – Helen's sister.

Also I don't know what will happen to the books and personal things. But to the extent possible I'd like for them to be distributed as you see fit. Some books might go to the school or church library.

Originally I had planned this for Nov. 1 – All Saints' Day.

But travel arrangements were delayed. I thought it would be an appropriate day for them to get to heaven.

As for me please let me be dropped from the congregation rolls. I leave myself in the hand of God's Justice and Mercy. I don't doubt that He is able to help us, but apparently He saw fit not to answer my prayers the way that I hoped they would be answered. This makes me think that perhaps it was for the best as far as the children's souls are concerned. I know that many will only look at the additional years that they could have lived, but if finally they were no longer Christians what would be gained.

Also I'm sure many will say, 'How could anyone do such a horrible thing?' – My only answer is it isn't easy and was only done after much thought.

Pastor, Mrs. Morris may possibly be reached at 802 Pleasant Hill Drive. Elkin – home of her sister. One other thing. It may seem cowardly to have always shot from behind, but I didn't want any of them to know even at the last second that I had to do this to them.

John got hurt more because he seemed to struggle longer. The rest were immediately out of pain. John ~~probably~~[252] didn't consciously feel anything either.

Please remember me in your prayers. I will need them whether or not the government does its duty as it sees it. I'm only concerned with making my peace with God and of this I am assured because of Christ dying even for me.

P.S. Mother is in the hallway in the attic – 3d floor. She was too heavy to move.

John[253]

This letter, along with several others, was found inside a locked filing cabinet. A note was left in plain sight on his desk, directing 'the finder' to the letters. Profiling the letter to his pastor, it seems List was a man already at peace with the crimes he had committed. He spoke of being removed from church duty rolls as though he were leaving for a brief trip and didn't want to burden those around him. His guilt was abolished by the belief that his family was in heaven.

Thirteen days after the murders, he had already made his way to Denver, Colorado, and created a new persona as Robert Peter Clark, even applying for a new social security number. He immersed himself in his new life and was an active member of his local Lutheran church within weeks of arriving. While the List family's remains went undiscovered in their home, a plane hijacking captured the nation's attention. A man calling himself D. B. Cooper hijacked a Boeing 727 over Portland, Oregon, on 24 November. He demanded $200,000 in ransom money and a parachute, claiming he would detonate a bomb he was carrying if authorities didn't comply. The ransom money was paid, and 'Cooper' parachuted from the plane, never to be seen again. Some would later speculate that Cooper and List were one and the same.

Four weeks into his new life as Robert Clark, List heard the news that, on 7 December 1971, police had finally entered his Westfield home. Neighbours had called police after seeing the light bulbs in the List home burn out one by one. Officers found Helen and her three children lying in sleeping bags in the ballroom, above them an original, multi-million dollar Tiffany glass ceiling, which could have saved the family from financial ruin and death. Alma's body was found in a closet in her third-floor private apartment.

By 10 December 1971, the entire country was looking for John List. His car was found at Kennedy Airport, but police and the FBI could find no trace of the man as the years progressed. In 1985, he married Delores Miller in Denver, a fellow Lutheran churchgoer. In his new life, he came across to neighbours as a friendly man and a devout church-goer.

In 1989, the television programme *America's Most Wanted* featured a story on the List murders, commissioning a sculptor to provide an image of what List would look like after 18 years. A former neighbour of 'Robert

Clark' saw the show and called police, giving them List's new name. FBI agents went to his home and spoke to his shocked wife. She told them how her husband lost job after job, and how she would nag him about his inability to provide a stable income. Agents obtained fingerprints that confirmed Clark was indeed John Emil List.

A few days later, on 1 June 1989, agents surrounded a Virginia accounting office, where John List was arrested. He proclaimed his innocence, but the fingerprints and the scar behind his ear were undeniable evidence of the man's true identity. After a nine-week trial, he was convicted of all five murders and sentenced to five consecutive life terms in April 1990. A psychiatrist at the trial stated that List's only motive was a 'midlife crisis'[254] and that he had obsessive-compulsive personality disorder. He could not see accepting welfare payments as an option and thought saving his family's souls by sending them to heaven was his only choice. His lawyer, Elijah Miller, called him a 'fragmented person … [who could] not see the grey areas, only black and white'.[255]

While in prison, List confessed to Jean Syfert, Helen's sister, that he had killed his family because 'he couldn't stand to be a failure'.[256] When questioned about why he didn't just commit suicide, he told a reporter that 'suicide would have barred him from heaven and that he hoped to be reunited there with his family.'[257]

Chapter 19
The Menendez Brothers

A background of parental abuse and hardship is a common theme in the childhoods of many of the killers in this book, but a tragic childhood is not a necessary prequel to murder. In the case of the Menendez brothers, it was an upbringing of wealth, greed and privilege, albeit, if the killers are to be believed, set against a background of possible abuse.

Serial killers have become a subject of fascination across the globe, with television shows, books and films being made about their lives. Mass murderers like the Columbine killers dreamed about the 'fans' they would have after they murdered and maimed the students of their high school. In the Menendez case, the televised murder trial of two young, handsome and wealthy defendants captured America's attention. It was the stuff of movies, and indeed, the case has since spawned at least two made-for-TV movies, two documentaries and eight books.

The Menendez brothers' trial was screened live across America on a daily basis. The case was even investigated and dissected on Hollywood entertainment programs. The main question everyone asked was: How did two young men, with the world at their feet, end up behind bars for the brutal murders of their parents?

The Menendez boys were not the first wealthy children to murder their parents. In 1992, 17-year-old Kristi Koslow hired her friends to murder her adopted father and stepmother. Her reasoning, when apprehended, was,

'I just wanted to get money.'[258] She was hoping to lay claim to a $12 million inheritance. And in 1980, Billy Rouse shot and stabbed his parents, Darlene and Bruce, while they slept, in their sprawling Libertyville mansion. All of the Rouse children were suspects, having much to gain financially from their parents' deaths, and it took police 15 years to extract a confession from Billy, the youngest of the children.

There were also brothers Neil and Stewart Woodman, who hired two other brothers, Steve and Robert Homick, to gun down their parents, Gerald and Vera, in their palatial Brentwood home in 1985. The brothers had taken control of their parents' company, which caused problems in their relationship with their parents. As the company spiralled into debt, the brothers learned of a half a million dollar insurance policy in their mother's name, which would help, to a small degree, with their financial problems. In the next chapter, the case of Jeremy Bamber is another example of a wealthy family dying at the hands of one of the children. Greed and privilege played a part in all of these crimes, and the Menendez case was no different.

The story starts with the ideals of a young Cuban man, Jose Enrique Menendez, who, with the encouragement of his parents, escaped Cuba to find his fortune in America. At 15, Jose was a successful athlete in his new promised land, excelling in sports such as swimming, basketball and soccer. He turned down a swimming scholarship at Southern Illinois University and instead married Mary 'Kitty' Louise Andersen. The newlyweds moved from Chicago to New York, and Jose gained a degree in accounting at Queens College, while also waiting tables.

Jose then began an ascent that would take him to the tree-lined streets of Beverly Hills. His first job was with Hertz, and this eventually led him to a role signing bands with RCA Records, including Duran Duran and the Eurythmics.[259] With this success, the family lived well in the suburb of Princeton, New Jersey. His two sons, Lyle and Erik, attended Princeton day school and rubbed shoulders with New York's elite.

When Jose was passed over for a promotion at RCA Records, he resigned on the spot, uprooting his family and moving to Los Angeles.

There, he was hired by International Video Entertainment, and took the company from debt to lucrative profits. After first living near Jose's place of employment, the family moved to their final home on Elm Avenue, Beverly Hills. It had a cream rendered facade, immaculate gardens and a circular driveway – it was a long way from Cuba. By now, Jose's two boys were teenagers. Lyle was attending Princeton, while his younger brother had transferred to Beverly Hills High.

By the time of his death, Jose Menendez was earning a million dollars a year, and was vocal about his disappointment in his sons. He often reminded them of his struggle to create the life they had, and that he had given up his own dreams of sports stardom to earn money when the family started out. He threatened to write them out of his will if they did not show respect to him, and responsibility with their money. To prove his point, he gave them strict allowances of $180 a month.[260]

While Jose had drive and ambition, his sons did not, particularly Lyle. According to the opening statement of the trial, 'Lyle Menendez was a failure. He knew it, his father knew it, and most painfully of all, he knew his father knew it.' For the relationship between father and eldest son, Lyle's suspension from Princeton was the final nail in the coffin.

Two months before the murders, Jose spoke to his brother-in-law about writing a new will, which would leave both boys out. He also told another family member, 'I've got to have a major talk with Lyle. He has got to get the message that we are not going to support them – we are not going to be supporting them for the rest of their lives.'[261] Eighteen-year-old Erik was obsessed with escaping his father's regime, but knew it was impossible for him to leave home without the funds to support his lifestyle. Erik also showed friends a movie script he had been writing, in which a young man murdered his overbearing father. While 21-year-old Lyle was away at university, Erik would spend hours on the phone to his brother, complaining about his lot.

Together, the two young men decided they'd had enough. Two days before the murders, they travelled out of the city limits to a sporting goods store in San Diego, and purchased guns using fake IDs.

The day of 20 August 1989 started out beautifully for the close-knit family. Chartering the Motion Picture Marine company yacht, the family cruised and fished together, leaving Jose and Kitty exhausted after a day in the sun. Later that evening, the two brothers having gone out to the movies, their parents retired to the den. The couple, who had been married for 26 years, ate bowls of berries and whipped cream for dessert and watched the James Bond film *The Spy Who Loved Me*.

At 10pm, Lyle and Erik rushed into the darkened study of their parent's home, carrying shotguns. The only light in the room was the flickering television. Jose and Kitty had more than likely fallen asleep in front of the television, as they had done on previous occasions, allowing the killers to ambush them.

According to the trial testimony, 18-year-old Erik claimed he saw a silhouette in the glare of the television and was reminded of his childhood, when his father would appear at his door. He claimed the image reminded him of times when he was abused by his father and that it caused him to shoot.[262] He aimed his gun at his father and fired. The sound woke Kitty from her slumber. She tried to flee as 21-year-old Lyle joined in, shooting at both parents.

When the bodies were found, they were peppered with shotgun shrapnel; all but one bullet had hit its mark. Jose Menendez, 45, had suffered five gunshot wounds. He'd had no time to react to the attack and was found with one leg still tucked up under the other, on the cream sofa in front of the television. Lyle had gone behind his father and fired a shot into the back of his head at point blank range. According to the trial transcript, the wound to the back of Jose's head was so destructive that, as the coroner removed the man's body from the crime scene, the remnants of his brain fell out of the skull cavity.[263]

Kitty had suffered nine gunshot wounds. She had reacted to the gun fire, falling down between the sofa and the coffee table, and had tried to crawl away while Lyle reloaded his gun. Lyle fired the final shot into her face. At trial, the prosecution called the murders an 'ambush in a storm of gunfire'.[264]

Both victims had also been deliberately shot in the knees.

In just a few seconds, Erik and Lyle had killed their parents.[265] After ensuring that they were dead, the two carefully collected every shell from the room, as well as the weapons. They then left to hide the shotguns, which have never been recovered.

They had planned to meet up with a friend to help provide an alibi for the night, but the evening's events had taken them longer than they expected, and their friend left the rendezvous point before the brothers arrived. Lyle called him and begged him to meet them at a restaurant. He then called a second time and asked him to meet them at their home, hoping to use him as a possible witness to the 'finding' of their parents. The friend said he would meet them at the restaurant, but again the brothers did not show up.

Lyle and Erik returned home to 'discover' their murdered parents, under the guise of collecting Erik's fake ID. Lyle, feigning hysteria, called 911.[266] The transcript of the call is as follows:

911 OPERATOR: Hello (UNINTELLIGIBLE) emergency.

LYLE MENENDEZ: Yes, police ...

911 OPERATOR: What's the problem?

LYLE MENENDEZ: We're the sons of ...

911 OPERATOR: What's the problem? What's the problem?

LYLE MENENDEZ: Someone killed my parents!

911 OPERATOR: Pardon me?

LYLE MENENDEZ: Someone killed my parents!

911 OPERATOR: Were they shot?

LYLE MENENDEZ: Yes!

911 OPERATOR: They were shot?

LYLE MENENDEZ: Yes! (UNINTELLIGIBLE)

911 OPERATOR: What happened?

LYLE MENENDEZ: Shut up! Erik, shut up!

911 OPERATOR: What happened? We have units en route. What happened?

LYLE MENENDEZ: I don't know!

911 OPERATOR: Who shot who?

LYLE MENENDEZ: (UNINTELLIGIBLE) I just came home!

911 OPERATOR: You came home and found who shot?

LYLE MENENDEZ: My mom and dad!

911 OPERATOR: Do you know if they're still in the house, the people that did the shooting?

LYLE MENENDEZ: Erik, get away from them!

The police arrived soon after the call to find both young men hysterical, curled up in the foetal position on the manicured front lawn. They were taken to the police station for questioning, where they gave almost identical statements through their tears. They told officers they had gone to see a Batman movie and had arranged to meet a friend afterwards, but had missed him, gone home and found their parents.

In most investigations, the first suspects are those closest to the victims. In this case, both boys helped police start elsewhere, diverting attention away from themselves. In their statements, both Lyle and Erik suggested that there could have been an organised crime connection. Since the victims had suffered shotgun wounds to the knees, an injury known as 'knee-capping' and often linked to organised crime, the brothers' story was believable. They were released shortly after making their statements.

The following day, after police completed initial crime scene investigations, the two boys carried the family safe to their attorney to have it unsealed. To boost their story about their parents being killed in a 'hit', Lyle hired a bodyguard to shadow his every move, claiming he was in fear for his own life. He also said he was considering buying a bulletproof limousine.[267]

Within days of the death of their parents, Erik and Lyle had gone on a spending spree that alarmed those around them, spending close to $1 million on Rolex watches, cars and clothing.[268] They purchased a restaurant, hired full-time tennis coaches and splurged on overseas holidays. They also moved out of the house owned by their parents and rented two apartments in Marina Del Rey, near where they had chartered the yacht on the day of the murders.

The lifestyle that the Menendez brothers were living showed little regard for their murdered parents and raised the suspicions of investigating police. The murders also began to weigh heavily on Erik, the more emotional of the brothers, who confessed his part in the crime to psychologist Jerome Oziel, telling him in a recorded interview on 31 October 1989, 'We did it.'[269] Due to doctor/patient privilege, the taped confessions could not be used, and the psychologist could not tell police what had occurred in his sessions. Once Lyle heard that his brother had confessed, however, he went and saw Oziel. On 11 December, both brothers told the doctor they had killed their parents. In their confessions, they did not mention any abuse.

Listening at the door of Oziel's office was a patient who had a relationship with the psychologist. She heard the brothers' confession and called police, telling them what she had heard. Soon afterward, Erik left the psychologist's office looking upset, followed by Oziel and Lyle. Lyle threatened Oziel about what had just been revealed, and Oziel later called the police, but it would be another three months before they had enough evidence to act. On 8 March 1990, six months after the murders, Lyle was arrested near the family home. Erik was arrested a few days later when he returned from a tennis championship in Israel.

The brothers' initial trial, in which abuse allegations were first raised, was held in 1993. The boys claimed they had feared for their lives and felt that they had no alternative but to kill their parents. During the investigation, other allegations of molestation were made against Jose Menendez. According to psychiatrist Dr Will Vicary, who testified at trial, 'There were allegations and they were investigated. They were followed up. People were interviewed and admitted they had been either molested or approached by the father sexually. However, because of their position – some of these people were in the entertainment business – they did not wish to make this a public statement, so this information, thus far, has not come out publicly.'[270]

After a hung jury in the first trial, both boys were sent to trial again, where they were found guilty of first degree murder, as well conspiracy to commit murder. Both were sentenced to life imprisonment. They were sent to different prisons, but have remained in contact via letters.

Regardless of the truth behind the molestation allegations, the brothers were 'quite mixed up and had a lot of psychological problems',[271] according to Dr Vicary. In their eyes, their similarly privileged friends had a lot of freedom, whereas they were raised under a tougher regime. They felt they deserved better and chose the most violent way to win that freedom, which ultimately led to their incarceration. According to the prosecution, 'It was their greed that got the better of them. It was greed that drove them to commit murder in the first place and it was the same greed that drove them to spend the money immediately.'[272]

Chapter 20
Jeremy Bamber

If money is the root of all evil and can compel two young men to murder their parents, then what does it take for a young man to murder not only his parents, but his sister and six-year-old twin nephews as well? In the Bamber case, the initial suspect was a pretty but disturbed young model, until the tables turned on the sole 'survivor' of the killings, who, like the Menendez brothers, didn't believe he should have to work for what was rightfully his.

As in the Menendez case, handsome and well-to-do Jeremy Bamber rang Chelmsford Police Station on the evening of 7 August 1985. He told the officer who answered the phone, 'You've got to help me. My father has rung me and said, "Please come over. Your sister has gone crazy and has got the gun."' He then told police that the line had gone dead.[273] Bamber's telephone conversation with police continued as he set the scene about his unstable sister, who had a history of mental illness. Police expected to find that a crazed woman had murdered her parents and children following a psychotic break. But as other family members began to scratch beneath the surface, the truth was far more sinister.

Ralph 'Nevill' Bamber married June in 1949, and they purchased the expansive property of White House Farm on the outskirts of Tollshunt d'Arcy, Essex. Nevill was the local magistrate and the couple were active members of their local church. When they discovered that they were unable to have children, the church helped them adopt Jeremy and Sheila. Though they had fulfilled their dreams of creating a family unit in their wonderful home, the two children would prove extremely difficult to manage in the strict religious upbringing the Bambers tried to enforce.

According to those who knew the Bamber family, they were decent people. Nevill was described as a good and fair man.[274] He was a regular participant in local shooting events and was known to be a good shot. He had quite a collection of guns and ammunition, including a .22 Anshutz automatic rifle that had a telescopic sight and sound moderator. Nevill preferred to keep the modifications on the rifle, as removing them required a screwdriver, and it took time to realign the sight. June was compulsive about her participation at her local church and there was some cause for concern when her participation turned into religious mania. Three years before the murders occurred, she was admitted to psychiatric hospital. The couple not only ran their own farm, but owned several other farming properties throughout the countryside, worth £435,000.

Jeremy was born in 1961, the illegitimate baby of a nurse who'd had an affair with a married stockbroker. Jeremy's adopted parents hoped their son would become active in the church, but he rebelled against them from a very young age, telling anyone who would anyone listen that he hated his adoptive parents. They sent him to boarding school, hoping the strict regime would help, but it just fed his resentment. His father allowed him to travel the globe, hoping he would find something to shape his life, but instead Jeremy found work smuggling drugs from the Middle East into England. He began fantasising about getting his hands on his family's wealth.

Sheila was older than her adopted brother by four years. She was born to a chaplain's daughter who'd had an affair with a young cleric. Sheila was emotionally frail and, like her adopted brother, rebelled against her strict religious upbringing. As a teenager, she worked as a model, but turned to drugs and alcohol and was admitted for psychiatric treatment. Sheila went on to marry Colin Cattell in 1977 and the couple had twin boys in 1979. Her mental health took a dramatic downturn again after the birth of the twins. She was admitted to hospital, where she was diagnosed as a paranoid schizophrenic.[275] Sheila's sons lived with their father, but they still saw their mother as often as possible. Her final hospital admission was four months prior to the murders, when she was suffering from religious mania.

Before the murders, Jeremy had moved out of the family farm and into a house his parents had purchased in Goldhanger, six kilometres away. He refused to work with his father on the farm, instead attending college in Colchester, where he met his girlfriend Julie Mugford. He also found work as a waiter.

Jeremy began telling friends about his ongoing fantasies of murdering his parents and sister. He told them he wanted to burn down the farm with them trapped inside, but then rethought that mode of murder, as it would destroy items of value in the house. He mused on whether he could hire a professional to murder them.

A few days before the murders, Sheila's six-year-old twins, Daniel and Nicholas, arrived to spend a few days with their mother. Then, the night before the murders, the farm's secretary Barbara Wilson called to speak to Nevill. She believed she had called in the middle of an argument, as the usually conversational farmer was abrupt, ending the phone call quickly.[276]

At 3.26am on 7 August 1985, Jeremy Bamber made a frantic call to the police, claiming he could not get hold of his family after receiving a distressing phone call from his father that his sister had 'gone crazy and has got the gun'.[277] The operator told Bamber to go the farm and wait for the police to arrive, but they passed him on the way. When Bamber arrived, almost two minutes after the police, he explained that his sister was in the house with a gun. He described her as 'a nutter' and said she'd been having treatment'. Police asked him why his father had called him and not the police, and Bamber explained that his father was a private man, who would have preferred not to involve authorities. When Jeremy was asked why he called the local constabulary, rather than emergency, he nonchalantly said that he thought it would make no difference.

Bamber told police about the guns that were in the house. He also told them he had loaded the .22 automatic rifle and left it on the kitchen table the previous night. He explained it was there so someone could grab it quickly to shoot the wild rabbits that had been destroying the crops. The police noticed the man's calm demeanour. Two hours later, once a tactical group had assembled to storm the house, Bamber finally became upset. He called his girlfriend Julie, who was driven to the farm by police to be with her boyfriend.

At 7.30am, police stormed the house and found the bodies. Nevill Bamber was in the kitchen, slumped over an upturned chair. He had been shot eight times, suffering two wounds to the right side of his face, and two more in the top of his head. He had also been shot in the mouth and jaw and his left shoulder and elbow. He had suffered two black eyes, a broken nose and bruising, and lacerations to the head, cheek and right arm. He had several defensive wounds consistent with being struck and burnt with a rifle. The room also showed signs of a struggle, with blood on various surfaces. A light was smashed, as well as several pieces of crockery. Nevill's watch had been knocked from his arm and was found under a mat in the kitchen, along with a piece of a gun's butt. The phone in the kitchen was off the hook.

June Bamber was in the main bedroom upstairs. Her body was in the doorway and covered in blood. She had been shot seven times, including one shot to the forehead. The other gunshot wounds were to her face, neck, forearm, chest and knee. She had been standing when she had first been attacked.

The bodies of the twin boys were found in their beds. Daniel had been shot five times in the head. Nicholas had been killed with three gunshots to the head.

Finally, Sheila was found lying on the floor near the bed in her room, with the blood-splattered .22 rifle lying along her abdomen. Her right hand was resting on the trigger and the muzzle was close to one of the two gunshot wounds in her neck. The rifle's silencer had been removed.

The coroner attended the scene to certify the deaths of the five family members and declared that Sheila's wounds were self-inflicted, giving credence to Jeremy Bamber's story that his crazed sister had killed them, and then herself. This quick finding meant that thorough investigations were not conducted of all of the firearms, and crucial evidence was not collected.

Three days after the killings, Jeremy and Sheila's cousin, David Boutflour, was not convinced that Sheila had committed the murders. He visited the White House Farm with other members of the family and located the silencer and scope for the .22 rifle that had been used in the shootings. David, who had been shooting with his uncle on previous occasions, noticed blood inside the silencer and sent it to police for investigating. Forensic testing on a flake of the blood matched Sheila's. The pathologist also tested the rifle's barrel and found no blood inside the gun. Sheila's hands were immaculate, with no evidence of the gunshot residue that would normally be found when someone has fired or loaded. The final test proved that that she was not the shooter; measurements of the gun with the silencer attached showed it would have been impossible for Sheila to place it under her chin and fire, as her arms were too short to reach the trigger. The case against her as 'mentally unstable daughter' had started to fall apart.

At the funeral, Bamber played the grieving son, sobbing into his girlfriend's shoulder as they walked behind the coffins of his family. He later told her, 'I should have been an actor,'[278] and claimed he had committed the perfect crime. It was then that Bamber's girlfriend went to police with the information they needed. She told them that Bamber had expressed a wish for his family to be dead and said they were ruining his life. In 1984, he expressed a desire to 'get rid of them all',[279] telling her that his 'father was getting old, his mother was mad [and] Sheila was mad as well.'[280] Jeremy talked compulsively about the killings and eventually confessed to Julie what he had done.

On the night of the murder, Jeremy had called Julie at 9.50pm, having spent the day planning and fantasising about the murders. He told her he was riled up and ready to act. In his words, it was 'tonight or never'.[281] Bamber dyed his hair, then rode his mother's bicycle to White House Farm. He put on gloves and sneaked into the farmhouse by using a window that had a broken lock. The latch looked like it was closed, but family members were aware that it was secret way into the house if all other doors and windows were locked. Once inside, Bamber unlocked the gun cabinet and took out the .22 rifle that had the silencer attached. It was then that his father heard a noise and went to investigate, only to be confronted with his adopted son holding the rifle. A fight ensured and Nevill was shot repeatedly, as well as being struck with the butt of the rifle. He was hit so hard that a piece of the rifle's stock broke off. Bamber grabbed the boxes of ammunition from the gun cabinet and headed upstairs.

He shot his mother as she got out of bed, having heard the sounds in the kitchen. He shot her again as she ran towards the bedroom doorway. Still alive, June slowly crawled towards the other bedrooms, but died when Bamber put the shotgun to her forehead and pulled the trigger.

Bamber walked into the boys' bedroom and found them sleeping. He shot them both in the head, killing them. He next moved to his sister's bedroom, where he found her sleeping, unaware of the carnage happening around her. He put the gun close to her chin and fired. The shot caused Sheila to fall from the bed. He then fired a second shot with the silencer pressed against her neck. He cleaned the gun and removed the silencer, placing it on his sister's body and rubbing her hands all over the barrel and trigger (once police began suspecting that the killings were not the work of Sheila, they uncovered Bamber's prints on the trigger). Then Bamber left the farmhouse and rode the bike home to his house in Goldhanger.

After Julie's interview, Bamber was arrested on 8 September 1985, one month and one day after the killings. He was interviewed for three days. He claimed that Julie had made the story up because he had dumped her, but confess to robbing a small caravan that his parents owned, stealing almost £1,000 in cash. He denied all knowledge of the murders and travelled to France after his release from police custody.

Like the Menendez brothers, Bamber enjoyed the good life while he was free. He spent his days at expensive restaurants, attending wine tastings and shopping, and purchased a sports car. But on his return to England, he was re-arrested and charged with all five murders.

At trial, Bamber was portrayed as a young man 'motivated by hatred and greed [who] had planned and carried out the killings'.[282] He was found guilty and sentenced to five life sentences. During sentencing, the trial judge called him 'evil almost beyond belief. It shows that you, a young man though you are, have a warped, callous and evil mind concealed behind an outwardly presentable civilised manner ... you fired shot after shot into them and also into the two little boys aged six who you murdered in cold blood while they were asleep in their bed ... I believe that you did so partly out of greed because, although you were a well-off young man for your age, you were impatient for more money ... You wanted to be master of your own life and to enjoy an inheritance, much of which would have come to you anyway in the fullness of time.'[283]

Like the Menendez brothers, Bamber felt restricted by the strict regimen and religious instruction of his parents. Like his older adopted sister, he fought against them often, moving away from home and ultimately travelling to escape. He rejected his adopted father's hard-working way of life, believing his parents and sister were undeserving of the wealth that had been afforded them. He was impulsive and impatient, but had planned to commit the murders for many years. As he said to his girlfriend, it was 'tonight or never'; he had seen an argument between his sister and father over the welfare of Sheila's sons, which would set the scene to frame Sheila. He had also raised concerns about his mother's mental health and was worried about how fit and healthy his father remained in his sixties; he knew that his inheritance was going to be a long wait.

The Menendez and Bamber murders had many similarities. In both cases, the killers were egotistical and overconfident. They told people they could commit the perfect murder and finally set about proving themselves right. Bamber had boasted that he could get away with murder, while Erik Menendez wrote a screenplay in which a young man killed his parents and got away with it. Yet in both cases, their ongoing talk about the murder of their parents was their ultimate undoing, coupled with crime scene evidence and their lavish spending habits.

Chapter 21
Marybeth Tinning

Marybeth Tinning was born Marybeth Roe to parents Alton and Ruth on 11 September 1942, in Duanesburg, New York. The first of two children, Marybeth spent most of her childhood being told that she was unwanted and unloved; her younger brother was the focus of the family, while Marybeth was shunned.[284] She was isolated from those around her, often being locked in a bedroom for entire days, and the only attention she received was physical abuse at the end of her father's flyswatter. She later recalled that if she cried, he would lock her in a closet.[285]

In court, she testified about her unhappy childhood, saying, 'My father hit me with a fly swatter because he had arthritis and his hands were not of much use. And when he locked me in my room I guess he thought I deserved it.'[286] She was extremely lonely as a child and attempted suicide multiple times while growing up.

At school, she was an outsider who did not fit in and had few friends. Most of the students were unaware that her 'strangeness' was due to a lack of social skills, which should have been taught in a caring home environment. Her loneliness at home and school was reinforced by outbursts of aberrant behaviour. She would act out, knowing that it was one way to get the attention she so desperately craved.

Tinning graduated from Duanesburg High School, where she had been elected president of the Future Homemakers of America Club,[287] a social club for those who wanted to be stay-at-home mothers. After high school, she worked several jobs, including as a nurse's aide at Ellis Hospital, as a waitress with Flavorland, and as a local bus driver.[288]

She said later that there were only two things that she ever wanted in life: 'to be married to someone who cared for me and to have children'.[289] Her wish would come true by the time she was 22, when she went on a blind date with Joe Tinning. In 1965, the couple married, and in May 1967, they were blessed with their first baby, Barbara. For once in her life, happiness had found Tinning. She doted on her newborn and many visitors came to see her and her baby daughter. In January 1970, they welcomed a second baby, a son named Joseph Junior.

Though Tinning enjoyed the attention she received from those who came to coo over her children, she was still denied her parents' love. Her father Alton had become ill and spent a lot of time in hospital. Tinning, being a dutiful daughter, saw him regularly but was always spurned.[290] In October 1971, while Tinning was heavily pregnant with her third child, Alton died of a massive heart attack. Having always been cold and abusive, Marybeth had hoped her father would show her love before the end, but it never came, and his sudden death caused far-reaching psychological issues from which she would never recover. She found that the sympathetic interest from others she received at his funeral was what she had yearned for her entire life, and that brought her the attention she wanted.

The day after Christmas 1971, Marybeth gave birth to her third child, a daughter named Jennifer. By now, those who had supported Tinning after her father's death in October had returned to their own lives, and were busy with Christmas. But death struck her family once again. On 3 January, the Tinnings rushed their newborn baby girl to Schenectady Hospital, where she was diagnosed with meningitis.[291] Multiple congenital brain abscesses were also found.[292] The eight-day-old baby died in hospital.

Once back at home, Tinning washed all of Jennifer's clothes and packed them away. She also disassembled the cot and packed up the baby's toys. The cleaning and packing up would later become part of Tinning's post-death ritual.[293] Friends and relatives flocked to the heartbroken woman, to console her and help with her two surviving children.

As the attention began to wane, tragedy struck the Tinning family once again. Seventeen days after Jennifer's death, Tinning rushed her two-year-old son Joseph Junior to the hospital. She told medical staff he had had a seizure and he was placed under close monitoring and observation for several hours. When nothing could be found to account for the seizure, he was discharged. Several hours later, Tinning returned with Joseph's limp body in her arms. She told doctors he had had a seizure again, causing the cot's blankets to wrap around his body and suffocate him. His death was attributed to cardiopulmonary arrest.[294] Again, she returned home to wash the toddler's clothes and pack away his belongings, and people rushed to be with her, deeply saddened and shocked by these two tragedies, happening so close together, and so soon after the death of her father.

On 1 March 1972, Tinning again rushed to the hospital with a child in her arms, claiming that four-year-old Barbara had had convulsions at home. Once again, the child was monitored and doctors could find nothing wrong. Barbara was discharged into the care of her mother and the following day, Tinning returned with the child, who was unconscious. She subsequently died without regaining consciousness. Doctors diagnosed the rare disease of Reyes Syndrome, which can cause encephalopathy (swelling of the brain), but no conclusive evidence or testing was sought. Tinning later recalled the death, in her own warped memories: 'While we were sleeping, she called out to me and I went in and she was having a convulsion. I guess I don't even remember whether we took her by ambulance or whether we took her, but anyway we got there and they did whatever they did.' As she had done following Jennifer and Joseph's deaths, Tinning washed and packed away all of Barbara's belongings, and wellwishers and mourners returned to the Tinning house.

Finding herself alone and childless again after Barbara's death, Tinning began working as a waitress. A month later, Marybeth and Joe decide to contact the Department of Social Services to express an interest in becoming foster parents. Looking at the tragic circumstances that had surrounded the family, the department understood the couple's desire to foster, rather than risk whatever condition had killed their own children. By the end of 1972, the Tinnings had fostered Robert, but he moved on in January 1973. They then took in another foster child, Linda, in 1973, but she was returned when the couple found out they were expecting another child. Timothy was born on 21 November 1973, but the joy of the new baby was shortlived. The couple rushed nine-day-old Timothy to the hospital, where he was pronounced dead on arrival. His death was declared to be from Sudden Infant Death Syndrome (SIDS).

The deaths of Joe and Marybeth's children started to chip away at the solid foundation of their marriage. They fought over money and Marybeth's failing mental health. Joe convinced his wife to seek psychiatric attention and she was admitted to hospital, but soon after returned home. Feeling she had been abandoned by her husband, she attempted to poison him with the barbiturate Phenobarbital, but Joe survived and told doctors he had attempted suicide.[295]

The couple called police in January 1974, claiming they had been burgled, but suspicion later fell on Marybeth following the theft of a family member's money. In late 1974, she confessed to a co-worker that she was pregnant again and that 'God told her to kill this one too'.[296] On 30 March 1975, Tinning gave birth to her fifth child, Nathan. While everyone around them hoped the fates of Tinning's previous four children would not fall to Nathan, on 20 September 1975, while Marybeth was out shopping with the baby, he died. According to Marybeth, she was driving to the store when he stopped breathing in his car seat. She drove to St Clare's hospital with the dead baby in her arms. Like Joseph, Nathan's death was attributed to SIDS and listed as acute pulmonary oedema.

For three years, the Tinning couple tried to move on from the tragedies that had struck them. They stopped having any children and nor did they foster any others. But in August 1978, the couple began adoption proceedings for newborn Michael, and in October had their sixth biological child, Mary Frances. At three months old, Mary Frances was rushed to hospital unconscious, but doctors were able to revive her. Her condition was listed as 'aborted SIDS'[297] and she was soon released home. A month later, she was again rushed to hospital in cardiac arrest, and doctors revived the child once more, but she was left with permanent brain damage. Mary Frances remained on life support for two days before dying.

On 19 November 1979, Tinning gave birth to Jonathan. At four months old, he was rushed to St Clare's Hospital, unconscious. He was revived but sent to a trauma hospital for further tests. When no diagnosis could be established, he was discharged. A few days later, he was again brought unconscious to the hospital, and died after fighting for life on a respirator for a month.

Though the family seemed to be cursed, the suspicion that a genetic anomaly was to blame was set aside when an adopted child died in similar circumstances. Tinning's two-year-old adopted son Michael was taken to a paediatrician on 2 March 1981, with Marybeth claiming the child would not wake up. The toddler was already dead when doctors examined him. Suspicion at last fell on Tinning, though no charges were yet laid.

For the next four years, the couple remained childless, as the rumours and innuendo died down. Then on 22 August 1985, Tinning gave birth to Tami Lynne. Four months later, the baby was dead. Instead of going to hospital, Tinning went screaming to a neighbour, who came inside to find the baby dead on the changing table. After the deaths of nine children in 13 years, police were at last called to investigate.

In April 1986, following tests on Tami Lynne's corpse, Tinning and her husband were arrested. Once in custody, Marybeth broke down and told police that she believed she was not worth 'anything in life'.[298] She confessed to three of the murders, but vehemently denied the others. In her handwritten confession, she wrote, 'I did not do anything to Jennifer, Joseph, Barbara, Michael, Mary Frances, Jonathon. Just these three: Timothy, Nathan and Tami. I smothered them each with [sic] pillow because I'm not a good mother.'[299] She was charged only with the murder of Tami Lynne.

At her trial, Medical Examiner Dr Michael Baden, an expert in SIDS, explained to the court, 'About three babies in a thousand die from crib death. The odds against two crib deaths in one family are enormous. The odds against three are astronomical ... There is no known genetic disease that can cause sudden death in healthy children ... A baby will not suffocate from being snarled in blankets and bed sheets.'[300]

After a six-week trial, Tinning was found guilty of the murder of Tami Lynne and sentenced to 20 years to life for the killing. According to experts who testified at her trial, she was a narcissist who was motivated by the attention she gained from her children's tragic deaths.

She has been refused parole since her eligibility in 2007. At a 2011 parole hearing, when asked what insights she had gained about herself, she replied, 'When I look back I see a very damaged and just a messed up person and I have tried to become a better person while I was here, trying to be able to stand on my own and ask for help when I need it ... sometimes I try not to look in the mirror and when I do, I just, there is no words that I can express now. I feel none. I'm just, just none.'[301]

Final notes

This book addresses family dysfunction and its effects on many facets of a person's life – in particular, the path to criminality that it may lead to. Indeed, the essence of the preceding chapters is about what creates a killer and what events in a person's life can eventually manifest in homicide. The killers listed herein cover a range of murderous campaigns, from serial killers prone to violence from an early age, to sexual deviants who murdered to hide their sexual crimes. There are those who kill their own family, or kill *with* their family members.

There are no hard and fast rules for what creates a murderer, but there are common themes, and many childhood 'red flags' are raised in this book. It seems possible that any one of us could have followed the same path, given the right (or rather, wrong) circumstances. Couples with a lust for rape and murder, sons who see their way to fortune through the murder of their parents, unstable teenagers, serial killers who feel rejected and unloved – to have a killer in the family is beyond the comprehension of most of us, but the age-old debate of nature versus nurture rages on.

In extreme cases, when murderers are born into generations of sexual violence and depravity, I must ask the disturbing question: what if the family in *Texas Chainsaw Massacre* really existed? Though the film claimed to be based on real events, the director and producer later stated that the cannibal family was based purely on the story of Ed Gein and his farmhouse full of body parts. Gein was a killer who, following the death of his mother, to whom he had devoted his whole life, tried to re-create her by stealing body parts from fresh graves. When he ran out of corpses, he murdered two women. The story was gruesome enough to give Gein a place in contemporary folklore, and to serve as inspiration for horror filmmakers.

Ed Gein features large in crime fiction and films. He was the model for skin-wearing serial killer Buffalo Bill in *Silence of the Lambs*, as well as the Leatherface character in *Texas Chainsaw Massacre*. His quiet, unnerving demeanour and infatuation with his mother were the basis for Robert Bloch's book *Norman Bates*, and the subsequent film *Psycho*. Gein found his place in infamy, as one of many killers who became the stuff of legend.

Still, the question remains. Could a family comprising generations of degenerates, sex offenders and murderers exist? There have been glimpses of such possibilities throughout time, from stories about the Borgia family and the Julio-Claudians of ancient Rome, to families that achieved success through murder and mayhem. But the killers listed herein are mainly from broken homes and lower socio-economic environments, where criminality is sometimes necessary in order to survive; a small child stealing food might lead to them committing larger thefts if they are not caught or chastised, and crimes can escalate from there. Yet in saying that, not all of those profiled in the book experienced poverty. The Menendez brothers, Bernardo and Homolka, and John List all had comfortable lifestyles before they committed murder.

Other killers experienced a conflict between general societal norms versus what went on in their own homes – deviant or abusive behaviour that children might consider normal without knowing what occurs in other families. Sexual deviance and predation is highly significant in the lives of many children who go on to become serial killers. In comparison with the general population, where 3% of people are sexually abused as children, that increases to 26% for serial killers.[302] The sexually motivated murders committed by Fred and Rose West, for example, were the culmination of generations of deviance and violence in their families, which resulted in the murders of at least 13 people. There are those killers who, like Fred and Rose

West, were born into families where incest was part of everyday life, and what seemed abhorrent to most was the norm for them.

The Kray brothers were taught early on to fight for what they wanted, both in the physical and metaphorical sense, but soon realised they could fight for more than just a day-to-day existence, and in this way greed fed many of the killers in this book. That same greed drove Manson and Jones, who as young children believed they had nothing. Manson spent most of his formative years in juvenile and adult detention facilities, while Jones was rejected by his father, and both men would draw a flock of believers around them. Their followers saw them as Gods, yet both ended up in disastrous circumstances, where the only possible result was death.

There are many ways in which a person might become a killer, and the possiblity of harbouring a killer in the family remains a very frightening one.

Bibliography

Books

Aggrawal, A 2010, *Necrophilia: Forensic and Medico-legal Aspects*, CRC Press.

Benford, T & Johnson, J 2000, *Righteous Carnage: The List Murders in Westfield*, iUniverse.

Bennett, W 2006, *Criminal Investigation*, Cengage Learning.

Britton, P 1997, *The Jigsaw Man*, Corgi.

Bugliosi, V et al 1992, *Helter Skelter*, Arrow.

Bulger, R et al 2013, *My James*, Macmillan.

Canter, D 1995, *Criminal Shadows: Inside the Mind of a Serial Killer*, HarperCollins.

Clarke, P et al 2011, *Extreme Evil: Taking Crime to the Next Level*, Canary.

Cullen, D 2010, *Columbine*, Grand Central Publishing.

Douglas, J and Olshaker, M 1996, *Mindhunter: Inside the FBI's Elite Serial Crime Unit*, Pocket Books.

Furio, J 2001, *Team Killers: A Comparative Study of Collaborative Killers*.

Hall, A 2008, *Monster*, Penguin.

Hatty, S 2000, *Masculinities, Violence and Culture*, Sage.

Howard, A et al 1994, *River of Blood: Serial Killers and Their Victims*, Universal.

Howard, A 2009, *Innocence Lost*, New Holland.

Howard, A et al 2009, *Predators*, New Holland.

Jones, A 2005, *Cruel Sacrifices*, Pinnacle Books.

Laws, DR et al 2008, *Sexual Deviance: Theory, Assessment and Treatment*,

Guilford Press.

Levine, P, Ph.D., et al, 2010, *Trauma Through a Child's Eyes: Awakening the Ordinary Miracle of Healing*, North Atlantic Books.

Masters, B 1997, *She Must Have Known*, Corgi.

McGregor, D 2007, *Massacre, Murder, Mayhem*, Lulu, p180.

Michaud, S & Aynesworth, H 1999, *The Only Living Witness*, Authorlink Press.

Pron, N 1995, *Lethal Marriage*, Ballantine Books.

Sullivan, K 2010, *The Bundy Murders: A Comprehensive History*, McFarland.

Vronsky, P 2007, *Female Serial Killers: How and Why Women Become Monsters*, Berkley Books.

Wambaugh, J 2011, *The Blooding*, Mysterious Press.

Wansell, G 1996, *An Evil Love: The Life of Frederick West*, Headline.

Whittaker, M et al 2007, *Sins of the Brother*, Pan.

Whittington-Egan, R & M 2011, *Murder on File*, Neil Wilson.

Williams, S 1998, *Invisible Darkness*, Bantam Books.

Wilson, C & Seaman, D 2011, *The Serial Killers: A Study in the Psychology of Violence*, Random House.

Journals

MacFarlane, B 1999, 'Horrific Video Tapes as Evidence: Balancing Open Court and Victims' Privacy', *Criminal Law Quarterly*, vol. 413, pp. 1–92.

Mitchell, H & Aamodt, M 2005, 'The Incidence of Child Abuse in Serial Killers', *Journal of Police and Criminal Psychology*, vol. 20, issue 1, pp. 40–47.

Moore, TJ, Glenmullen, J & Furberg, CD 2010, 'Prescription Drugs Associated with Reports of Violence Towards Others', *PLoS ONE* 5(12): e15337. doi:10.1371/journal.pone.0015337.

Sansone, R & Sanson, L 2008, 'Bully Victims: Psychological and Somatic Aftermaths', *Psychiatry*, vol. 5, no. 6, pp. 62–64.

Newspapers and magazines

1990, 'I know what has been done is wrong', *New York Times*, 29 March, www.nytimes.com/1990/03/29/nyregion/i-know-that-what-has-been-done-is-wrong.html.

1993, 'John List's sister-in-law acts as consultant for film to be aired Tuesday on murders', *The Westfield Leader*, 18 February.

2004, 'Profile: Marc Dutroux', *BBC News: Europe*, 17 June, http://news.bbc.co.uk/2/hi/europe/3522367.stm.

2004, 'Marc Dutroux, Belgium's Most Hated Man', *Agence France Presse*, 29 February, accessed via www.accessmylibrary.com/coms2/summary_0286-20510635_ITM.

2007, 'Fred and Rose West: Multiple Murderers', *H2G2*, 30 January, http://h2g2.com/approved_entry/A18532514.

2007, 'Menendez brothers on trial: Testimony begins', *CNN Court TV Archive*, posted 31 December, http://edition.cnn.com/2007/US/law/11/26/court.archive.menendez1/.

2007, 'Menendez brothers on trial: Erik testifies he feared parents', *CNN Court TV Archive*, posted 31 December, http://edition.cnn.com/2007/US/law/12/10/court.archive.menendez5/index.html.

2009, 'Josef Fritzl: a monster caged', *The Scotsman*, 21 March, www.scotsman.com/news/josef-fritzl-a-monster-caged-1-1305181.

2012, 'Documentary captures Melinda Loveless' only on-camera interview', *Newswire Today*, 22 February, www.newswiretoday.com/news/106629/.

Abrahamson, A 1993, 'Lyle Menendez went on spree after killings, witnesses say', *LA Times*, 28 July, http://articles.latimes.com/1993-07-28/local/me-17696_1_lyle-menendez.

Aitkenhead, D 1995, 'I'm so like my dad, says Stephen West', *The Independent*, 17 December, www.independent.co.uk/news/uk/home-news/im-so-like-my-dad-says-stephen-west-1526097.html.

Bibby, P 2012, 'An adrenalin-filled thrill kill', *WA Today*, video, 7 June, http://media.watoday.com.au/news/national-news/an-adrenalinfuelled-thrill-kill-3356932.html.

Boorstin, R 1987, 'Schenectady Child Suffocation Case Goes to Jury', *New York Times*, 6 July, www.nytimes.com/1987/07/16/nyregion/schenectady-child-suffocation-case-goes-to-jury.html.

Dale, A 2012, 'Matthew Milat sentenced to 30 years jail for 'cold blooded' murder', *The Daily Telegraph*, 8 June, www.news.com.au/national-news/matthew-milat-sentenced-to-43-years/story-e6frfkvr-1226388884080.

Dalton, D 1998, 'If Christ came back as a con man', *The Gadfly*, October issue, www.gadflyonline.com/archive/October98/archive-manson.html.

Debelle, P 2003, 'Snowtown killers jailed until death', *Sydney Morning Herald*, 30 October, www.smh.com.au/articles/2003/10/29/1067233251741.html.

Dunne, D 1990, 'Nightmare on Elm Drive', *Vanity Fair*, October, www.vanityfair.com/magazine/archive/1990/10/dunne199010.

Gavin, R 2011, 'Rare Glimpse into child killer's mind', *Times Union*, 11 February, www.timesunion.com/local/article/Rare-glimpse-into-child-killer-s-mind-1007994.php.

Horton, M 2009, 'Adopted daughter hires friends to kill stepmother and father', *Examiner*, 5 February, www.examiner.com/article/adopted-daughter-hires-friends-to-kill-stepmother-and-father.

Icke, D 2007, 'Satanic ritual abuse: Where have all the children gone?', *Illuminati News*, December 16 accessed September 2008, www.illumianti-news.com/Articles/35.html.

Keel, P 2010, 'From the archive: Essex family murders trial', *The Guardian*, 20 October, originally published 29 October 1986, www.guardian.co.uk/theguardian/2010/oct/29/archive-essex-family-murders-trial-1986.

Kluger, J 2013, 'Brothers in Arms: Sibling Psychology and the Bombing Suspects', *Time Magazine*, 19 April, http://science.time.com/2013/04/19/siblings/.

Letrent, S 2013, 'A killer in the family', *CNN Online*, 31 March, http://edition.cnn.com/2013/03/31/living/a-killer-in-the-family.

Moore, M 2008, 'Josef Fritzl admits locking mother in bricked-up room at dungeon house', *The Telegraph*, 29 October, www.telegraph.co.uk/

news/3281656/Josef-Fritzl-admits-locking-mother-in-bricked-up-room-at-dungeon-house.html.

Paterson, T 2009, 'How cruel I was: Fritzl finally admits killing son', *The Independent*, 19 March, www.independent.co.uk/news/world/europe/how-cruel-i-was-fritzl-finally-admits-killing-so n-1648399.html.

Rayner, G & Gammell, C 2009, 'Josef Fritzl changes plea to guilty after daughter Elisabeth faces him in court', *The Telegraph*, 18 March, www.telegraph.co.uk/news/newstopics/joseffritzl/5011197/Josef-Fritzl-changes-plea-to-guilty-after-daughter-Elisabeth-faces-him-in-court.html.

Ryder, A 2012, 'Shanda Sharer's mum and murderer form unlikely alliance', *Wave 3 News*, 22 May, www.wave3.com/story/18573121/shanda-sharers-mother-and-murderer-form-unlikely-alliance.

Scheikowski, M 2012, 'Milat gets 43 years for slaying Aboriginal friend', *Tracker*, 8 June, http://tracker.org.au/2012/06/milat-gets-43-years-for-slaying-aboriginal-friend/.

Stout, D 2008, 'John E. List, 82, killer of family members, dies', *New York Times*, 25 March, www.nytimes.com/2008/03/25/nyregion/25list1.html?_r=0.

Thomas, J 1997, 'Hometown witnesses paint McVeigh likeable as a child', *New York Times*, June 10, www.nytimes.com/1997/06/10/us/hometown-witnesses-paint-mcveigh-likable-as-a-child.html.

Toppo, G 2009, '10 years later, the real story behind Columbine', *USA Today*, 14 April, http://usatoday30.usatoday.com/news/nation/2009-04-13-columbine-myths_N.htm.

Wainwright, R & Totaro, P 2009, 'A dangerous mind: what turned Martin Bryant into a mass murderer?', *Sydney Morning Herald*, April 27, www.smh.com.au/national/a-dangerous-mind-what-turned-martin-bryant-into-a-mass-murderer-20090427-ajk4.html.

Wright, S, Sims, P & Freeman, S 2010, 'Revealed: the horror image drawn by Jon Venables just weeks before he killed James Bulger', *Daily Mail*, 9 March, www.dailymail.co.uk/news/article-1256190/Revealed-The-horror-drawing-Jon-Venables-weeks-killed-James-Bulger.html.

Websites

2001, 'Ronnie and Reggie Kray', Crime File, Crime & Investigation Network, www.crimeandinvestigation.co.uk/crime-files/ronnie-and-reggie-kray/crime.html.

Aamodt, M 2012, 'Serial Killer Information Centre', Department of Psychology, Radford University, http://maamodt.asp.radford.edu/Serial%20Killer%20Information%20Center/Project%20Description.htm.

Butle, A & De Coninck, D 1997, 'Dutroux and Nihoul suspected of the murder of Christine Van Hees in 1984', http://old.radicalparty.org/belgium/x1_eng2.htm.

Casey, V et al, Jeffrey Dahmer timeline, Department of Psychology, Radford University, http://maamodt.asp.radford.edu/Psyc%20405/serial%20killers/Dahmer,%20Jeff.htm.

'Charles Manson', FBI Records: The Vault, Federal Bureau of Investigation website, http://vault.fbi.gov/Charles%20Manson.

'Columbine High School', FBI Records: The Vault, Federal Bureau of Investigation website, http://vault.fbi.gov/Columbine%20High%20School%20.

Crime Library, truTV, Time Warner, www.trutv.com/about/index.html.

Dutroux Case and X-Dossier victims-witnesses, originally at www.isgp.eu/dutroux/Belgian_X_dossiers_victims_and_witnesses.htm, copy now available at https://wikispooks.com/ISGP/dutroux/Belgian_X_dossiers_victims_and_witnesses.htm

'Eric Harris and Dylan Klebold', *Criminal Minds* wiki, http://criminalminds.wikia.com/wiki/Eric_Harris_and_Dylan_Klebold.

Franklin, K 2008, 'Forensic psychology angles in the Fritzl case,' *Forensic Psychologist* blog, 8 May, http://forensicpsychologist.blogspot.com.au/2008/05/forensic-psychology-angles-in-josef.html.

Gado, M 'She is a wicked woman!', *Crime Library*, www.trutv.com/library/crime/notorious_murders/women/marybeth_tinning/13.html.

Kinsolving, L 1972, 'The Prophet Who Raises the Dead', *San Fransisco*

Exmainer, 17 September, http://jonestown.sdsu.edu/AboutJonestown/PrimarySources/Kinsolving1.htm.

Lambert, T, 'The Case of Colin Pitchfork', *Local Histories*, www.localhistories.org/pitchfork.html.

Le Meurtre de La Champignoniere (Murder of a Mushroom), http://sites.google.com/site/tueriesdubrabant/lemeurtredelachampignonnière.

Lightfoot, A, Easterling, B & Herman, S, Colin Pitchfork timeline, Department of Psychology, Radford University, http://maamodt.asp.radford.edu/Psyc%20405/serial%20killers/Pitchfork,%20Colin.pdf.

Linder, D 2002, 'The Charles Manson Trial', University of Missouri-Kansas City Faculty of Law, http://law2.umkc.edu/faculty/projects/ftrials/manson/mansonaccount.html.

Linder, D 2006, 'Oklahoma City Bombing Trial', University of Missouri-Kansas City Faculty of Law, http://law2.umkc.edu/faculty/projects/ftrials/mcveigh/mcveightrial.html.

Ramsland, K 2012, 'Imagining Ted Bundy', *Psychology Today*, www.psychologytoday.com/blog/shadow-boxing/201208/imagining-ted-bundy.

Ross, R 2001, *The Jonestown Massacre*, 'Cult Education and Recovery', Rick A. Ross Institute, www.culteducation.com/jonestown.html.

Scott, S 'Death of James Bulger', Crime Library, www.trutv.com/library/crime/notorious_murders/young/bulger/6.html.

'Terror hits home: The Oklahoma City bombing', *Famous Cases and Criminals*, Federal Bureau of Investigation website, www.fbi.gov/about-us/history/famous-cases/oklahoma-city-bombing.

Film and television

A look back at the Menendez brothers murder case 2003, television program, Larry King Live, CNN, 20 August, transcript: http://transcripts.cnn.com/TRANSCRIPTS/0308/20/lkl.00.html.

Fred West: Born to Kill 2012, television program, Channel 5, 26 July.

Interview with Melinda Loveless 2012, television program, Eyewitness News, Nightbeat, Channel 13, Indianapolis, March 14.

Jonestown: The Life and Death of Peoples Temple 2006, motion picture, Firelight Media Inc, distributed by Seventh Art Releasing (USA, theatrical).

Most Evil: Cult Leaders 2007, television program, Discovery Channel, 14 October.

Most Evil: Murderous Women 2006, television program, Discovery Channel, 27 July.

Real Crime: Cracking the Killer's DNA Code, television program

Ted Bundy: The Mind of a Serial Killer 1995, television program, A&E Biography.

The Krays: The Final Word 2001, television program, Mission Television Productions, 1 October.

The Massacre at Columbine High 2004, television program, Zero Hour, The History Channel.

Court transcripts

US v McVeigh [1998] USCA10 1002; 153 F.3d 1166; 98 CJ C.A.R. 4652 (8 September 1998)

R v Milat & Klein [2012] NSWSC 634 (8 June 2012)

R v Bunting and Others (no. 3) No. SCCRM-01-205 [2003] SASC 251 (29 October 2003)

R v Martin Bryant (22 November 1996)

R v Pitchfork, [2009] EWCA Crim 963 (14 May 2009)

R v Bamber [2002] EWCA Crime 2912 (21 December 2002)

Opening statement of David Conn at retrial of both Menendez brothers

T vs The United Kingdom – 24724/94 [1999] ECHR 170

V vs The United Kingdom – 24888/94 [1999] ECHR 171

Other

Articles from *The Westfield Leader*, 1971 onwards.

Author interviews with Ivan Milat.

Lawson, B, Lillard, K & Mayer, T, Ted Bundy timeline, Department of Psychology, Radford University, http://maamodt.asp.radford.edu/ Psyc%20405/serial%20killers/Bundy,%20Ted%20-%202005.pdf.

Heckel, J, Drum, T & Gravitt, K, John Justin Bunting timeline, Department of Psychology, Radford University, http://maamodt.asp.radford.edu/ Psyc%20405/serial%20killers/Bunting,%20John%20Justin.pdf.

Letter sent from Timothy McVeigh to Congressman John J. LaFalce (D-NY), 16 February 1992.

Paul E. Mullen's psychiatric report on Martin Bryant.

REB Doomed – Eric Harris' online AOL blog.

Schnitker, T and Nissen, W, *Who Was the No Name Maddox Child*, powerpoint presentation, harmsc.pbworks.com/f/Who+Was+the+No+Name.ppt.

Endnotes

1   Interview with Arthur Shawcross

FRED AND ROSE WEST

2   Wansell, G 1996, *An Evil Love: The Life of Frederick West*, Headline, p27.
3   Fred West, Wikipedia (accessed July 2007).
4   Wansell, G 1996, *An Evil Love: The Life of Frederick West*, Headline, p73.
5   Ibid.
6   Fred had confessed and recanted the confession to Mary's murder multiple times.
7   Wansell, G 1996, *An Evil Love: The Life of Frederick West*, Headline, p85.
8   Ibid, p89.
9   Mae was born May June West on 1 June 1972
10   Wansell, G 1996, *An Evil Love: The Life of Frederick West*, Headline, p107.
11   Ibid, p129.
12   Ibid, p138.
13   Ibid, p143.
14   Masters, B 1997, *She Must Have Known*, Corgi, p395.
15   Wansell, G 1996, *An Evil Love: The Life of Frederick West*, Headline, p158.
16   Masters, B 1997, *She Must Have Known*, Corgi, p395.
17   Ibid.
18   Wansell, G 1996, *An Evil Love: The Life of Frederick West*, Headline, p189.
19   Ibid, p196.
20   Howard Ogden in *Fred West: Born to Kill* 2012, television program, Channel 5, 26 July.
21   *Fred West: Born to Kill* 2012, television program, Channel 5, 26 July.
22   Fred West in *Fred West: Born to Kill* 2012, television program, Channel 5, 26 July.
23   Ibid.
24   Ibid.
25   Ibid.
26   Ibid.
27   Wansell, G 1996, *An Evil Love: The Life of Frederick West*, Headline, p12.
28   Fred West in *Fred West: Born to Kill* 2012, television program, Channel 5, 26 July.
29   Ibid.
30   Ibid.
31   Ibid.
32   *Fred West: Born to Kill* 2012, television program, Channel 5, 26 July.
33   Aitkenhead, D 1995, 'I'm so like my dad, says Stephen West', *The Independent*, 17 December, www.independent.co.uk/news/uk/home-news/im-so-like-my-dad-says-stephen-west-1526097.html.

HOMOLKA AND BERNARDO

34 Laws, DR et al 2008, Sexual Deviance: Theory, Assessment and Treatment, Guilford Press, p398.

35 MacFarlane, B 1999, 'Horrific Video Tapes as Evidence: Balancing Open Court and Victims' Privacy', *Criminal Law Quarterly*, vol. 413, pp. 1–92.

36 Williams, S 1998, *Invisible Darkness*, Bantam Books, p40.

37 MacFarlane, B 1999, 'Horrific Video Tapes as Evidence: Balancing Open Court and Victims' Privacy', *Criminal Law Quarterly*, vol. 413, pp. 1–92.

38 Williams, S 1998, *Invisible Darkness*, Bantam Books, p64.

39 MacFarlane, B 1999, 'Horrific Video Tapes as Evidence: Balancing Open Court and Victims' Privacy', *Criminal Law Quarterly*, vol. 413, pp. 1–92.

40 Williams, S 1998, *Invisible Darkness*, Bantam Books, p109.

41 Ibid, p110.

42 Ibid, p119.

43 Ibid, p183.

44 Vronsky, P 2007, *Female Serial Killers: How and Why Women Become Monsters*, Berkley Books, p328.

45 Pron, N 1995, *Lethal Marriage*, Ballantine Books, p260.

46 Furio, J 2001, *Team Killers: A Comparative Study of Collaborative Killers*, p109.

47 Pron, N 1995, *Lethal Marriage*, Ballantine Books, p307.

48 Ibid, p322.

TED BUNDY

49 *Ted Bundy: The Mind of a Serial Killer* 1995, television program, A&E Biography.

50 Lawson, B, Lillard, K & Mayer, T, Ted Bundy timeline, Department of Psychology, Radford University, http://maamodt.asp.radford.edu/Psyc%20405/serial%20killers/Bundy,%20Ted%20-%202005.pdf.

51 *Ted Bundy: The Mind of a Serial Killer* 1995, television program, A&E Biography.

52 Ibid.

53 Ramsland, K 2012, 'Imagining Ted Bundy', *Psychology Today*, www.psychologytoday.com blog/shadow-boxing/201208/imagining-ted-bundy.

54 Lawson, B, Lillard, K & Mayer, T, Ted Bundy timeline, Department of Psychology, Radford University, http://maamodt.asp.radford.edu/Psyc%20405/serial%20killers/Bundy,%20Ted%20-%202005.pdf.

55 Ramsland, K 2012, 'Imagining Ted Bundy', *Psychology Today*, www.psychologytoday.com blog/shadow-boxing/201208/imagining-ted-bundy.

56 Sullivan, K 2010, The Bundy Murders: A Comprehensive History, McFarland, p83.

57 Michaud, S & Aynesworth, H 1999, *The Only Living Witness*, Authorlink Press, p173.

58 Ibid, p138.

59 *Ted Bundy: The Mind of a Serial Killer* 1995, television program, A&E Biography.

60 Michaud, S & Aynesworth, H 1999, *The Only Living Witness*, Authorlink Press, p138.

61 Ibid, p139.

62 *Ted Bundy: The Mind of a Serial Killer* 1995, television program, A&E Biography.

63 Dr Dobson in *Ted Bundy: The Mind of a Serial Killer* 1995, television program, A&E Biography.

THE MILATS

64 Shears, R 2012, 'Nephew of notorious Australian backpacker murderer killed friend with battleaxe in the SAME forest his uncle preyed on victims', *Daily Mail*, 8 June, www.dailymail.co.uk/news/article-2156367/Matthew-Milat-nephew-notorious-Australian-backpacker-murderer-killed-friend-battleaxe.html

65 Interviews with the killer by author.

66   Ibid.
67   Howard, A 2009, *Innocence Lost*, New Holland, p180.
68   Ibid.
69   This sighting would prove significant later.
70   Howard, A 2009, *Innocence Lost*, New Holland, p174.
71   Interviews with the killer by author.
72   Letrent, S 2013, 'A killer in the family', *CNN Online*, 31 March, http://edition.cnn.com/2013/03/31/living/a-killer-in-the-family.
73   Scheikowski, M 2012, 'Milat gets 43 years for slaying Aboriginal friend', *Tracker*, 8 June, http://tracker.org.au/2012/06/milat-gets-43-years-for-slaying-aboriginal-friend/.
74   R v Milat & Klein [2012] NSWSC 634 (8 June 2012)
75   Bibby, P 2012, 'An adrenalin-filled thrill kill', *WA Today*, video, 7 June, http://media.watoday.com.au/news/national-news/an-adrenalinfuelled-thrill-kill-3356932.html.
76   Dale, A 2012, 'Matthew Milat sentenced to 30 years jail for 'cold blooded' murder', *The Daily Telegraph*, 8 June, www.news.com.au/national-news/matthew-milat-sentenced-to-43-years/story-e6frfkvr-1226388884080.

THE SNOWTOWN KILLERS
77   Debelle, P 2003, 'Snowtown killers jailed until death', *Sydney Morning Herald*, 30 October, www.smh.com.au/articles/2003/10/29/1067233251741.html.
78   Heckel, J, Drum, T & Gravitt, K, John Justin Bunting timeline, Department of Psychology, Radford University, http://maamodt.asp.radford.edu/Psyc%20405/serial%20killers/Bunting,%20John%20Justin.pdf.
79   Ibid.
80   Ibid.
81   Wilson, C & Seaman, D 2011, *The Serial Killers: A Study in the Psychology of Violence*, Random House, p372.
82   R v Bunting and Others (no. 3) No. SCCRM-01-205 [2003] SASC 251 (29 October 2003)
83   Ibid.
84   Ibid.
85   Wilson, C & Seaman, D 2011, *The Serial Killers: A Study in the Psychology of Violence*, Random House, p369.
86   R v Bunting and Others (no. 3) No. SCCRM-01-205 [2003] SASC 251 (29 October 2003)
87   Suzanne Allen's death was found to be from indeterminate causes.
88   Debelle, P 2003, 'Snowtown killers jailed until death', *Sydney Morning Herald*, 30 October, www.smh.com.au/articles/2003/10/29/1067233251741.html.
89   R v Bunting and Others (no. 3) No. SCCRM-01-205 [2003] SASC 251 (29 October 2003)
90   Ibid.

TIMOTHY MCVEIGH
91   Sansone, R & Sanson, L 2008, 'Bully Victims: Psychological and Somatic Aftermaths', *Psychiatry*, vol. 5, no. 6, pp. 62–64.
92   Joseph Hartzler's opening statement in the Timothy McVeigh trial.
93   'Terror hits home: The Oklahoma City bombing', Famous Cases and Criminals, Federal Bureau of Investigation website, www.fbi.gov/about-us/history/famous-cases/oklahoma-city-bombing.
94   Thomas, J 1997, 'Hometown witnesses paint McVeigh likeable as a child', *New York Times*, June 10, www.nytimes.com/1997/06/10/us/hometown-witnesses-paint-mcveigh-likable-as-a-child.html.

95   'Terror hits home: The Oklahoma City bombing', Famous Cases and Criminals, Federal Bureau of Investigation website, www.fbi.gov/about-us/history/famous-cases/oklahoma-city-bombing.

96   Joseph Hartzler's opening statement in the Timothy McVeigh trial.

97   'Terror hits home: The Oklahoma City bombing', Famous Cases and Criminals, Federal Bureau of Investigation website, www.fbi.gov/about-us/history/famous-cases/oklahoma-city-bombing.

98   Linder, D 2006, 'Oklahoma City Bombing Trial', The Oklahoma Bombing Conspirators, page, University of Missouri-Kansas City Faculty of Law, http://law2.umkc.edu/faculty/projects/ftrials/mcveigh/mcveightrial.html.

99   Thomas, J 1997, 'Hometown witnesses paint McVeigh likeable as a child', *New York Times*, June 10, www.nytimes.com/1997/06/10/us/hometown-witnesses-paint-mcveigh-likable-as-a-child.html.

100   Letter sent from Timothy McVeigh to Congressman John J. LaFalce (D-NY), 16 February 1992.

101   Linder, D 2006, 'Oklahoma City Bombing Trial', The Oklahoma Bombing Conspirators, page, University of Missouri-Kansas City Faculty of Law, http://law2.umkc.edu/faculty/projects/ftrials/mcveigh/mcveightrial.html.

102   US v McVeigh [1998] USCA10 1002; 153 F.3d 1166; 98 CJ C.A.R. 4652 (8 September 1998).

103   Linder, D 2006, 'Oklahoma City Bombing Trial', The Oklahoma Bombing Conspirators, page, University of Missouri-Kansas City Faculty of Law, http://law2.umkc.edu/faculty/projects/ftrials/mcveigh/mcveightrial.html.

104   US v McVeigh [1998] USCA10 1002; 153 F.3d 1166; 98 CJ C.A.R. 4652 (8 September 1998).

105   Ibid.

106   Ibid.

ERIC HARRIS AND DYLAN KLEBOLD

107   Eric Harris' diary entry.

108   Kluger, J 2013, 'Brothers in Arms: Sibling Psychology and the Bombing Suspects', *Time Magazine*, 19 April, http://science.time.com/2013/04/19/siblings/.

109   Ibid.

110   Ibid.

111   Cullen, D 2010, *Columbine*, Grand Central Publishing, p32.

112   'Eric Harris and Dylan Klebold', *Criminal Minds* wiki, http://criminalminds.wikia.com/wiki/Eric_Harris_and_Dylan_Klebold.

113   Dylan Klebold's diary entry.

114   REB Doomed – Eric Harris' online AOL blog.

115   *The Massacre at Columbine High* 2004, television program, Zero Hour, The History Channel.

116   Moore, TJ, Glenmullen, J & Furberg, CD 2010, 'Prescription Drugs Associated with Reports of Violence Towards Others', *PLoS ONE* 5(12): e15337. doi:10.1371/journal.pone.0015337.

117   'Columbine High School', FBI Records: The Vault, Federal Bureau of Investigation website, http://vault.fbi.gov/Columbine%20High%20School%20.

118   Eric Harris' diary entry.

119   Dylan Klebold's diary entry.

120   'Columbine High School', FBI Records: The Vault, Federal Bureau of Investigation website, http://vault.fbi.gov/Columbine%20High%20School%20.

121   Ibid.

122   Toppo, G 2009, '10 years later, the real story behind Columbine', *USA Today*, 14 April,

http://usatoday30.usatoday.com/news/nation/2009-04-13-columbine-myths_N.htm.

123   Dylan Klebold's diary entry.

124   Bennett, W 2006, *Criminal Investigation*, Cengage Learning, p345.

125   Available from various online sources; see Youtube for actual recording.

CHARLES MANSON

126   Schnitker, T and Nissen, W, *Who Was the No Name Maddox Child*, powerpoint presentation, harmsc.pbworks.com/f/Who+Was+the+No+Name.ppt.

127   Bugliosi, V et al 1992, *Helter Skelter*, Arrow, p189.

128   Linder, D 2002, 'The Charles Manson Trial', University of Missouri-Kansas City Faculty of Law, http://law2.umkc.edu/faculty/projects/ftrials/manson/mansonaccount.html.

129   Ibid.

130   Bugliosi, V et al 1992, *Helter Skelter*, Arrow, p190.

131   Ibid, p198.

132   Ibid, p197.

133   Schnitker, T and Nissen, W, *Who Was the No Name Maddox Child*, powerpoint presentation, harmsc.pbworks.com/f/Who+Was+the+No+Name.ppt.

134   Bugliosi, V et al 1992, *Helter Skelter*, Arrow, p437.

135   Most Evil: Cult Leaders 2007, television program, Discovery Channel, 14 October.

136   Dalton, D 1998, 'If Christ came back as a con man', *The Gadfly*, October issue, www.gadflyonline.com/archive/October98/archive-manson.html.

137   Bugliosi, V et al 1992, *Helter Skelter*, Arrow, p5.

138   Ibid, p114.

139   Ibid.

140   Ibid.

141   Ibid.

142   Linder, D 2002, 'The Charles Manson Trial', University of Missouri-Kansas City Faculty of Law, http://law2.umkc.edu/faculty/projects/ftrials/manson/mansonaccount.html.

143   Ibid.

144   Ibid.

145   Ibid.

146   Bugliosi, V et al 1992, *Helter Skelter*, Arrow, p549.

147   Douglas, J and Olshaker, M 1996, *Mindhunter: Inside the FBI's Elite Serial Crime Unit*, Pocket Books, p121–2.

148   Ibid.

149   Ibid.

JIM JONES

150   Jim Jones recordings.

151   Ibid.

152   Ibid.

153   Kinsolving, L 1972, 'The Prophet Who Raises the Dead', *San Fransisco Exmainer*, 17 September, http://jonestown.sdsu.edu/AboutJonestown/PrimarySources/Kinsolving1.htm.

154   *Jonestown: The Life and Death of Peoples Temple* 2006, motion picture, Firelight Media Inc, distributed by Seventh Art Releasing (USA, theatrical).

155   Ibid.

156   Ross, R 2001, The Jonestown Massacre, 'Cult Education and Recovery', Rick A. Ross Institute, www.culteducation.com/jonestown.html.

157   Ibid.

158   *Jonestown: The Life and Death of Peoples Temple* 2006, motion picture, Firelight Media Inc, distributed by Seventh Art Releasing (USA, theatrical).

159   Ross, R 2001, The Jonestown Massacre, 'Cult Education and Recovery', Rick A. Ross
       Institute, www.culteducation.com/jonestown.html.
160   *Jonestown: The Life and Death of Peoples Temple* 2006, motion picture, Firelight Media Inc,
       distributed by Seventh Art Releasing (USA, theatrical).
161   Most Evil: Cult Leaders 2007, television program, Discovery Channel, 14 October.
162   *Jonestown: The Life and Death of Peoples Temple* 2006, motion picture, Firelight Media Inc,
       distributed by Seventh Art Releasing (USA, theatrical).
163   Ibid.
164   Ibid.
165   Ross, R 2001, The Jonestown Massacre, 'Cult Education and Recovery', Rick A. Ross
       Institute, www.culteducation.com/jonestown.html.

MARC DUTROUX

166   Le Meurtre de La Champignoniere (Murder of a Mushroom), http://sites.google.com/
       site/tueriesdubrabant/lemeurtredelachampignonnière.
167   Butle, A & De Coninck, D 1997, 'Dutroux and Nihoul suspected of the murder of
       Christine Van Hees in 1984', http://old.radicalparty.org/belgium/x1_eng2.htm.
168   2004, 'Profile: Marc Dutroux', *BBC News: Europe*, 17 June, http://news.bbc.co.uk/2/hi/
       europe/3522367.stm.
169   The two surviving victims, Laetitia Delhez and Sabine Dardenne, were photographed
       during their abuse sessions. The photographs were not found during subsequent searches,
       suggesting the photos may have been given to others. Dutroux Case and X-Dossier
       victims-witnesses, originally at www.isgp.eu/dutroux/Belgian_X_dossiers_victims_and_
       witnesses.htm, copy now available at https://wikispooks.com/ISGP/dutroux/Belgian_X_
       dossiers_victims_and_witnesses.htm
170   The reported number of videos confiscated differs from a mere few to a few thousand.
171   Dutroux Case and X-Dossier victims-witnesses, originally at www.isgp.eu/dutroux/
       Belgian_X_dossiers_victims_and_witnesses.htm, copy now available at https://
       wikispooks.com/ISGP/dutroux/Belgian_X_dossiers_victims_and_witnesses.htm
172   Icke, D 2007, 'Satanic ritual abuse: Where have all the children gone?', *Illuminati News*,
       December 16 accessed September 2008, www.illumianti-news.com/Articles/35.html.
173   Dutroux Case and X-Dossier victims-witnesses, originally at www.isgp.eu/dutroux/
       Belgian_X_dossiers_victims_and_witnesses.htm, copy now available at https://
       wikispooks.com/ISGP/dutroux/Belgian_X_dossiers_victims_and_witnesses.htm
174   Ibid.
175   Ibid.
176   2004, 'Marc Dutroux, Belgium's Most Hated Man', *Agence France Presse*, February 29,
       www.accessmylibrary.com/coms2/summary_0286-20510635_ITM.

JEFFREY DAHMER

177   Aggarawal, A 2010, *Necrophilia: Forensic and Medico-legal Aspects*, CRC Press, p127.
178   Levine, P, Ph.D., et al, 2010, *Trauma Through a Child's Eyes: Awakening the Ordinary
       Miracle of Healing*, North Atlantic Books.
179   Casey, V et al, Jeffrey Dahmer timeline, Department of Psychology, Radford University,
       http://maamodt.asp.radford.edu/Psyc%20405/serial%20killers/Dahmer,%20Jeff.htm.
180   Howard, A et al 1994, *River of Blood: Serial Killers and Their Victims*, Universal, p108.
181   Casey, V et al, Jeffrey Dahmer timeline, Department of Psychology, Radford University,
       http://maamodt.asp.radford.edu/Psyc%20405/serial%20killers/Dahmer,%20Jeff.htm.
182   Clarke, P et al 2011, Extreme Evil: Taking Crime to the Next Level, Canary.
183   Casey, V et al, Jeffrey Dahmer timeline, Department of Psychology, Radford University,
       http://maamodt.asp.radford.edu/Psyc%20405/serial%20killers/Dahmer,%20Jeff.htm.
184   Howard, A et al 1994, *River of Blood: Serial Killers and Their Victims*, Universal, p180.

COLIN PITCHFORK

185   Lightfoot, A, Easterling, B & Herman, S, Colin Pitchfork timeline, Department of Psychology, Radford University, http://maamodt.asp.radford.edu/Psyc%20405/serial%20killers/Pitchfork,%20Colin.pdf.

186   R v Pitchfork, [2009] EWCA Crim 963 (14 May 2009).

187   R v Pitchfork, [2009] EWCA Crim 963 (14 May 2009).

188   Britton, P 1997, *The Jigsaw Man*, Corgi, p153.

189   Cracking the Code Documentary

190   Joseph Wambaugh *The Blooding*

191   Britton, P 1997, *The Jigsaw Man*, Corgi, 532.

192   R v Pitchfork, [2009] EWCA Crim 963 (14 May 2009).

193   Lambert, T, 'The Case of Colin Pitchfork', *Local Histories*, www.localhistories.org/pitchfork.html.

194   Canter, D 1995, *Criminal Shadows: Inside the Mind of a Serial Killer*, HarperCollins, p50.

MELINDA LOVELESS

195   2012, 'Documentary captures Melinda Loveless' only on-camera interview', Newswire Today, 22 February, www.newswiretoday.com/news/106629/, accessed March 2013.

196   Ryder, A 2012, 'Shanda Sharer's mum and murderer form unlikely alliance', *Wave 3 News*, 22 May, www.wave3.com/story/18573121/shanda-sharers-mother-and-murderer-form-unlikely-alliance.

197   Interview with Melinda Loveless 2012, television program, Eyewitness News, Nightbeat, Channel 13, Indianapolis, March 14.

198   2012, 'Documentary captures Melinda Loveless' only on-camera interview', Newswire Today, 22 February, www.newswiretoday.com/news/106629/, accessed March 2013.

199   Jones, A 2005, *Cruel Sacrifices*, Pinnacle Books, p22.

200   Jones, A 2005, *Cruel Sacrifices*, Pinnacle Books, p26

201   Interview with Melinda Loveless 2012, television program, Eyewitness News, Nightbeat, Channel 13, Indianapolis, March 14.

202   Ibid.

VENABLES AND THOMPSON

203   T vs The United Kingdom – 24724/94 [1999] ECHR 170.

204   Scott, S 'Death of James Bulger', Crime Library, www.trutv.com/library/crime/notorious_murders/young/bulger/6.html.

205   Wright, S, Sims, P & Freeman, S 2010, 'Revealed: the horror image drawn by Jon Venables just weeks before he killed James Bulger', *Daily Mail*, 9 March, www.dailymail.co.uk/news/article-1256190/Revealed-The-horror-drawing-Jon-Venables-weeks-killed-James-Bulger.html.

206   Ibid.

207   Ibid.

208   V vs The United Kingdom – 24888/94 [1999] ECHR 171.

209   T vs The United Kingdom – 24724/94 [1999] ECHR 170.

210   V vs The United Kingdom – 24888/94 [1999] ECHR 171.

211   Ibid.

212   Bulger, R et al 2013, My James, Macmillan.

213   Ibid.

214   T vs The United Kingdom – 24724/94 [1999] ECHR 170.

MARTIN BRYANT

215   Mass murder, Wikipedia.

216   Wainwright, R & Totaro, P 2009, 'A dangerous mind: what turned Martin Bryant into

a mass murderer?', *Sydney Morning Herald*, April 27, www.smh.com.au/national/a-dangerous-mind-what-turned-martin-bryant-into-a-mass-murderer-20090427-ajk4.html.

217 Paul E. Mullen's psychiatric report on Martin Bryant.

218 Ibid.

219 Ibid.

220 Ibid.

221 Wainwright, R & Totaro, P 2009, 'A dangerous mind: what turned Martin Bryant into a mass murderer?', *Sydney Morning Herald*, April 27, www.smh.com.au/national/a-dangerous-mind-what-turned-martin-bryant-into-a-mass-murderer-20090427-ajk4.html.

222 Port Arthur Massacre, Wikipedia.

223 Howard, A 2009, *Innocence Lost*, New Holland, p221.

224 Ibid.

225 Hatty, S 2000, Masculinities, Violence and Culture, Sage, p44.

226 Ibid.

227 At the time, police were unaware that the Seascape's owners were already dead.

228 McGregor, D 2007, *Massacre, Murder, Mayhem*, Lulu, p180.

229 R v Martin Bryant (22 November 1996).

THE KRAY BROTHERS

230 *The Krays: The Final Word* 2001, television program, Mission Television Productions, 1 October.

231 Ibid.

232 Pearson, J 1995, *The Profession of Violence: Rise and Fall of the Kray Twins*, HarperCollins.

233 *The Krays: The Final Word* 2001, television program, Mission Television Productions, 1 October.

234 Ibid.

235 Ibid.

236 2001, 'Ronnie and Reggie Kray', Crime File, Crime & Investigation Network, www.crimeandinvestigation.co.uk/crime-files/ronnie-and-reggie-kray/crime.html.

237 Ibid.

238 *The Krays: The Final Word* 2001, television program, Mission Television Productions, 1 October.

JOSEF FRITZL

239 Rayner, G & Gammell, C 2009, 'Josef Fritzl changes plea to guilty after daughter Elisabeth faces him in court', *The Telegraph*, 18 March, www.telegraph.co.uk/news/newstopics/joseffritzl/5011197/Josef-Fritzl-changes-plea-to-guilty-after-daughter-Elisabeth-faces-him-in-court.html.

240 Ibid.

241 2009, 'Josef Fritzl: a monster caged', *The Scotsman*, 21 March, www.scotsman.com/news/josef-fritzl-a-monster-caged-1-1305181.

242 Ibid.

243 Hall, A 2008, *Monster*, Penguin.

244 Ibid.

245 Moore, M 2008, 'Josef Fritzl admits locking mother in bricked-up room at dungeon house', *The Telegraph*, 29 October, www.telegraph.co.uk/news/3281656/Josef-Fritzl-admits-locking-mother-in-bricked-up-room-at-dungeon-house.html.

246 Ibid.

247 Franklin, K 2008, 'Forensic psychology angles in the Fritzl case,' *Forensic Psychologist* blog, 8 May, http://forensicpsychologist.blogspot.com.au/2008/05/forensic-psychology-

angles-in-josef.html.

248 Hall, A 2008, *Monster*, Penguin.

249 Paterson, T 2009, 'How cruel I was: Fritzl finally admits killing son', *The Independent*, 19 March, www.independent.co.uk/news/world/europe/how-cruel-i-was-fritzl-finally-admits-killing-so n-1648399.html.

JOHN LIST

250 Benford, T & Johnson, J 2000, *Righteous Carnage: The List Murders in Westfield*, iUniverse, p69.

251 'List trial begins', *The Westfield Ledger*, 25 January.

252 Word crossed out in original.

253 1990, 'I know that what has been done is wrong', *New York Times*, 29 March, www.nytimes.com/1990/03/29/nyregion/i-know-that-what-has-been-done-is-wrong.html.

254 Stout, D 2008, 'John E. List, 82, killer of family members, dies', New York Times, 25 March, www.nytimes.com/2008/03/25/nyregion/25list1.html?_r=0.

255 'List trial begins', *The Westfield Ledger*, 25 January.

256 1993, 'John List's sister-in-law acts as consultant for film to be aired Tuesday on murders', *The Westfield Leader*, 18 February.

257 Stout, D 2008, 'John E. List, 82, killer of family members, dies', New York Times, 25 March, www.nytimes.com/2008/03/25/nyregion/25list1.html?_r=0.

LYLE AND ERIK MENENDEZ

258 Horton, M 2009, 'Adopted daughter hires friends to kill stepmother and father', *Examiner*, 5 February, www.examiner.com/article/adopted-daughter-hires-friends-to-kill-stepmother-and-father.

259 Dunne, D 1990, 'Nightmare on Elm Drive', *Vanity Fair*, October, www.vanityfair.com/magazine/archive/1990/10/dunne199010.

260 Opening statement by David Conn at Menendez trial.

261 Ibid.

262 2007, 'Menendez brothers on trial: Testimony begins', *CNN Court TV Archive*, posted 31 December, http://edition.cnn.com/2007/US/law/11/26/court.archive.menendez1/.

263 Opening statement of David Conn at trial of both Menendez brothers

264 Ibid.

265 2007, 'Menendez brothers on trial: Erik testifies he feared parents', *CNN Court TV Archive*, posted 31 December, http://edition.cnn.com/2007/US/law/12/10/court.archive.menendez5/index.html.

266 From 911 call transcript.

267 Abrahamson, A 1993, 'Lyle Menendez went on spree after killings, witnesses say', *LA Times*, 28 July, http://articles.latimes.com/1993-07-28/local/me-17696_1_lyle-menendez.

268 *A look back at the Menendez brothers murder case* 2003, television program, Larry King Live, CNN, 20 August, transcript: http://transcripts.cnn.com/TRANSCRIPTS/0308/20/lkl.00.html.

269 2007, 'Menendez brothers on trial: Erik testifies he feared parents', *CNN Court TV Archive*, posted 31 December, http://edition.cnn.com/2007/US/law/12/10/court.archive.menendez5/index.html.

270 *A look back at the Menendez brothers murder case* 2003, television program, Larry King Live, CNN, 20 August, transcript: http://transcripts.cnn.com/TRANSCRIPTS/0308/20/lkl.00.html.

271 Ibid.

272 Ibid.

JEREMY BAMBER
273   R v Bamber [2002] EWCA Crime 2912 (21 December 2002).
274   Ibid.
275   Ibid.
276   Ibid.
277   ·Ibid.
278   Whittington-Egan, R & M 2011, Murder on File, Neil Wilson.
279   R v Bamber [2002] EWCA Crime 2912 (21 December 2002).
280   Ibid.
281   Ibid.
282   Ibid.
283   Keel, P 2010, 'From the archive: Essex family murders trial', *The Guardian*, 20 October, originally published 29 October 1986, www.guardian.co.uk/theguardian/2010/oct/29/archive-essex-family-murders-trial-1986.

MARYBETH TINNING
284   *Most Evil: Murderous Women* 2006, television program, Discovery Channel, 27 July.
285   Gado, M 'She is a wicked woman!', *Crime Library*, www.trutv.com/library/crime/notorious_murders/women/marybeth_tinning/13.html.
286   Ibid.
287   *Most Evil: Murderous Women* 2006, television program, Discovery Channel, 27 July.
288   Boorstin, R 1987, 'Schenectady Child Suffocation Case Goes to Jury', *New York Times*, 6 July, www.nytimes.com/1987/07/16/nyregion/schenectady-child-suffocation-case-goes-to-jury.html.
289   Gavin, R 2011, 'Rare Glimpse into child killer's mind', *Times Union*, 11 February, www.timesunion.com/local/article/Rare-glimpse-into-child-killer-s-mind-1007994.php.
290   *Most Evil: Murderous Women* 2006, television program, Discovery Channel, 27 July.
291   Leggett, J 1986, 'Grand Jury Investigating Deaths of At Least Two Tinning Children', *Schenectady Gazette*, 18 June.
292   Ramirez-Gaston, D, Sutphin, K and Thompson, B, Marybeth Tinning timeline, epartment of Psychology, Radford University, http://maamodt.asp.radford.edu/Psyc%20405/serial%20killers/Tinning,%20Marybeth%20_2012_.pdf.
293   *Most Evil: Murderous Women* 2006, television program, Discovery Channel, 27 July.
294   Ramirez-Gaston, D, Sutphin, K and Thompson, B, Marybeth Tinning timeline, epartment of Psychology, Radford University, http://maamodt.asp.radford.edu/Psyc%20405/serial%20killers/Tinning,%20Marybeth%20_2012_.pdf.
295   Ibid.
296   Ramirez-Gaston, D, Sutphin, K and Thompson, B, Marybeth Tinning timeline, epartment of Psychology, Radford University, http://maamodt.asp.radford.edu/Psyc%20405/serial%20killers/Tinning,%20Marybeth%20_2012_.pdf.
297   Ibid.
298   *Most Evil: Murderous Women* 2006, television program, Discovery Channel, 27 July.
299   Leggett, J 1986, 'Grand Jury Investigating Deaths of At Least Two Tinning Children', *Schenectady Gazette*, 18 June.
300   Gado, M 'She is a wicked woman!', *Crime Library*, www.trutv.com/library/crime/notorious_murders/women/marybeth_tinning/13.html.
301   Gavin, R 2011, 'Rare Glimpse into child killer's mind', *Times Union*, 11 February, www.timesunion.com/local/article/Rare-glimpse-into-child-killer-s-mind-1007994.php.

CONCLUSION
302   Mitchell, H & Aamodt, M 2005, 'The Incidence of Child Abuse in Serial Killers', *Journal of Police and Criminal Psychology*, vol. 20, issue 1, pp. 40–47.

UK £12.99
US $16.99